SOUND HERITAGE

SOUND HERITAGE
Voices from British Columbia

Saeko Usukawa
and the Editors of the
Sound Heritage Series

Douglas & McIntyre
Vancouver/Toronto

Douglas & McIntyre Ltd.
1615 Venables Street
Vancouver, British Columbia V5L 2H1

Canadian Cataloguing in Publication Data

Main entry under title:

Sound heritage

  Selected from issues of Sound heritage
series.
  ISBN 0–88894–443–8

  1. British Columbia — History — Sources —
Addresses, essays, lectures. 2. British
Columbia — Biography — Addresses, essays,
lectures. 3. Indians of North America —
British Columbia — History — Sources —
Addresses, essays, lectures. 4. Oral
history — Addresses, essays, lectures. 5.
Oral biography — Addresses, essays, lectures.
I. Usukawa, Saeko, 1946–   II. Sound
heritage series.
FC3803.S68 1984   971.1   C84–091303–6
F1086.S68 1984

Design by Barbara Hodgson
Typeset by Evergreen Press Ltd.
Printed and bound in Canada by D. W. Friesen & Sons Ltd.

Contents

PART I: THOSE WHO CAME BEFORE

Ruins of a Haida raven totem at Yan, Queen Charlotte Islands, circa 1915. Photograph by Edward S. Curtis, courtesy Provincial Archives of British Columbia / 78388

LEGENDS AND HISTORY OF THE NATIVE PEOPLES

*B*efore the arrival of the non-Indians, the native peoples did not have a system of writing; all traditional knowledge was passed on from one generation to another by word of mouth. This body of knowledge, or "oral tradition," was often the reasoned explanation of events for which there was no immediate understanding. It was also the means by which their history was transmitted.
— Randy Bouchard and Dorothy I. D. Kennedy

The Flood, a True Story

Edited by Randy Bouchard and Dorothy I. D. Kennedy, British Columbia Indian Language Project

*S*torytelling played an important role in Lillooet oral tradition. Such terms as "myths," "legends," "tales" and "narratives" have been used to describe the storytellers' accounts. The Lillooet term *sh-KO-qual* is most often translated by older Lillooet people as "true story"; the term *sh-pi-TACK-with* is most often translated as "legend." However, the Lillooet do mot make a clear-cut distinction between what they consider are true stories and what they consider are legends; the older people believe that the events described both in legends and in stories actually occurred. For example, the Lillooet feel that the account of "The Flood" is a true story, yet it precedes the Lillooet legendary (mythical) age.

BAPTISTE RITCHIE: This is a true story that has been told to the Mount Currie people for many, many years. When I was young, the old people told me this story many times.

A long, long time ago one of my ancestors, whose name was *In-CHEE-nim-kan*, received some advice from the Great Chief. He was told that the land was going to flood and almost all of the mountains would be covered with water. The Great Chief gave *In-CHEE-nim-kan* some instructions: "Bind together all of the driftwood that you can find; use young willow saplings to do this."

After he had gathered all the people together, *In-CHEE-nim-kan* told them what the Great Chief had told him: "Twist cedar bark and red willow into a long rope, for we will have to anchor onto the top of *In-SHUK-ch* [a mountain at the southeast end of Lillooet Lake]. When you have made enough rope, the Great Chief will tell me."

The Great Chief told *In-CHEE-nim-kan* to advise the people that they should collect all the salmon roe they could when the fish came up the river. *In-CHEE-nim-kan* had control of the salmon run, because he made the fish weir.

Although he could not see the Great Chief, *In-CHEE-nim-kan* believed in the advice that he received from him.

After the people had filled the raft with anchor ropes, *In-CHEE-nim-kan* told them to load the salmon roe onto it. He knew that it would be a long time before the water receded. The Great Chief was taking care of the people whom he had placed on earth. *In-CHEE-nim-kan* knew that the salmon roe would provide enough nourishment until they were able to gather food after the flood.

The brother of *In-CHEE-nim-kan* began to question what he was doing: "Why did you place all of that rope on the raft? Look at all the space that it has taken!" *In-CHEE-nim-kan* looked at his brother and replied, "I have been given my orders from the Great Chief. When the flood comes, my raft will float over to *In-SHUK-ch* mountain and I will anchor onto the peak." "Why don't you use animal hides to braid into a rope? It won't take up as much space. I am going to braid a rope that is the same length as yours, but is made from hides." The brother of *In-CHEE-nim-kan* made a raft and a long rope of animal hides.

A man named *Kush-TEE-tsa,* who *In-CHEE-nim-kan* accepted as a brother, took his daughter and son to *In-CHEE-nim-kan* and asked him to look after them. All of the children who were old enough to take care of themselves were allowed on the raft.

It began to rain. It rained and rained, and the water rose until they could no longer hold the raft. All the canoes and rafts flowed with the water. The children who hadn't been put on the raft sat on logs and in smaller canoes. Eventually, they reached *In-SHUK-ch* mountain.

In-CHEE-nim-kan told his brother to anchor to *In-SHUK-ch:* "When the water goes down, you will need a long rope to keep you secured until the raft finally rests." They both fastened their ropes to *In-SHUK-ch.* It is not known how long the people were anchored to the mountain peak, but *In-CHEE-nim-kan*'s brother's anchor rope, which was made from animal hides, stretched until it broke. His raft floated away, because the water was moving very fast.

The water receded quickly, and *In-CHEE-nim-kan*'s raft floated down until it stopped on a sloping area of the mountain. This was where the Great Chief had told *In-CHEE-nim-kan* they would land. Everything was covered with mud. *In-CHEE-nim-kan* decided that the children of *Kush-TEE-tsa* would best be able to provide for themselves at Skookumchuck, so he left them there. The descendants of these children are today called "Stager" [the anglicized pronunciation of *Kush-TEE-tsa*]. *In-CHEE-nim-kan* placed the people where he felt that they could best take care of themselves. Everyone had enough dried salmon roe to keep them from going hungry.

After a while *In-CHEE-nim-kan* returned to Mount Currie; the meadows here were better after the flood. He found that a lot of the people had moved to Mount Currie, because their own land was now covered with rocks. They settled along the Lillooet River.

Before the white people came to this land, there were prophets who were the leaders of our people. They received advice from the Great Chief; we now call him God. *In-CHEE-nim-kan* was one of these prophets. I, Baptiste Ritchie from Mount Currie, now have the name *In-CHEE-nim-kan*.

How the Animals and Birds Got Their Names

Edited by Randy Bouchard and Dorothy I. D. Kennedy, British Columbia Indian Language Project

Immediately after the Flood, the world was inhabited by "animal-people," the Lillooet believed. These beings had both animal and human (Lillooet Indian) attributes. The world at this time was considered to be in a different state, so it was necessary for it to be changed for the "coming people" — the Lillooet Indians.

CHARLIE MACK: This is a legend about what happened after the Great Flood. There were only a few people who survived. Most of the animals and birds perished. The chief told the people, "We are going to try to revive all the animals and birds. I am ordering you to tell this to all those who are not here."

The wolf was a person at this time. The chief said to him, "You must go out and gather the people and tell them what we are going to do." So the wolf went around to the people and did what the chief asked. He told the people that they would have to bring back the deer and all the other animals and birds.

A group of Lillooet Indians near Lillooet, B.C., in 1867 or 1868.
Photograph by Frederick Dally, courtesy Provincial Archives of British
Columbia / 71720

When the wolf had done what he could, there were still some people on the other side of the mountain who hadn't heard the plan. The chief sent his sons up the mountain, because he thought that they were the only ones who could make it through the fresh snow there. They tried but they couldn't make it.

The chief said to the porcupine, who was also a person at this time, "You are the oldest brother we have. You better go up over the mountain and get those other people." He replied, "Chief, you have tried all the strong men. So you think that I could do it? All right, I'll go and get those people." So the porcupine started to climb, taking his time, ploughing through the snow. He got to the top of the mountain and rolled down to the bottom. He climbed up again, but once at the top, he rolled down again.

When the porcupine finally reached the other people, he said, "We are having a big meeting, and the chief wants everyone to come and listen. The rest of the people are over there waiting." All right," said the people, "are you going to take us back with you? You know the way." The porcupine said that he would. "Follow me, we will go down there."

There was a good trail where the porcupine had rolled down earlier. He cleared the way by curling into a ball and rolling down through the snow. The people followed him and rolled down the deep, fresh snow. He got all the people down.

The chief was pleased that the porcupine had brought all the people down. "We are going to have a special gathering," he said. "Tonight we will sing in the big underground house."

The chief gathered all the people. "My dear people, I have been thinking. Now there are no animals and birds. We are going to try to revive them. We were saved because we were able to float around until the flood waters went down. All the animals and birds died; they couldn't make it. Everything that we lived on, died." They all began to sing their guardian spirit songs. Everyone sang. One person said, "I am going to be a bluejay," and he made the noise of a bluejay. The people said that he could be Bluejay.

Another person made the sound of a magpie. The chief and the people said that he could be Magpie, as they had a lot of use for that bird.

Another person said, "I am going to be a deer, a fawn." He imitated the sound of a fawn, and the people were satisfied; he was to be Deer.

Another person became a woodpecker. He made the noise of this bird. The chief agreed that he could be Woodpecker.

There were a lot of people at the special gathering, and they all turned into animals or birds. The porcupine said, "I am the oldest brother; I am going to be Porcupine." Then he sang Porcupine's song.

Underground Homes of the Lillooet

Edited by Randy Bouchard and Dorothy I. D. Kennedy, British Columbia Indian Language Project

Traditionally, the Lillooet lived in villages clustered alongside rivers, streams and lakes. Prior to the 1900s their economy was that of a fishing, hunting and gathering society that was seminomadic during the food-harvesting periods. Although men from a certain village, or villages, might frequent particular hunting areas, hunters from other villages generally would not be forbidden to use these same areas. The same was true for berry-picking and root-digging areas, which were utilized by women. In the late fall, after all the necessary food had been stored away for winter usage, the people would move into underground houses, where they would live until spring.

BAPTISTE RITCHIE: My dear friends, I am telling these stories so that you will know the ways of our ancestors. A long time ago the people in this area lived in underground houses, which we call *shi-EESH-ti-kin*. Near the Birkenhead River and the Lillooet River, there are still many large depressions in the ground where once there were underground houses.

One of the largest underground houses was built by a man named *Ee-pa* at a place called *Ha-TLO-la-wh* on the north side of the Birkenhead River, several miles up from its mouth. *Ee-pa* was an ancestor of some Mount Currie people who are still living today.

Very few people can remember how a *LEEL-wat* [Mount Currie Lillooet] underground house was constructed. Unlike other peoples' underground houses, there were never any posts inside the Mount Currie ones. The opening at the top of the larger houses was approximately four feet [1.2 m] by six feet [1.8 m] wide, but the rain and snow never went inside, because the fire was directly below this opening. The house pits were made very shallow in the meadow areas, so that water from under the ground would not seep into them.

After the pit was dug, logs were laid across the top of it, at ground level. Successive layers of logs, with the logs of each layer shorter than the layer below, were laid on top of this base [forming a pyramidlike structure]. Hot rocks were used to burn notches near the ends of each log, so that they would fit together snugly. The space left at the top was both the smokehole and the entrance. At its highest point, the underground house was between eight and nine feet [2.5 m to 2.8 m] above ground level. Planks were split from red cedar trees and placed over this log framework. The cracks between the logs and between the cedar planks were filled with cedar bark, and the framework was then covered with dirt.

In the old days the people had to work together to be able to build an underground house. Only those people who helped build it would be allowed to live in it. Those people who would not work together with the others would have no choice but to spend the winter in shelters which had been constructed as summer lodges.

Inside the pit which had been dug, they constructed a platform about one foot high, completely around the house, five feet in from the edges of the pit. This platform was called *ee-YAI-wash*. It was on this platform that the people slept, using boughs and pounded inner cedar bark as mattresses. Hides from mountain goats and other animals were used as blankets. Sometimes it was so crowded that the people had to sleep with their heads at the sides of the pit and only the width of the platform in which to stretch out. The special hunters, called *Tu-WEET*, shared their surplus animal hides with the other people.

A cedar log served as a ladder leading from the floor of the pit up through the smokehole. Notches [used as steps] were burned into the log with hot rocks.

Cattail plant leaves were woven into mats by the women; they also made eating mats from inner cedar bark, but wooden bowls were used most often to eat from. Community work was extremely important, for if someone didn't help, he was excluded in the winter.

There were often twenty or thirty people living in one underground house.

A fire for cooking was made for an hour in the morning and an hour at night. The women placed hot rocks in water contained in watertight baskets to cook each family's meal. Although only two cooking fires were made each day, the underground house was always warm.

The people moved into these underground houses in the late fall and stayed until the leaves came out on the trees. Then they built plank houses. Four posts were sunk into the ground, and cedar planks, which were about two feet [0.6 m] wide and four inches [10 cm] thick, were fastened between them. When the people went up into the mountains, they would live in a rock crevice or in a lean-to. There was always a lot of building material to be found along the banks of the rivers.

My ancestors had control of the salmon run. When the fish came up the river, they blocked the stream until everyone caught enough fish for their winter storage. Then the logs were pulled out of the river and left on the bank until the next year.

The people were well taken care of because they listened to their leaders.

My uncle, Old Joe, *In-k-CHEE-lick*, was the last person from this area to be born in an underground house. You can still see the pit where that undergound house was, across from my house at Mount Currie.

How We the Native People Lived

Edited by Janet Cauthers

The long memories of these informants include vivid recollections of life within native cultures still relatively untouched by the white world. They give detailed accounts of daily life, the methods used to provide food and shelter and the celebrations that marked their lives. Chief William Matthews and Chief Solomon Wilson of the Masset and Skidegate Haida respectively, Mrs. Ralph Hall of the Carrier people and Mrs. Edward Joyce of the Kwakiutl document both the cultures themselves and the ways in which they changed with the coming of European society.

The Haida and Kwakiutl people, though different in many respects, belong to the Pacific Northwest coastal culture based on the abundant wealth of land and sea and having a highly complex, stable society, with very rich and elaborate social and

Haida Indians at Yan, Queen Charlotte Islands, in 1881. Photograph by Edward Dossetter, courtesy Provincial Archives of British Columbia / 33613

religious beliefs. The Carrier are a hunting and fishing people of the northern interior of British Columbia who have assimilated many of the economic and social characteristics of the coastal Tsimshian.

MRS. EDWARD JOYCE: There were quite a lot of community homes, you know, those big Indian community houses, similar to what they're building at Alert Bay now. They had the totem poles at the door.

And then as a child, we didn't have any private quarters. It was little open compartments where we slept on the side of the building. And then during the time that we had to eat, we used this centre part, with the fire. They cooked right in the centre part, with the opening where the smoke went out, and our family was in there and we ate. Of course, we cooked right in the centre of the floor; and then we had something similar to the chesterfield only about three times as long, and of course it was boards, all boards. There were the cupboards on each end, where you kept your food or your dishes and things like that, you know.

The food itself was kept in great big wooden cedar boxes. And it was mostly always dried fish, dried berries and things like that we had. Eulachon oil was always mixed with what we ate, you know. And myself, I think that was really nice. I even long for it yet, but my husband doesn't. He wasn't brought up to understand how to eat all that. I think if we eat it now today, it would be so much better for a lot of us. The way they used to eat their food, you know, it was all natural food. Natural, got from nature, you know. Deer was smoked and kept for the winter, and clams and everything, seaweed, wild crab apples, wild rice and porcupine, beaver — that's a delicacy if you know how to cook it. I just can't describe it to you unless you know what it tastes like. If you haven't eaten it, you wouldn't know; but ourselves, we've eaten it and I like it.

People say all the Indians did eat was dried fish and things like that, but it wasn't so. To my own idea we had so much variety all the year round that could be dried and kept for the winter. Berries, blueberries, blue huckleberries and red huckleberries could be dried. Salmonberries could be dried, and we dried seaweed.

Where mother came from was Mackenzie Sound, and we used to go, after the eulachon work was over, and take the seaweed and work on it for pretty near a month and dry it. It's dark brown colour. Well, we pull it off the rock. It's a lot of work but it's worth it, because we used to trade with a lot of people that came down from the interior. They'd trade with us with their soapberries, because we don't get soapberries down here and we love them, too.

The seaweed itself, we cook it when we first get it, and it does get green. Most of it was barbecued before it was smoked. Like the deer meat and the clams, you put it on sticks, about so long, then you put it by the fire and barbecued it first before you smoked it. Delicious. After it is smoked, it has its own salt flavour to it, you notice yourself. Whatever you get out of the sea seems quite salty. I guess that's where

*Probably Westcoast (Nootka) Indians, with halibut drying on poles, 1902.
Photograph by Charles S. Sely, courtesy British Columbia Provincial
Museum, Ethnology Division / PN–4740*

they got their salt from. I don't ever remember hearing of them
getting salt anywhere else. Just the sea itself.

When the seaweed was ready to get, each family went out and got
it. When the clams were ready to get, they all knew when they were
ready and they went and got them. So pretty well everybody in the
village went after it. And if they didn't, they might have got something else they like. They might have got more dried berries and then
they'd trade with you if you had seaweed. They had boxes when I was
quite small. I remember it well, but later on they had barrels and then
they started, of course, canning and bottling things like you white
people do now. 'Course it's frozen now. But it was dried that I
remember as a child. It was all dried.

[The house] was just plain cedar boards, you know, maybe thick, twice as thick as my hand. I guess you've seen pictures of them, but they were that thick, and no insulation of any sort. I guess that's why young people of today have so many colds, because everything is insulated. But we were always more or less used to this cold. It didn't affect us. I think we were healthier for it. I don't remember until I started going to school that I ever got cold as a child. We didn't have these horrible colds that we got when we got into this Home. And did we ever get it!

According to your family legends, you had either a crow or a thunderbird or an eagle and then maybe you might have totem poles on each side of the door outside. The eagle isn't really a class, as you mean. The eagle is a standing among the Indians. I'm not an eagle; my sister is an eagle. She was born in the family; the oldest girl in the family is an eagle or the oldest boy is an eagle. She was the oldest in the family, so she became an eagle as soon as she got old enough. It's in certain families. Not all families have it. It's hers, anyway, but they do have ceremonial things that they go through, like she has to have a name given to her, her eagle name. And they give a potlatch, and she becomes an eagle. She's the second eagle from Kingcome. Our cousin from Kingcome is the first. But I'm not an eagle. I'm not entitled to it unless she wants to pass it to me, but she'd pass it on to her oldest child, now. And the oldest child passes it on to his. That's the way it works, and not everybody becomes an eagle.

When the white people come, they all started painting their family crests and stuff. As far as crests go, well, we have so much of it. As I said, my dad was from Port Rupert as well as from Gilford Island, as well as Kingcome, and he had so many in the family. I guess around the time when the white people first come there, he was in that tribe that was so respected or so high class that his great-great-grandfather went from village to village and he could choose any woman he wanted, chiefs' daughters. And he could say, "Well, I want her," and you couldn't refuse him. Didn't matter whether he had twenty wives, or whatever the case may be; that was the custom. So that's why we've got so many relatives all up and down the coast.

You have a back door as well as a front door — there's a front double door. Say our people want, or one of the family is going to give, an Indian dance or a potlatch; they used these two doors and they opened it every time when each one comes in. Well, that's like the society people among the whites. You announce who comes in each time they come in. [The back door] is for the dancers that come. They use that to bring in their costumes and their masks and stuff. That's what that's for.

[There was] very little light, as I say. It wasn't tight, you could see, because the opening would be about half the width of this room right now, and it was never covered. We never noticed the rain or anything like that. If it snowed, I don't quite remember, but the fires must have been going most of the time, because I know there's quite a bit of

Masked Kwakiutl dancers, circa 1914. Photograph by Edward S. Curtis. Courtesy Provincial Archives of British Columbia / 74499

snow up at Kingcome. You get about six or seven feet of snow every winter, and you get snow for three or four months up there.

CHIEF WILLIAM MATTHEWS: You see, each tribe has a crest they belong to. The raven clan, raven crest, has several subcrests. They have the grizzly bear and the shark. And the eagle, my tribe, they have one subcrest. We're eagles and then we have the beaver. The beaver was inside this big building here, about eight feet long — the image of the beaver. He had a big stick up out of the ground in his mouth and all kinds of decorations on him. That's the only one I know. See, the prominent crests are raven and eagle, and then there are other subcrests. But the mainland people, they've got several crests. Some are wolves and things like that. But on this island these two crests are the prominent crests, the eagle and raven. And we had four eagle tribes on this island, prominent tribes, and five raven tribes on this island; nine tribes altogether. They were all related by marriages, you see, because they have to marry across.

My father's name, I don't adopt his name according to our custom; but I adopt my uncle's name who is eagle, because I am going to be his successor.

Of course, they intermarry with other tribes. I'm an eagle. I'm not supposed to marry an eagle woman. Marry raven woman. And then a raven man is not supposed to marry a raven woman, he must marry an eagle woman across. And then my children don't claim my property. My sister's son who is eagle, you see, is my successor; and of course, my wife's raven, and her children are raven. They've got their own uncle to succeed. So they couldn't cross the line.

If I want my children to be recognized among the high-class people, I raise a totem pole; and their crest is on that, my children's. And then from that day on other tribes will recognize my children. Even if I pass away, my children are part, and that's the guarantee of the totem pole. Then another totem pole represents a story, the whole history. Then another totem pole represents a memorial, you know, and so on. Since they couldn't record language in writing, that's the nearest thing, that carving of totem poles. . . .

[When a pole was raised] all the guests and the hosts dressed up in their regalia, the best they got, and they sang, too, you know; they had different songs for different things. They made a big event of it, you know. So they weren't playing, they meant business, because this thing that they put up will be given lots more honour in the years to come. His children will be honoured, and his successors will be recognized and invited to different places.

Now, if I put up a totem pole or any big event, I invite all the chiefs, honourable people. I give them goods and all, blankets and clothing, even firearms. And one man said it was an investment, just like you put your money in the bank. They said in the years to come, many years to come, these chiefs, each one of them, when they do anything that's important, they will invite me. And what I contributed is coming back from each chief. They put away things like you put in the bank. All your life, you know, you get the result, and your children are recognized, your nephews. So that wasn't done just to build themselves up. All those things are done for some purpose.

Before I was born, a missionary from England came here on a sailing ship right round Cape Horn: Archdeacon Collison, him and his wife and his children, before I was born, fully one hundred years ago. And when he landed here, they were still raising these totem poles, and he objected to that. When they spent so much property on that thing, he took it for granted that they were worshipping those images and things. So he didn't favour it. He said they shouldn't do it any more. You waste too much property on that thing, giving things away, valuable things away.

Of course, our people took that religion, Christianity, very seriously, and from that day on they start to cut them down. And I saw two cut down. And when they chopped it down, they made a big event of it. The last two that was here, they cut down. Of course, a few remained that they sold out to the American side. I don't know where the others went, especially that beaver that was inside here. It wasn't easy for them. No. It was hard for them to do away with that thing which they value so much, which represented so many things.

When the missionary didn't want it, 'course they had to comply with him. Oh, my people took this religion very seriously, you know. Today they don't care. The church is empty. Of course, they were civilized then. So many other denominations, other organizations, came in here, you know. And a lot of our people are in the habit of trying something new. They're human; they'll go follow you if you organize something here, something new. They're human.

CHIEF SOLOMON WILSON: Each different village has their own story, their own different family crests, and nobody else can touch that crest. A raven can't wear eagle, and eagle can't wear raven. If you belong to the finback clan, nobody else can wear it, outside. If somebody tries it, lots of goods change hands. That's a thing that the white people call potlatch. Potlatch means to *give* to somebody. And now, missionaries come around and say this potlatch was no good and all that; but when it comes right down to their thing, when they ask for donations, they say give until it hurts, and yet it's the same thing. Potlatch and give is just the same.

MRS. RALPH HALL: They would do all their work in the summertime, prepare for the winter; and in the winter they would find places where they could set up camp sheltered from the north wind, and that's where they would spend the winter. In the evenings the men would tell stories around the campfire, and if the food got short, the men would go out and go hunting for food. That's how they spent the winter. They weren't exactly roaming. They all kept together for safety, because they were always raided from the other villages. It was mostly the Chilcotins and the Beaver Indians from the north who raided the village. Some of our language is spoken down in the Quesnel area. They took women and children captives, and they brought them down. They were very warlike.

Each family brought up their own family and taught them to do the right things. The head men, of course, advised the people on how to behave, and if they didn't do things right, they would tell them they shouldn't do this.

They knew that there was a Supreme Being in the old days, even though they were not Christians. They didn't say he was the Creator. There was a Being that they knew, and they said this: "One is watching you and listening to you if you don't talk right and don't do things right. This Being is watching you." Yes, this Being is supposed to be all-powerful.

They brought their children up to do everything. They showed them how to hunt and fish and get along. They had to rely on themselves for survival and they taught their children.

The Meeting of Captain Cook and Chief Maquinna

Edited by Barbara S. Efrat and W. J. Langlois

The following narratives have been passed down from one generation to another through oral tradition. Within a nonliterate society, oral traditions relating to history may be passed down with only minimal changes in content. The society may, as is the case with the native Indians of this area, rely upon the memory of one or more elders to know the history of the tribe and to teach it carefully to subsequent generations. It has been documented that oral traditions, though modified slightly in the transmission, can be a sophisticated means of recording history.

Due to the impact of western society on the native Indians of British Columbia, the oral traditions of the Indians have suffered a decline. Only recently, after decades of suppression by western society, has there been an attempt by this same western society to understand and help preserve these traditions. Today many of these traditions have been forgotten and others altered by the influence of written accounts of history.

Interested readers might find it valuable to compare some of the following accounts with the published journals of Capt. James Cook.

MRS. WINIFRED DAVID: My husband wasn't all Clayoquot. One of his grandparents, his grandmother, was part Nootka, and that's how come she knew this story about when Captain Cook first landed in Nootka Sound. The Indians didn't know what on earth it was when his ship came into the harbour. They didn't know what on earth it was. So the chief, Chief Maquinna, he sent out his warriors. He had warriors, you know. He sent them out in a couple of canoes to see what it was.

So they went out to the ship and they thought it was a fish come alive into people. They were taking a good look at those white people on the deck there. One white man had a real hooked nose, you know. And one of the men was saying to this other guy, "See, see . . . he must have been a dog salmon, that guy there, he's got a hooked nose." The other guy was looking at him, and a man came out of the galley and he was a hunchback, and the other one said, "Yes! We're right, we're right. Those people, they must have been fish. They've come alive into people. Look at that one, he's a humpback. He's a humpback!" They call it *ča•p̓i*, they're humpback fish. So they went ashore and they told the big chief: "You know what we saw? They've got white skin. But we're pretty sure that those people on the floating thing there, that they must have been fish. But they've come here as people."

And they couldn't understand each other, you know. They didn't know what those white men were saying and they were talking Indian too. So the chief told them to go out there again and see, you know, try to understand what those people wanted and what they were after. And they went out again, and Captain Cook, he must have told his crew to give those Indians some biscuits, pilot biscuits, thick white pilot biscuits. So they gave them pilot biscuits, and they started saying among themselves that they're friendly. Those people up there are friendly. We should be nice to them. And they started talking Indian and they told them to go around the sound, you know. They started making signs and they were talking Indian and they were saying *nu·tka·ʔičim nu·tka·ʔičim*, they were saying. That means, you go around the harbour. So Captain Cook said, "Oh, they're telling us the name of this place is Nootka." That's how Nootka got its name. Because those Indians were saying *nu·tka·ʔičim nu·tka·ʔičim*, they were saying. They were telling them to go around the harbour. So ever since that, it's been called Nootka. But the Indian name is altogether different. Yeah. It's Yuquot, that Indian village. So it's called Nootka now, and whole of the west coast [of Vancouver Island], we're all Nootka Indians now.

PETER WEBSTER: Nootka? That's a new word thought of when the explorers tried to explore *muwačath*, Friendly Cove. We say they explored North America or Vancouver Island. But they didn't. They were led into a shelter, these ships. They got stuck. They were anchored out in the open Pacific, and a bunch of Indian people took off with a whaling canoe, maybe a dozen men, and they directed these ships that couldn't get in, 'cause they didn't know, they were told to come around that point, *nutkšiʔa· nutkšiʔa· nutkšiʔa·*, where the lighthouses stand today. And maybe the *mamatńi* [white man] standing at the railing of the ship thought, ah, that must be Nootka, Nootka, although what they were told was to come around that point and get into the harbour. So that's when that word Nootka came in. And I don't agree with that word, because, you know, it's not right. And we're called Nootkans from Port Renfrew to Kyuquot.

GILLETTE CHIPPS: I am going to tell you about when the first white man appeared in Nootka Sound. The Indians were dancing around the island — they called the schooner an island. They said there's an island, because big trees on it. Big trees on it. They say Indian doctors go out there singing a song, find out, try to find out what it is. Rattling their rattles around the schooner, go around, all see a lot of white men standing aside, goes on the other side, sees all kinds of white man, too. All different kind of faces. Pale face white man, they said it was the dog salmon; and oh, that's a spring salmon, I think they said was a Spanish, dark colour. Maybe it was the same men on the other side when they go around the other side, the same person but different places.

Chief Maquinna of the Nootka Indians in 1778. Engraving by John Webber, courtesy Provincial Archives of British Columbia / 7931

That is what I think myself. So anyway, they seen lots of cohoes aboard that boat. Red-faced men, big nose, and so they said it was coho. That was when the first white man appeared in Nootka Sound in the schooner.

They invited Captain Cook and his engineer and his cook, and I think it was two sailors, with them to go ashore, 'cause the chief, Chief Maquinna, called him in. Captain Cook said all right. They got in the big house, Maquinna's house, big smokehouse. It was a big one. A lot of people go in there, and they start dancing and eating.

They started dancing in the smokehouse. A lot of people stayed throughout the day towards the morning. Mate Tom was going to sleep, half-awake during the dancing in the smokehouse. Don't know what to do. Can't get the man out, 'cause Captain Cook says, wait, wait, it's not finished yet. He was right. Got to wait until he is finished. So they dance all night into the morning until they finished. From all parts of the inlet all chiefs got to finish singing. Anyway, I guess they had a good time. Captain Cook sort of wake his mate; he was a blacksmith, Tom. Yes, he was a blacksmith on the schooner. That's what he was.

PETER WEBSTER: I wouldn't say the first ship, but I do know that it was seen southeast side of Estevan Point. This Hesquiat seen something strange out in the open Pacific, looks like house poles out there. They went out in their canoe to see what it was. They saw these guywires for each mast. The blocks look like skulls. Us old people would say an Indian word that means "skull of a dead human," just the bones. And this is what they thought it was, dead people that was aboard that ship. And then the mast, yes, the mast; somebody composed a song right away while they were still on the ocean.

The song says: "I got my walls of a house floating on the water." Since those ships were found floating on open Pacific, we started calling the white people *mamatni,* regardless of what nationality, even the white people that have never been on the water. In Europe I'd still call them *mamatni.* But *mamatni* means that you are living on the water and floating around, you have no land.

Forming Tender Ties:
Fur Trader Frederick Thornberg

Edited by Bob Bossin

The letters and writings of Frederick Christian Thornberg were bequeathed to his youngest son, who passed them on to Les Hammer of Port Alberni. Mr. Hammer undertook the lengthy task of typing the trader's voluminous handwritten notes. He then gave the typescript to Thornberg's granddaughter, Flora Leavitt. We are indebted to Mr. Hammer and Mrs. Leavitt for the preservation of these remarkable documents.

I am Frederick Christian Thornberg, born in Stege on Moen Island, Denmark, on the 31st December 1841, midnight, half past 11 o'clock, half hour more would be the new year.

At 17 years of age I was ordinary Seaman on board a Danish Bark calet the Thye. A few days out of Egypt a heavy gale struck us and we were trowen on our beam ends. All three masts crashet overboard. At break of day, a brig paset close by us and seen Our fix and she hove to.

A few days after this, this Brig brought us in to the Isle of Malta. There I soon had a chance to ship in an English craft. I could talk as good English then as I do now when I writes this, because I had a good Education. But I have bean for so many years trading with Indians and having to talk their Languits that I forget.

I arrivet in Esquimalth harbour, Vancouver Island, 22 February 1862. . . .

In the beginning of the month of June 1867 I marriet, Indian facion, a native Woman, Cicely Horthylia. We had one child live. Second Child was O.K. but orders came to have Children vacinadet and she got sick and died. Third Child was still born in Victoria. My wife, Horthylia, died in 1883. I was at that time just off the West Coast, Vancouver Island, British Columbia.

I Fred Thornberg took charge of Clayoquot Station in 1874 buying furs, Seals and Dogfish Oil, the chief trade. I traded through a hole in the End of the Building. It was two feet high and about a foot 6 inches wide and two Indians could just stand and look in with their elbows and breasts leaning on the bottom part of the hole. A small counter was just inside the hole. On the outside was a small veranda so that the Indian would be out of the rain when he came to trade. I could not talk the Indian dialect and very few of the Indians understood the Hudson Bay company trade giberits called Chenook — but I soon learnet to talk the Indian Dialect. I had great help from a middle aget Indian name Gwiar.

One day I wanted to make a better and stronger fence around my small yard and garden, so I askt Gwiar if he would make me some strong 5 feet cedar pickets. He said he had to goe up the Inlet to a small Lake where there was good Cedar Trees. Two days after, he came back. I went over to his shack and he lay in bed and he looket very bad. I askt him if I could doe any thing for him. He replyet no, the medicine you have will doe me no good. Up in that Lake in the Eavening I seen a

Jhe-haa. That means an Indian Devil and if anyone sees him it is a very bad sign. Gwiar was positive that he would die very soon. In three Days he was death. No Indian came over from the Clayoquot tribe to do as all West Coast Indians done — hoist the death up in a tree, because Gwiar had bean the Father of Tweens. His boddy was just rolet up in the blankets and mats on which he died and they put it in a canoe and took it to the other side of the Island and there was there an overhanging rock that partly formet a small cove close to the beatch and lots of underbrush growen there and it hidet this cave and they laid the death Gwiar there.

I forgot the year, but it was before 1880, some of the Nootka Indians had bean to Seattle in a large Canoe and coming back one of the Indians brought the small pox with him. 90 died in Nootka Sound of the pestilence. I heard report from the Clayoquot Indians that the Nootka Indians had threaten to kill all white men that was on the West Coast then and there was only three of us. The Nootka and Hesquiat Indians had said that we white men (only 3) had put small pox in Bottles with water and pouret some water in to theire rivers and drinking water so that all the Indians would die and then we the white men would have all the Land on the West Coast. Indians on the West Coast were very superstitious and if one of those Witch Doctors startet in Lying Hateret against the white race, then every Indian — in those early years the 70 to 80-ties — would believe what this Witch Doctor said. Indians today, 1913, is not much better, but will denie it, if anyone ask them.

In February 1885, I Frederick Thornberg took charge of Ahousat small trading store. I did not like to live alone, so I lookt around for a Wife. There was one of the unmarriet Indian Women callet Lucy.

I had seen this woman a few times in Clayoquot. She had come there with her Father, Ha-a-pes, a very old man, and she helped him to pack up to the Oil Shed. I askt her and him if it was true what I had been told that this old man's wife had left the old man and livet with another man.

Yes, the old Man replyet, my own son Grutlass thrashed his owen Mother. The old man was near crying.

Then Lucy told me why. Grutlass' mother-in-law died but the husband was alive and he wanted to have Grutlass' Mother. The old Woman said no, she would not doe that. Then Grutlass' Wife threatened to leave Grutlass unless his Mother left Ha-a-pes and went to live with her Father. So Grutlass gave his mother a pounding with his Fist until she gave in and done it.

When the Rev. Father Braband [Augustus Joseph Brabant] came there to stay for a month to teatch the Indians Christianity someone soon told him about this. So he got some Indians to help him and he brought this old Woman before him and some of the Indians held her fast and with a sharp pair of scissors the Priest cut all her haire off her head, the same way as the West Coast Indians uset to doe when any of their relatives dies. That was real punishment bothe for the old Woman and the others that was to blame for it.

In April 1885 I marriet Indian facion Lucy Ha-a-pes. She had two large scars right on the top of her Head. No haire growed there but she tried her best to hide it when combing her hair or tying it. This is how she got them. Her boss, the brother Grutlass, had a little son and he took a cold. Grutlass at oncet consulted with the Witch Doctor, Thus-kure. After feeling the Boys stomack and singing over it, Thus-kure said the little Boy would die, unless he doctoret it good and strong. But he would doctor the Boy only for a certain fee. He wanted Lucy for his Slave and concubine. Grutlass was quite willing, but Lucy said No and posetive No and she would sooner die than have anything to doe with this Witch Doctor. One day, the little Boy cryet very much and Grutlass got afraid. He lookt around for his Sister Lucy and he seen her down by the beatch at pretty low water. Going down to the Beatch on his way he picket up a large hardwood wedge. When he got down to his Sister Lucy, he commandet her to goe at ones to the House of the Witch Doctor. She refuset. He then struck her across the head with this wedge twice and she went down like a log and lay still and Grutlass never gave a look at his Vickteam, but at ones turnet off and went up to his house and left his Sister for Dead on the Beatch. Those that seen what Grutlass had done was afraid to go near her on account of this Witch Doctor, and if no one had goen to pick her up and carry the boddy away from where it lay, the tide coming in would have completely coveret her Boddy and she would have been drownet, even if she was not really dead, only stunet. But old Chief Maquinna seen from his place Grutlass and his sister Lucy on the beatch and her falling and Grutlass leaving her there. So he went along the beatch and when he came up to this young woman she lay as if dead and the blood was running out of her head and soaking in to the sand. After inspecting her better, he thought that there was still plenty of life in her, because he could feal on her head that the skull was not crushet. So he picket her up and carriet her to his house and shut his dore and with the help of his wife they done for this Lucy the best they know how and she got at last out of her stubbor and in time she got allright and the two wounds healet up, and I Fred Thornberg seen them because she later on was my wife and the Mother of five of my Children.

She died April 20, 1901, poisoned by eating small Mussels. I was too late to save her.

NOW YOU ARE MY BROTHER: EARLY MISSIONARIES

*T*he efforts of the early missionaries to Christianize the Indian peoples of British Columbia met with qualified success. While a large percentage of the Indians found something to attract them in the Christian message, many appear to have resisted missionary attempts to completely substitute European religion for their Indian culture. The continued presence of the medicine men and the resurgence of Indian cultural activities in recent years are witness to this resistance. The relationship between the churches and the Indians, however, remains. Missionaries still work throughout the province, continuing the historical process begun in 1858. But there are significant differences. The attitudes of the missionaries have changed. As one put it, "I go to visit people, not push religion on them"; another points out that although in the past missionaries used to be "tin gods on pedestals," that has now changed.

It is easy to condemn the ethnocentricity of the early missionaries that was responsible to a large extent for the decline of Indian languages and culture. Even today's missionaries have sometimes felt responsible for what was done in the past. But recent writings reveal that the Indian peoples were capable of sound judgement and discernment with regard to the offerings of white civilization and were not merely helpless victims falling before a conquering society.

— Margaret Whitehead

The "Romantic" Missionary: Robert Tomlinson

Edited by Margaret Whitehead

Because of historical interest in William Duncan, other Church Missionary Society missionaries have received scant attention, even though their lives were equally interesting, informative and, in the case of Robert Tomlinson's at least, far more romantic. He followed in the footsteps of his father, who was a disinherited eldest son to whom religion meant more than money; he was an impetuous lover who married into Victorian high society; he was a medical intern who provided the only white medical services in hundreds of square miles, and he was a staunch evangelical who, in support of his friend, gave up the income from the Church Missionary Society that provided for himself and his family.

As might be expected, the picture of Tomlinson that emerges from interviews with members of his family is one of a man, if not of heroic proportions, at least of exceptional qualities. Yet, to one of his contemporaries, Bishop George Hills, Tomlinson was a man "full of Irish fanaticism . . . very impetuous and ignorant of the courtesies of civilized society." It cannot be denied, however, that regardless of the bias of his family, Robert Tomlinson's life was always interesting and colourful, and epitomized the romantic aspect of frontier life.

AGNES "KATHY" JOHNSON (Robert Tomlinson's granddaughter): My grandfather's grandfather was a well-to-do man in Ireland. He was a Catholic, a very strong Catholic. He had a lot of land and property, and money too. My grandfather's father was his oldest son and when he was young he became converted to the Protestant way of religion. His father objected and he said, "If you turn Protestant, you will be disinherited." So he turned Protestant and he became an Anglican rector in Catholic Ireland. When my grandfather was young, there were seven boys in the family, and of course, his father being an Anglican minister in a Catholic country, they were pretty hard up.

The mother — my grandfather's mother — had tuberculosis. 'Course they didn't know too much about it in those days. My grandfather said he was going to study medicine so he could learn to find out what caused it and how to cure it. So they said, "We can't afford to send you to college." He said, "If you can't afford to send me to college, I'll get to college some other way."

Robert Tomlinson worked his way through medical training by working initially as a livery boy and later as a tutor to other students. The young Irish boy's interest in tuberculosis resulted in an unexpected diversion from his MD program. When he was still an intern, his father received information from the Church Missionary Society that William Duncan needed a doctor, as many of the Indians in British

Robert Tomlinson, missionary to the Nass and Skeena river areas, sometime in the 1870s. Courtesy Provincial Archives of British Columbia / 41743

Columbia were dying of tuberculosis. Robert Tomlinson looked upon this as a call from God and, leaving his internship incomplete, sailed for the Pacific Northwest, bringing whatever knowledge he had gained to do what he could to help the people.

KATHY JOHNSON: When my grandfather came over from Ireland, he had to stop in Victoria to wait for Mr. Duncan to come down and get him. And, of course, it was in the local paper that he had come to come up north. My grandmother's uncle was the archbishop [Archdeacon Woods] down there and they invited him to stay at their house. My grandmother was staying there; she was teaching school in a ladies' school for children in Victoria. They got to know each other and they liked each other, and she wanted to come with him.

MRS. ROBERT TOMLINSON, JR. (Robert Tomlinson's daughter-in-law): My father-in-law was going off in the north as missionary and he thought it would be a very good thing to have a wife. So he went to Mr. Woods — Richard Woods was his name — and he asks for the hand of his daughter. She was then sixteen. I guess Grandpa Woods thought he had gone nuts altogether. He said, "Go up there and find out what you're takin' a woman to, and if in a year you're of the same mind, you come down and my answer might be quite different. But you're not takin' Alice up there at this stage of the game." So he had to be content with that.

After consulting with Duncan, Robert Tomlinson went to begin his missionary work on the Nass River, where he founded a mission at Kincolith. The following spring, Tomlinson returned to Victoria to marry Alice.

MRS. ROBERT TOMLINSON, JR.: In a year he came down with five Indians. You know, the Indians had dugout canoes — they were Nishga' Indians — but there was not ribs in them. My father-in-law thought in order to bring his wife up he sure was going to have a canoe that was safe from the elements if they got into a storm. So he made ribs and then he made thwarts. Before that the Indians never had thwarts. So he fixed seats in the canoe. The Indians thought that was an awfully good idea, so after that, when they fixed their canoes, they put seats in. Before that they sort of knelt down and paddled.

    Well, he was all ready to take her back the next day, because he didn't want these Indians lying around — what would he do with them? Grandfather Woods said, "No. The ladies want to make a wedding, and it'll take at least two or three weeks before her dress is made." So he set the Indians to work cutting out a road. The place where they lived was called Garbally, which is "house on a hill," and the road still is called Garbally Road [in Victoria]. They cut that road so that grandfather could bring his bride back to the house in the carriage.

Robert and Alice Tomlinson were married at St. John's Anglican Church, and according to Mrs. Robert Tomlinson, Jr., Dean Cridge, a close friend of the family, "walked all the way down to the end of the arm to kiss the bride good-by." During the nine years the Tomlinsons spent at Kincolith, there were outbreaks of war between the Haidas and the Tsimshians, and on several occasions a gunboat was sent from Victoria to the Nass to bring the Tomlinsons out, but they refused to leave. Their confidence that they would not be harmed was based, at least in part, on a strange coincidence.

ROBERT TOMLINSON, JR. (Robert Tomlinson's son): When Father was an intern in the hospital in the old country, he was always losing his laundry when it was sent out to the wash. So he decided to get some indian ink and mark all his laundry with his name. After he got through with that he still had a lot of ink left over, so he thought — going out as a missionary — he might as well have the dove as his crest. And so he made a drawing of a dove on his handkerchiefs and on his linen, and of course being in indian ink, that dove was pretty well black.

    When he was in the mission at Kincolith, he had two boys staying with him at the mission house. He gave them free room and lodging, and in return they were to look after everything, washing included.

The boy at the washtub saw the picture of what he thought was a raven and he came to the conclusion that the missionary came from the same crest as he did.

So he calls to his brother, and away the two go down as hard as they could to the other end of the town to tell the relatives that the *shemar-get* — as they called the missionary — was one of their relatives. He belonged to the same crest, the raven. There are four crests, or clans, somewhat similar to fraternal orders, amongst the Indians.

So they all traipsed back, and with their signs and the little English they had learnt, and the little Indian father had learnt, between the lot of 'em he understood they wanted to know: Was that his crest? Yes, that was his crest. So they had a feast, and it was announced that the *shemarget* belonged to the raven clan, and so the raven clan had always to look after him. That stood him in good stead many a time later on. Saved his life.

When he brought a bride, of course the bride had to belong to some other crest, because nobody could marry anybody in their own crest, so she was adopted by the eagles. And all the children belonged to the mother's crest so, therefore, when I was born, I became an eagle. That stood me in good stead many and many a time in later years, being an eagle.

MRS. ROBERT TOMLINSON, JR.: When I went up there, I couldn't marry an eagle — he was flying too high for me! So the finback whale adopted me. So I was wallowing in the water. Uncle John — I called him — made a potlatch, or feast. He adopted me into the finback whale crest and gave me two bracelets, which I prize very much.

Although Tomlinson's aim was to develop a second Metlakatla at Kincolith — an aim that was partially fulfilled — his medical training and the lack of any other medical man forced him into the role of itinerant doctor. This meant that he was away every year for several months at a time. He travelled to Metlakatla, throughout the Nass and Skeena river areas, and even, on occasion, as far as Wrangell, Alaska. Alice Tomlinson had to adjust to a very different life as a missionary's wife.

MRS. ROBERT TOMLINSON, JR.: She would be alone for months at a time, with nothing but the Indian women up there. They were Nishga Indians, so Robert, my husband, as a boy learned the Nishga language and could rattle it off before he could talk English, because they had girls in the house working for them, working with them so Grandma could teach the girls how to do things. She had never done much sewing herself, because they were pretty well protected. They came from Ireland and they belonged to the gentry in Ireland and moved over here. So she'd never done much housework and she'd never knitted in her life. But now she had to teach the Indians how to knit a sock.

The only way she could learn how to knit a sock was to unravel a sock that was made by machine. The heels are turned entirely different than a homemade sock. So she and my father-in-law figured out how these socks were made, and so they taught the Indians how to knit. So the Indians up the Skeena and on the Nass knit their socks with the heels the same way as the boughten socks, which comes in from the side. The homemade comes square up. And, of course, they had to make their own candles; they had to do a lot of things that she had never done in her life.

While Alice Tomlinson was adjusting to a pioneer existence, her husband was gaining Indian trust through his medical skills. His main opposition was the medicine men upon whose traditional role the missionary was intruding. Tomlinson also had to accept that the Indians would not always respond to the services he provided, as white patients might.

KATHY JOHNSON: When he went up the Nass River — one of the first trips he made up the Nass River — he stopped at a village, and they brought him a boy that was dying with TB, and he told them he could do nothing for him because he was dying. And he explained how the lungs were like bags, and that the TB had eaten holes in the lungs, and that he wouldn't live very long. When he came back to the village that he had passed through, one of the Christian natives came to meet him and told him, "Don't go into the village, because if you do, they will kill you. They think that you made the sickness because you knew all about it." He said, "I'm going anyway."

So he went, and this fellow told him, "They're going to invite you to a feast, and at the feast they're going to kill you." So he went down to the place where they were preparing the feast, and they had bearskins hanging around the walls, bearskins to sit on on the floor. And they had kind of a stupid boy — a teenager, but rather stupid — tending the fire while they were waiting for everything to cook. So he says to this boy, "What's this?" The boy said, "It's a bearskin." He said, "What's a bear?" So the boy started to tell him all about what a bear was, how it hibernated and what it ate and so on. "Well," he said, "you must have made the bear." "Oh no, I never made the bear." "Well," he said, "how do you know?" "My father told me, my uncle told me, my grandfather told me about the bear." He kept arguing with this boy that he made the bear.

Finally, the head men came in and they all backed the boy up that he never made the bear. They *all* knew about the bear. Then he turned round and told them how *his* people had told *him* about the sickness; and he wanted to know more and he went to school and he learned more about it. He'd come there to help them, but when it got too bad, he couldn't do anything. But he was going to try and help them beat the system. And the head chief took a knife out of his blanket and handed it to him by the handle and he said, "I was going to kill you, but now you are my brother."

MRS. ROBERT TOMLINSON, JR.: They had a little hospital in Kincolith, the first hospital that was built up north. The Indians brought their own blankets.

If an Indian was sick, he didn't sleep on any bed. He didn't sleep on any bed, anyway, but if he was sick he certainly wasn't going to sleep on a bed and let the bad spirits under the bed. So they brought their own blankets and Grandmother administered chloroform — there was no ether in those days — and my father-in-law operated. He operated on a man for appendicitis, just with Alice giving him chloroform. She was the only person who could help at all.

ROBERT TOMLINSON, JR.: One time he removed a bullet from an Indian, although he was ill himself. He got right out of bed and travelled from Kitwanga up to Hazelton, made the trip in one day. But he was so tired when he got up there — then the Indian was resting easily — so he thought it would be better for all concerned if he waited till he had a little sleep and tackled the job by daylight instead of lamplight. He used one of the old Hudson's Bay clay pipes, brand new one. He sterilized the pipe for a probe. The lead marked the stem of the clay pipe where the bullet was. The bone just scratched it, but the lead of the bullet marked it so he could measure it, and then he cut and extracted the bullet out of that. It was lodged in between the bones back of his, oh, in his shoulder blade, in there somewhere.

If anybody called in a medicine man while Father was treating an Indian, that was the end. He never interfered with the medicine man. If the medicine man interfered with him, well, that's where he stepped out.

It was forty-six years Father practised medicine and surgery with the Indians — not only of British Columbia, but many of the Indians from the Tlingit tribes [in Alaska] used to come over to Kincolith and be treated of bullet wounds and so forth. But for forty-six years Father treated and he never charged one single Indian for his services. I don't know whether he charged any whites or not; he may have charged some whites, but mighty few of them. But that was always considered some record, never to charge an Indian anything for medicine or service.

He used to buy his medicines and give the medicine free. He was told that the Indian department would supply him medicine. All he had to do was make out an order and send it down to the Indian department, and they'd fill the order and send it to him. There was no sense in him paying for the medicine himself when he gave his services. So he tried it when he was at Kincolith. A box of medicines came along, all right enough, and he opened up the medicine and he looked and he says, "I didn't order that and I didn't order that; I did order so and so." He had a copy of his order and he went down the list.

So he wrote and asked why they didn't fill the order as he had ordered it. Oh, the medicine he had ordered was too expensive. This was a much cheaper medicine; it was plenty good enough for the Indians. He just nailed a lid onto that box and from that day until the day of his death he never ordered another ounce of medicine from the Indian department.

Indian Memories of Mission School

Edited by Margaret Whitehead

Mary Englund was born in Lillooet, the home of her mother's people, in 1904. Her father, a French-Canadian, named her Marie Anne. Until she was about six years old, the family lived at what is now Bralorne, approximately thirty-five miles west of Lillooet, but when her father died in 1910, the family returned to the Indian reserve. An older brother and two sisters had attended and left the Indian residential school at Mission before Mary and a younger brother were taken there in 1912. The school was run by the Oblates, who had charge of the boys, while the Sisters of St. Ann had charge of the girls. Mary has strong memories of her school days; some things she remembers with pleasure, some she recalls with bitterness. Still a faithful Catholic and lay spiritual leader, she is nevertheless quite candid about her school experiences.

MARY ENGLUND: By this time [1912] we were old enough — my brother and myself — to go to the boarding school. There was no school around, so the priests used to come and collect the children to go to school, like from Fountain and Lillooet and Bridge River and all around. That was Father Rohr and Father Chirouse and all those. They'd come around once or twice a year and they'd count out the children and take stock, I guess you might as well say. And then they would say when you were ready to go to school. Your parents had to supply you with clothes such as shoes, underwears, and before that, when my older sisters and brother went to the school, they had to have blankets and sheets and everything. So mother figured since she already supplied all that, that would be there, so we didn't have to take any. So the priest said we didn't have to take any, just our clothes. But even at that our clothes were pretty skimpy.

Life was tough. It wasn't very nice, you see, because my mother was alone. My grandmother really kind of kept an eye on us, looked after us and kept us together. Because Mother had to go out and work. However, we managed to get along. There was my uncle, then there was my grandmother; you see, we all lived in the village. We each had our own house, but everybody took care of one another. If Grandmother wasn't around, my uncle, who was the chief, then he took care of us. Everybody looked after one another more or less. Of course, Mother was home a good part of the time, but there was times she had to leave us, otherwise we never got anything to eat.

Father Chirouse picked us up when the train came to Lillooet. I was really excited, because we'd never been anywhere outside of going here.and there to one reserve and another, either in a canoe or boat and on horseback. It was something really exciting to go on the train. We were left alone so many times we never had the tendency to say, "Well, I'm sorry I'm going to go away and leave my mother," because we were alone most of the time. And I couldn't understand why they were cryin'. My brother and I, we enjoyed it, you know. We enjoyed the train ride as far as that went. It was fun. It was something new. It was the old steam engines. Father Chirouse was the one that took us. He was awfully nice. I remember he talked to us and then he'd go further and get in the other seats, and we'd look over to see what he's doing. We were able to open the windows and look out to see what we were passing. It was really fascinating until we got to Squamish, and then we had to go on a boat, and by this time it was dark. After we got to Vancouver, I remember walking along the street with *big buildings* — fascinating — we couldn't understand all these big buildings. Finally, we got on another train and we finally got to Mission. And then we had to walk. I thought we'd *never* get there.

Then I had to leave my brother. I couldn't understand why I had to leave him in this other building while I went to the other building. You see, there was a big building where the boys lived, and then you went along and there was a big church, and then you went along and that's where the girls lived. These were three-storey buildings. There was the main floor and the second floor, and on the third floor we slept, all the girls slept. And I remember when I got there I couldn't figure out why I had to leave my brother . . . and I kept asking, but they said that he had to stay with the rest of the boys. I wanted to know why.

I had never seen a nun in my life. So these people, with their covered-up heads and white around, and then their black robes and black veil — how the Sisters of St. Ann dressed — I couldn't figure out why they had to wear such clothes. And I used to ask the girls, "Why's she dressed like that?" "Because she's a sister." "Well, what's a sister?" They told us we had to stay there for a whole year; well, I didn't know what a year was. That was the other problem: "When's the year going to end?"

So anyway, this one big girl — she'd been there quite a while — she took me over to this other building. Way at the back of the convent was another big building, where they did all the washing and you did your bath, and there were square wooden tubs. You heat the water and you filled it, and that's where you had to have your bath. You didn't go to bed — when you first got there — without your bath. Every girl that came in, they had to be taken to the laundry and put through the wash. And then you had to take all your clothes off and leave them there, and then they gave you other clothes to put on. Sort of a uniform. They were white blouses; they buttoned at the back, and there was a sort of a jumper with frills around the sleeves and buttoned at the back — 'course I couldn't button them, so I had to have somebody to help me — and underwears and long black stockings, and underwears down to the ankle and then the black stockings over it. Oh my! It didn't please me. I very seldom had these big long johns on — I would call them now, long underwear — and then these big black stockings on, because at home we never wore any of those things. We had little panties on down to the knees with little frills around, and I couldn't figure out these long things and then these stockings over. And then we had to have garters to hold them up. Then black shoes with little high-top laces . . . the only shoes I had were boys' lecky boots in those days and I thought, oh boy, I was dressed up. Because we at home hardly ever wore any shoes. We wore moccasins and we ran all summer barefooted. I really was uncomfortable. But they were handy when it came cold.

But oh my, was I *ever* homesick. You know, home wasn't much; in fact, the nuns didn't call it home, they called it our *camp*. And that used to hurt me. It still does when I think about it. When we'd talk about going home, they'd say, "You're not going home, you're going back to your camp." That was their impression of the reserve. Well, in a way they were right, because the homes we had in those days were made out of great big log houses. And the house we got into didn't even have a floor in it. It was just dirt floor. Then we used to have to every so often go out and chop boughs and put them on the floor to keep the dust down, until Mother was able to get some lumber and put the floor down. You know, we were raised in a hard way, so going to school and going in the convent, it was very unusual.

This one girl, she was very good to me. Apparently, she had come from the same reserve I did, but I don't ever remember her. So anyway, she was awfully good with me. She helped me in the mornings to dress. We were given a basin and a towel, toothpowder and toothbrush and a comb. That was ours. We had little squares in the washroom, and the washroom was quite a length and all window in front, so the sister could look in from the dormitory. And this great big galvanized trough with the cold water, cold taps, and in there were the basins. You filled up your basin then you went over to the counter — no hot water, all cold water — then you had to scrub your teeth in the sink, then you had to wash your basin and put it underneath the counter. You had to fold up your towel and take it with you and put it at the head of your bed. And there was squares for your comb and your toothbrush and toothpowder. So that was our gadgets.

An older girl saw to it that you were dressed. Then, of course, it took us time to put on these long stockings and high boots, and laces. And your hair had to be braided at the back and put up in a knob. You couldn't have one little hair hanging on your face. It had to be smoothed back. So she used to help me comb my hair. She'd wet my hair and comb it and braid it here and braid it there, then she'd braid it at the back and roll it up and pin it up. That was the way we were supposed to have our hair. At home we got up, washed our face, and we didn't think of combing our hair; we just took it and tied it up and that was it.

We lived a simple life, you know, and then to go into these places where we didn't know that we didn't have to talk. That was another

Indian girls leaving the church at St. Mary's Mission in Mission, B. C., circa 1913. Courtesy Mary Englund

big thing. Everything was *silent*. You lived by the bell. The bell rang, you shut up. Not another word. And here we'd keep on talking, us that were new, and we had to be shushed and shaken and what not. Then we had to go in lines, you see, one behind the other, go upstairs. No matter where you went, you were in line. You never moved until the bell rang. There was a little bell always, no matter where you went. Or one of those desk push-bells.

I never forget that night when we first went there. We were outside in the yard, and this bell rang inside. I said, "What's that for?" "Oh come on, come on. We've got to go for supper." So away we went and had supper. We got in there. "Don't talk, don't talk. No, don't talk, just get in line. No, not one word." And then we went into the dining room, and they put us in certain places, and then the grace was said. The bell rang, then you sat down. Great big long tables — there must be twenty on each table — and the benches and galvanized plates — or tin plates, as we called them — the same with saucers. And we had a fork and a spoon. There was never much of knives, because you didn't get no butter and you didn't get no meat to cut up; everything was grounded up. And green tea. We never got no milk except skim milk to put in your tea. Of course, me — I was not knowing the rules — I was talking to this girl who was with me. She told me what to do: "You don't talk before the bell rings and you don't talk after the bell rings, either." So we kept on talking;

the bell was ringing, and we were still talking, and she'd come over and shush me up.

'Course the sisters were pretty good in a way, too, you know. If they knew you were new and didn't know the rules, they'd say, "Here! You remember now, you're not supposed to talk after the bell rings?" I remember this one sister, her name was Sister "V," she'd great big eyes, you know. She was a French nun. My, she was *miserable.* She'd roll her eyes around. Gosh, we had to watch for her. This Sister "V" was a real needle in the side, and you know the Indians, they have a name for everything, and the owl always has a big eye, you know, and so this nun we all called her *chkilulek,* the owl.

You got up around five-thirty in the morning. The bell rings, and you had to get up. You had to go and wash and dress and get your hair combed and make your little — we had little cots, and the mattresses were full of straw — and you had to make your bed, make it really neat. You can't just slip-slop, everything had to be tight. If you didn't make your bed right, the nun would come along and pull all the sheets and blankets off, and you had to make it over. You had to fold up your nightgown and put it under your pillow. You had a little closet to hang your clothes in. If those weren't neat in there, you either had to kneel down somewhere in some corner or kept silent at the dining room mealtime.

After breakfast each one had their offices to go to. They called them offices, that was jobs. A certain amount of girls went to the dormitory; they had to put white spreads on the beds. A certain amount of girls went to the kitchen, a certain amount of girls stayed in the dining room and washed the dishes. See, there was fifty-one girls, and there was certain ones that swept the halls and cleaned the halls. My first job was in the classroom. I went with these two big girls to go to the classrooms; they were to clear the classroom out. There was one classroom, and we had shifts. The middle ones went to school in the morning; the big girls went to the sewing room. We had to clean the boards, clear the brushes and dust everything, dust the desks and swept the floors. . . .

Everybody went to catechism eight-thirty in the morning until nine, and then there was school. The older girls went to the sewing room and they mended socks and underwear and whatever there had to be mended, and that's where I made my first encounter with a nun, too. She would give us those long black stockings — sometimes they wore off on the heel or the toe — and you'd stick your hand in there and they'd give you a darning needle and you'd mend them, darn them, in other words. I didn't want to darn in one place because it was thin, so I just mended the hole and that was it. We had to go and show them to the sister when we had finished, and she'd stick her hands in the sock and work her finger out. If her finger went through, it was just too bad. You had to do it over again. She put her

Knitting and sewing lesson being given to native children by the Sisters of the Child Jesus at St. Joseph's Mission, Williams Lake, B. C., circa 1900. Courtesy Public Archives of Canada / C–56765

finger through my sock, and I don't know what I said to her, but she got really annoyed at me. She says, "Now stick your hand out." She had great big scissors and she hit me. I was really annoyed. I didn't cry at first, and she looked at me, and I don't know what she saw in my face, but I know she looked terrible to me. I went and sat down and I banged down. You know how you do when you get mad. She says, "Come back here. You kneel right there and finish your sock." On my knees! I didn't have no thread in my needle, so I just sat there and sucked my needle.

But later on when I got a little higher and a little older, I used to go to the sewing room in the morning, and she started teaching us how to run the machines and sew. First it was aprons — we all had to wear aprons — so she gave me this material, she cut it out — she never let us cut it out — and then she showed us where to sew, and your stitching had to be straight. So I started this zigzag. She'd make me rip it over, and I'd sit there and cry and rip, and the names I didn't call her. 'Course to myself. It never came out, because I didn't dare. I didn't trust nobody; you couldn't in a convent, you know. You'd say one thing, and this girl might go and tell Sister, and you got punished for it, so you had to say things to yourself that you didn't like.

We weren't allowed to speak our language in school. We had to speak English right from day one. I was pretty well bilingual, you might as well say. When we first moved to the reserve, we couldn't talk Indian, either. We had to learn from the kids we played with, and during this time while we were on the reserve we kept pretty well, at least I did, to our language, and we talked in Indian, too. So it didn't bother me too much, although it was kind of different, and you got mixed up. It was a difficult situation. See, they had different Indian dialects. Along the Fraser Valley they had the Stalo and the Thompson, and us here was the Chehalis. We talked differently than they did. So if we talked to them, it was all English. Even if we could talk with one another, the nuns wouldn't allow it. Of course, there was a lot of us that could talk the same language; you take from Fountain to Pavilion down to Mount Currie, we all talked the same language. When we were alone in some corner, we did talk our own language, and if the sister caught us, it was, "You talk English!" That's where a lot of girls kind of forgot their language. If you're there, stayed there a certain length of the time, you forget certain words in Indian. You couldn't explain yourself too much in Indian as you would in English. They said it was better for us to speak English, because we could learn English and read and write better if we kept our English, if we spoke English instead of talking Indian.

When the principal came over — Father Rohr, he was French — they'd sit and talk French, and we knew very well they was talking about us, all of us, and we resented that very much. They wouldn't allow us to talk Indian, but they could talk French. We used to tell them that: "How come you can talk in French in front of us, and you wouldn't allow us to talk Indian in front of you?" And, of course, they got after us for that. You weren't allowed to question. Oh yes, they weren't very nice in that respect.

Of course, all the parents thought that was great, you see, that we should talk English and be able to write, so that we'd be able to write letters when we got home, to do things for the Indian people. You were something great when you come home: "Oh, she can write now." They were kind of proud of us in a way, once you were able to write your name, your mother's name, your father's name and whoever was in the family. We were doing all right. They were proud of you then. I remember my grandmother — I don't know how old she was, but she was partly blind and she was all crippled with arthritis — she'd pat us on the head, because we can write.

We were not to tell our parents what went on in the school. That was another rule. We were not allowed to discuss what goes on in school when we go home. We never got sugar at school, no sugar in our porridge or in our tea, so when we went home, I guess this one girl was telling her parents how she never got sugar at school. When she got back to school, she was really reprimanded by the principal, Father Rohr. And he didn't go about it in a nice way. He went about it in a way very insulting, telling you what you did in your *camp* and what you told your father and mother and the tattletales. And your parents never had anything to say of what you were doing in the school, because they didn't know. I was told I was not to tell my mother of what went on. Whatever we did outside the school when we went home, if it wasn't just what it should be, we heard about it when we got back to the school. We were punished for it. If the girls that went to school with you saw you in the village with so-and-so, if they had anything against you or felt jealous of you in any way, they'd tell the sister, and you'd get reprimanded for it. But I was lucky; there was nobody else from my village, just me.

But you didn't dare rebel: whatever they said was gospel. There was two girls that got dismissed while I was there. That was a terrible thing. I don't know, sometime in September or October I think it was, they ran away from school. We were staying up quite late that evening until nine o'clock. We were having games and so on, and all at once these girls disappeared. And come line-up time to get ready to go to bed, they weren't there. Boy, that was terrible for us. We were concerned, you know. So anyway, we went to bed. We thought maybe they're just hiding downstairs somewhere. And once you go to bed, once you get up in the dormitory, there's a trap door that goes over the stairs, and that's got a great bolt that Sister puts in there. Nobody can get through there. So you were locked up there. I often think afterwards, when I got older, what would we do if the bottom part of the building got burnt? How would we get out of there? But anyway, they were brought back about a month or so later on. They were found and brought back, and their parents were notified. And they really got reprimanded. They not only got reprimanded, I remember, they went to bed one evening, and there was one big husky sister, she came up and she had a great big — you know, they used to use the razor straps for shaving? Well, she had one of those with a wooden handle on it. They laid on their stomach on the bed, and they really went to work on them. I don't know how many straps they got, but we were all crying; everybody was sniffling and crying. That strap was used on very serious occasions.

They gave you notes. Like in school you have certain notes, if it's "A" you're perfect, "B" you're not too good, "C" you're gettin' worse, and "D" you're very poor and you need reprimanding and you need the strap or something. I lost my note; this was really funny, I was working in the kitchen. I used to work in the pantry helping the sister. She was grinding up this meat to make meatballs for *their* table — they had a dining room by themselves — so I cleaned up the meat grinder. 'Course I had scraps of meat left and I came down into the kitchen. Sister was French, she could hardly talk English. There was a pot of hash on the stove for the girls, ground-up meat and potatoes and everything was in that big pot of hash, so I went and I asked her what was I to do with this handful of scraps of meat. Instead of saying "hash," she said, "Put it in your ass." And I started to laugh, and oh, she was annoyed at me. She went right away and told Sister Superior, and of course I lost my note for that. We were reprimanded because we're not to condemn the nuns because they couldn't speak very good English, and they reminded us that we weren't perfect in English, either, because we spoke Indian.

Every occasion that comes up like a principal's birthday, like Father Rohr's birthday, or he'd go away and he'd come back; and we'd have a welcoming party, and the sister would write out a speech, and you had to read that to the priest. And there was always somebody to read that big speech, you had to read this in long sheets, you know, and you had to read *every word perfect*. I read it several times, but my cousin, she was always getting chosen to read this, and you had to practise that. You had to practically memorize it in order to make a perfect recitation. Sister "V" would say, "Now, if you weren't an Indian girl you could do that perfectly well, better; a white girl, she would go over that very well, nicely."

They were always degrading us because we were Indian. We didn't come from homes, we came from *camps*, and we didn't know how to live. We ate rotten fish, so they didn't seem to be particular in what they gave us to eat. They never let us forget that we were *Indian*, and that we weren't very civilized, that we were more or less savages. The other nuns weren't too forward with their mentioning of Indians, but this particular nun, Sister "V," she looked after us in the recreation room and she looked after us in the dining room — once in a while the other nun would come and take her place — and she looked after us in the dormitory. She was constantly with us, which I think was too much of a strain for her. If they had changed places, I think it would have eased her tension a little more, and she wouldn't have been so hateful towards us.

There was a couple of sisters that really showed their affection. One was Sister Mary André. Whenever I met her in the hall, she'd put her arms around me and she really showed that she was a happy-go-lucky person. And then there was our teacher, Sister Mary Hildegard. You were privileged if you could go down town with the sisters, if they had something to do down town, to go and mail letters or go and pay bills, and you were privileged if you were chosen to go with the sister. We'd go down town, and you see, you were not to touch them, but the minute we got outside the door and out the yard, she'd hold my hand. Oh, it was really a privilege.

Most of them were pretty nice. Like our teacher, she was pretty nice, but we were told that we were expected to stand up, and if we didn't, she used to report us to Sister Superior. We were called rude if we didn't stand up whenever any of them entered. Same way if you passed them in the hall or anywhere, you're to stop and bow your head. They were really up on the pedestal. I guess it was good training in a way. I don't know. They sure put themselves somewhere where you couldn't touch them. You couldn't reach them and you had to bow to them, that's something I could never . . . it made me to a certain extent very bitter by the time I left school.

Another thing that made me very rebellious was the punishment. They used prayer to punish you. If you were late or you disobeyed in one way or another, you knelt down and you said ten Hail Marys or ten Our Fathers or something like that. Well, saying these things was against your nature. You know it wasn't a praying thing, and therefore I rebelled against it. I couldn't see the sense of using prayer as a punishment.

And going in the chapel, you couldn't look at the next person. We wore veils and we went in there with our hands folded; and even if we nudged, there's a nun watching way at the back and she saw everything that went on. You got your ears pulled or you got a slap in the face. On special occasions we wore great big veils that came down. You wore that and you had uniforms to go with that, and we thought that was great to wear a great big long veil. You were an angel or something. They were pinned in our hair and they had to stay there. But I guess it was a way of teaching you respect. You were not to look around, but there were little instances as you came in the church, because the boys sat on one side and we sat on the other. It got so the older girls, the minute you'd come in, a certain boy would cough, and of course some girl would answer. Finally, the nuns would catch on: "Who was that that did that?" And of course nobody didn't dare tell. No, you were a tattletale if you told. You were not to talk to a boy unless it was your brother. And you were not to have any way of showing any kind of signs or anything to a boy. . . .

When you went home, you missed the companionship of the others. You felt alone. Although the family was there, my brothers were there, my older brother, my uncle, my grandmother — we always had an uncle live with us, because he was blind — but you were lonely. At least I was, and children on the reserve were not of your . . . oh, they were *people* you know, but they weren't like the ones you had in the convent. So it was different. You talked to them, they were nice to you, they wanted to know what the school was all about. And we'd go swimming. Things were different, but Mother always tried to make life easier for us. She always had a garden. We'd weed the garden, and then when we got through, the horses were saddled, and we packed up lunch and we went up in the hills picking berries. We spent our holiday that way. We'd come down and then we'd get ready before we went back to school. There was washing and ironing and getting ready and bathing and hair washing. Then we'd hit the train. We never felt that we were leaving somebody to get on that train; we were anxious to be on our way. We never thought that, well, maybe we should say good-by to Mother, she'll feel bad.

She died while I was in school. But then we weren't allowed . . . once you had no parents, there was no home to go to, you weren't allowed out of the school. I wasn't allowed out, anyway. My younger brother and myself, we stayed in the school. We did have family at home, but after my mother died, we weren't allowed to go home. We weren't even allowed to go to the funeral, which hurt me very much, because I was old enough to understand. So there I was, kind of left with my two brothers to look out for. My one brother was two years younger than me, and the little one, he was just eight or nine years old.

Nursing Sisters

Edited by Margaret Whitehead

SISTER TERESA BERNARD: I was born in St. Jules de Maria, in the county of Bonaventure, Gaspé Bay, in 1914. And we were a family of eleven. I went to the country school, which was an English and French school, all the grades from one to six. That was the highest grade we could go. So I stayed in grade six from twelve to sixteen; to have a teacher certificate, I had to wait till I be sixteen. At sixteen, I went to Carleton — they had a normal school — where I was there for one year, and after I took the government test for elementary school diploma.

I'd always had the idea of being a sister. I didn't work for it, you know. I went out and I had a boy friend and all this, but it always bothered me a little bit. So I had in my mind I was just going to try — and come back! So I packed my things and I said, "Now, you don't touch my things, because I'll be back." I entered the Sisters of Christ the King, because my older sister had already entered. So I'd no preference but the fact that she was there. I said, "It doesn't matter where." I was just willing to try. It still bothered me a lot when I was a novice. I was very independent and I didn't care, because I still had home in my mind. When I made my first profession, all these bad ideas and everything went away.

They just asked me, "Would you like to take a nursing course?" In those days we always say yes. So I went to Montreal and I trained at Hôtel Dieu. I enjoyed my course. The order was just started in 1928, and in maybe '36 they send two or three sisters to Japan. They were the first ones. They were teaching, and the war broke out, and we had no communication. My own sister, she left for Japan. We had four sisters teaching at Nelson, the concentration camp for Japanese. They closed that in '44, so they sent back all those Japanese east. In those days Mother Foundress could not send any in mission fields in

Japan. You couldn't go anywhere. During that time, the Indian missions started. So two sisters from Nelson and I and another sister from Montreal, we all met here in Vancouver. Bishop Duke wanted some sisters for Anaham. But I had, you know, the false impression that everybody had, the Indians are people that you should not mix with; Indians are people that you should not trust too much — although my own town was near a reserve, and my father was very friendly with them.

So we got to Anaham, and there was not an Indian on the reserve. They were nomad. They would all disappear in those days. There was not a soul on the reserve. There was just a little house full of flies. There was a tiny little house belonging to the Oblate father, and the Indians had built another little log house on the side. This house was only three rooms. In front there was like a parlour, and two little rooms in the back. It was too small. And the flies! You were opening your mouth, and the flies would get in before you put in the meat.

And we went in the church and we seen . . . oh, we were not used to that, you know. The bishop had been there in June, and see, his throne was still there, and they had put decoration at Christmas all over the church. It was all hanging down all over. And after, they never made the cleaning, and there was cobwebs everywhere. We didn't understand the Indians' customs, because we shouldn't have touch that. It's true. We went in the church and we clean up. We took everything down, which we shouldn't have done. Now, I see all the mistakes we made. Reminds me of that Irish song, "The English came to show us their ways." Well, it's the same. We went there with the idea of show them how to live and show our ways.

We arrived there about August twenty-seven — the end of August — school was supposed to start the beginning of September. Sister Marie des Anges and Sister Stanislaus, the two of them were teachers. There was nobody there. Nothing was built, and September was going on. The week after, they all came down from the meadow, from nowhere. They were all camping; there was hardly any houses. They all had tent and they tented around us. It was just like a village of little tents.

And after, they started. And the way they work, you know, they work five, six, would work together, and the others were all sitting there and talking together. They will work for maybe an hour or so and they will exchange. But they just had five hundred dollars for that, that was just the material. They were not getting very much in those days from the government. So they put the walls and they put the windows and they put the roof, but the inside, it wasn't finished. So when the five hundred dollars was over, they all went home. You know, it's cold, it's forty below out there. So we said, "We can't stay like this." There was a saw, there was some paper, so we started to put paper on some walls — building paper — when we were all

The Sisters of Christ the King building a hen house at their home on Anaham reserve, circa 1945. Courtesy Sister Teresa Bernard

finished that, they got some kind of beaver board or something like this, and Father Bede from Williams Lake he came up and he covered up all the inside of that building.

After we had these quarters, we slept there; so the two little rooms we didn't need it, so we said we will make a chapel with one. We had no tabernacle or no altar, so I said, "I'll have to make one." First time it was all crooked, you know, but after I could saw very well. So that was my first masterpiece!

There was two classrooms, those who had already been to school — they were about twelve, I think — and in the other one there were maybe forty — they had never been to school. They were all different ages. So this was okay, and we went on, but these people were not used to stay on the reserve. They had meadows far away and they had cattle and they used to hunt. When they used to go, they used to bring the whole family. So they hadn't thought about this. They didn't know when they had asked for a school that they would have to stay down and look after the children, or keep the children home, down for school. But Christmastime came, and the snow, but they said they had to go and feed their cattle. So after Christmas we had maybe six in the school.

After a while, little by little, they stayed longer on the reserve, and they are just a few families that kept their children from an education. Some had had an education before, but some of those didn't. They couldn't see the reason to have an education. Shoot a moose, shoot a squirrel, you don't need to know to read and write. They didn't believe in it. Said it was just wasted time for them.

Bishop Duke always had in his mind to start an Indian community, and we got a little girl — Sister James from Nanaimo, I think; she was only a postulant. He wanted to have a native community, so in '45 the bishop ask Father Sutherland to go in all the residential schools — and there were lots in those days — and make propaganda. So in that year a whole bunch of girls came — five or six — but they didn't stay very long. Some came from Mission, one from Pavilion, another was from North Van. Andy Paull, his girl, well, his daughter, didn't stay very long. Of that group, two stayed: one named Sacred Heart, and the other was named Incarnation. They took the habit.

They stayed maybe a year, two years; one after the other, they left. We had another one from Smithers. That one made profession. Bishop Duke send her on a propaganda tour to pick up some other girls, and she went to some place — in Le Pas, Manitoba, they have a Métis congregation — so she, instead of finding him some recruits, she joined their community. Bishop Duke was very, very happy with all these recruits and he thought that they would grow up in the community in no time. So he decided to build the convent.

I don't think they realized too much what they were to relinquish. They had no idea what was religious life. We would go and make our prayers, and they would be by themselves and they will run after the boys on the reserve. The Chilcotin boys would call them Shuswaps if they want to insult them. But they didn't realize too much what was religious life.

At the beginning it was funny. We started a nursing home — that old building down there — at the beginning I didn't have any experience. You know, you train in a hospital. In a hospital you have young doctors, you're not supposed to give any medication without being prescribed, you are not supposed to do anything without it's ordered; and you are sent way back in the field, all by yourself, there's nobody to help you. At the beginning I find it so hard.

And besides that, I was French. I had studied in French and to translate all this in English, I didn't know the medical words. You train and you learn all the technique and the words that go with it.

And the Indians in those days, they didn't know very many English. They knew maybe four, five words. So I was trying to get the message to them. It was *so hard,* and I didn't know them. They'd bring the children and after they'd stay around the house to see if the child was crying. They don't trust us. But it didn't take very long. It was the other way round. They would bring them all. They would want to go to stampede, and *all* their baby were sick, you know.

Sister Bernard — another sister the same name as I — she was driving for me. Every time we would go for the sick — they would call me in — and I would visit them in those reserves. Redstone, Stoney, oh, any place in the Chilcotin. There's not a place I didn't go. Riske Creek, Nemiah Valley, impractical places they were — Eagle Lake. And never anything happened. I have in my mind, you know, that Obedience send me there and He wants me to do it, and I'm going to do it and this is all. Oh, I went some terrible places.

Just got lost once. I was taking a baby home, and an Indian put a mark at the road where to turn off. When finally I find a guide, he said, "Now, can you take me to my camp?" It was getting quite dark. I said, "Well, yes. I suppose." Put the baby on a horse, and by the time he gets home with the baby, he's going to be sick again! And coming back, there was no road, and I got stuck one place and I could hardly see the road. I was alone, you know. Usually I wait for my companion — another sister used to come with me — but she wasn't ready. I was impatient in those days, I didn't wait.

They were still believing quite a bit in the medicine man. And they would — not doing it openly — but they would go and get the medicine man, and sometimes I know I had to wait at the door, and they will tell me, "Oh well, they're doing something inside. You can go after." And after they will say, "You can go," but they had used a medicine man first; and after, me. And after they would probably call the priest. They wouldn't take any chance. No, they would use every possible means.

I admire the simplicity in their religion. Very simple, very strong. Like holy water. Well, I like holy water, but I cannot have that faith that they have in holy water. And I'm sure holy water did miracle for them, because they never went to the meadows without having gone to the priest and have holy water blessed. And I'm sure even holy water made miracles for them, got them better in the meadows when they were all by themselves. They would have that faith.

PART II: SETTLING THE FRONTIER

One of the Brown brothers on the Lardeau Creek–Duncan trail. Brothers Cy, Hemlock and Hughie Brown were among the first prospectors in the area. *Courtesy George Palethorpe*

DREAMS OF FREEDOM: SPECIAL COLONIES

When William Duncan established Metlakatla near the mouth of the Skeena in 1862, he did so to create a sanctuary for his Tsimshian parishioners. Metlakatla was, Duncan believed, distant enough from Fort Simpson and the various nearby Indian villages to ensure there would be little outside influence. At Metlakatla they would worship and live in the way they chose, free individuals.

Although no one could have known it at the time, Duncan's action would be repeated by others numerous times in the forthcoming years. Many of these colonies would be created for exactly the same reasons. The Bella Coola Valley was settled by Norwegian immigrants from the United States in 1894. Danish settlers, many also from the United States, began to develop land at Cape Scott in 1896. In 1901, Finnish settlers began to build Sointula on Malcolm Island. A group of Doukhobors from Russia bought land in the Kootenays and moved there from their settlements in Saskatchewan in 1908.

— Gordon Fish

Into a Wild Country: Norwegians at Bella Coola

Edited by Gordon Fish

The beginning of a severe depression in the United States in 1893 caused many farmers in the Midwestern states to lose their properties when they were unable to make payments on debts and mortgages. In Minnesota and the Dakotas, where many Scandinavians had settled in the latter part of the nineteenth century, a group of Norwegians became interested in making a fresh start elsewhere. Leading one search for a better area was Rev. Christian Saugstad, a Lutheran pastor in Minnesota. He was actively looking into the possibility of establishing a colony where his congregation would be able to live a happy and virtuous life away from the evils of the world. It seems likely that he saw, or heard about, an article on Bella Coola written by Bernhart Fillip Jacobsen, a Norwegian, who had been to the valley early in 1884. Jacobsen described the area in favourable terms and even suggested that it would be a suitable place for a colony.

MILO FOUGNER: Most of the people that went to Bella Coola were from Minnesota, North Dakota, South Dakota, [Iowa, Wisconsin] and some of predominantly Scandinavian areas in the Red River Valley. And 1894 was the middle of one of the worst depressions, I guess, that the United States had ever experienced. It was getting harder and harder to sell their wheat. They had several poor crops, they had hail and this, that and the other thing, and they didn't have the wheat that we have nowadays. There was rust, and they were plagued by a number of things, and their economic position was pretty bad.

Reverend Saugstad, who was, amongst other things, I think, an idealist, probably had been thinking for some time about establishing a colony of almost morally perfect people, in an ideal situation away from temptation.

He was to be the leader. So he and two others, Mr. [A.] Stortroen was one, came out to the West, and they examined several possibilities. One, the American government offered them the Yakima Valley and said that they would put in irrigation if Saugstad's group would settle. Then they came to Victoria, and they [the B. C. government] offered them land in the Fraser Valley. And then he and B. F. Jacobsen went up to Bella Coola.

Jacobsen at that time was collecting curios for a museum in Germany and could speak the Bella Coola language; in fact, he could speak two or three Indian dialects fluently and had been on the coast some time. They looked the situation over, and more and more Reverend Saugstad realized that here was the Shangri-la that he was looking for. He could herd his people in there, and they could be supervised, and he could make the valley into a garden.

TED LEVELTON: Now, my personal opinion is, they either wore dark glasses or couldn't see at all, because, frankly, I would never have come here when I think of what the country was like when we arrived here. What he could see in the place I'll never know. But anyway, he came back and painted a very glowing picture of the conditions here. There was lots of fish, there was lots of game, there was wild fruit and there was good land and lots of timber. Well, I quite agree with him there — there was lots of these things that he mentioned, mind you — but for a man to move in here with just his bare hands, into a wild country, no transportation whatever except a boat every two months in those days, and that was uncertain. . . . If the weather was bad, they didn't come in here.

He [Reverend Saugstad] came back here and then got busy, and that summer they signed up about eighty-five people. Among them was my dad, Erasmus Levelton. He was a man who had been raised in the timbered country. He'd done quite a number of years fishing the

Lofoten Islands, out where the fishing is really tough. You fish in the winter there; you go out there with the cold gales howling and ice and things. Anyway, he got fed up with that kind of life and decided to migrate. We migrated to the United States in the summer of 1892 and went to Minnesota, where a number of relatives had moved in previous years.

ANNIE LEVELTON: Dad didn't like Minnesota. He wasn't used to the flat prairie country and he wanted to go where there was the sea; he was used to that.

TED LEVELTON: They left Minnesota and went up to Winnipeg, where they got on the CPR, and the CPR took them into Vancouver. They had to go from Vancouver to Victoria, because that was where the provincial government was, your land department and all that.

MILO FOUGNER: They boarded the old side-wheeler *Princess Louise* and headed for Bella Coola. On the way there they drew lots for land, and it had been decided that first of all they would draw lots for land, a quarter section of land each. Then the four chaps who had drawn the same section, quarters in the same section, banded together, and the idea was that they would build a temporary shelter on the section and the four of them would work together improving their individual properties. This worked out very nicely.

There was no dock there, of course. The Indians came out to meet them in canoes at the mouth of the river, and the colonists were all very surprised that standing right up in one of the Indian canoes was a very, very blonde-haired girl. It turned out she was Bertha Thorson, a daughter of an old sea captain [Thore Thorson] who had retired in Bella Coola. He had come there just prior to the colony and he later joined the colony. It sort of perked them up a bit to see some of their kind there.

Although the colonists were scattered along the valley, the centre of the community was about twelve miles (19 km) from the sea. Originally called Christiania, the community later became known as Hagensborg, the location of Hagen Christensen's store.

The first winter was a hard one. The colonists cut a road from Bella Coola, at the mouth of the Bella Coola River, to Hagensborg.

On 6 May, more colonists arrived. Some were families of the men in the first group, and others were Norwegians from different areas of the American Midwest.

TED LEVELTON: We came up here on a boat called the *Danube*. I can remember the old whistle just about scared us to death. We were standing around, you know, watching the shoreline gradually coming closer, and then, all of a sudden, this whistle let out a terrific blast out, and we kids just about jumped out of our shoes! As soon as the steamer blew its whistle, these Indians all came boiling down in their great big old spoon canoes and surrounded the ship. They had heard about these people coming in and they figured, "Well now, here's a dollar or two for us, you see; we'll be able to take these people ashore."

They would take a whole canoe-load from the boat down there up to the village for a dollar. It'd take three men when the tide was out, because there was a rather rapid current in that river, and they'd have the boat loaded with trunks. There used to be a village on the bank; great big old houses. They would be forty feet wide and probably a hundred feet long — terrific big houses.

When we landed here, Dad already had a house built, and we walked right up six miles that same afternoon. I can remember going up. I was not quite six and I can remember my legs were getting pretty tired by the time I got up there.

ANNIE LEVELTON: Father had a cabin — luckily. He was the only one who really had a good cabin, so we had a home to go to, but it was alarming after having been on the prairies to see those huge trees, you know. And my mother, oh, she just couldn't get reconciled to the fact that she left a beautiful home in the old country, in Norway, with servants and all that sort of thing to look after all us little ones, and to arrive up here and. . . . Oh dear, she didn't know what to do.

ANNIE ENGEBRETSON: My father was Jacob Johnson Lumaas. He came to the States in 1869 and he worked in Wisconsin in the timber. So he was a logger, a hand logger. Then he had a farm in Cookston, Minnesota, then his wife died and his children died and there was only one left — that was me. And I was not very strong, so he thought he'd change climate and he wanted to go back to logging. That's the reasons he came here. He came in 1894. I'd thought it would be all right if it could make me strong and healthy. I was thirteen.

We landed at [John] Clayton's store. There was about forty of us, mostly women and children and two or three men.

I can picture them leaving Clayton's. They all had packs on. My father had my blanket, I had my suitcase, and the little children were riding on top of the packs on the men, and there was a long string of us went up. The trail was narrow, crooked. We crawled on trees across the creeks; especially we had to cross a big river, that they call Nusatsum; it [the bridge] was just poles and my father led me across. We all got as far as what we call Hagensborg now. My uncle, Ole Gaarden, lived this side of Snootli [Creek], and we stayed at his place.

BERTHA NYGAARD: I came in the spring of 1895 with my parents. My dad was headed for California; then Reverend Saugstad met him on the street in Minnesota and persuaded him to join the colonists. And that's what he did. He said, "We want men like you, great big husky men."

My first memories of Bella Coola are of the Indians poling us up the river. I was frightened, and they were chanting. They only had blankets around them. The old Hansen place was where we landed, and poor mother — there were five of us — said she was standing out there, she didn't know where to go or what to do, and my dad was then pitching a tent under some trees for the night. And Mrs. Hansen said, "Come with me, this house can hold a few more," and when we got there it was just full of people!

TED LEVELTON: When you're a kid of six, it was a grand place to run around, climb trees and chase squirrels and all this kind of stuff.

You could raise good crops when you got the land cleared, but boy, it was all backbreaking work. The ground was grubbed with a grub hoe. There were no horses or ploughs, and the patches were too small, anyway, for a horse even to turn around on. You'd grub out a little spot for a garden and another little patch for potatoes, and that was it for the first few years. It was the women and the children that did most of this, because the men had to get out and hustle. Most of them who came here, I would say, were down to practically their last dollar when they arrived here. I know certainly my dad was.

ANNIE ENGEBRETSON: They all had to work and they were all together in bunches then, you see. My father started to cut logs for his own house. He just split the cedar logs. I shingled the roof. We were busy all the time. I helped to pull on the crosscut saw, dig up the devil's club and things. I got strong!

ANNIE LEVELTON: We kids all helped clear land. We had to work from the time we were quite small. Of course, Father was a builder of no mean ability.

TED LEVELTON: Luckily, he was a good woodsman, a good man with a broadax. He could build just about as nice a log house as you'd want to set eyes on. And he was also a fairly good carpenter, so he got a certain amount of work building homes for others here. That's the way he made a few dollars.

BERTHA NYGAARD: My father was a tailor in Minnesota. In Bella Coola he was supposed to be a farmer, but he didn't know anything about farming. He had hands like a woman because he'd done nothing but light work, but he made a success of whatever he undertook. We ended up having one of the biggest ranches there.

MILO FOUGNER: I suppose transportation was their biggest problem. My dad says in one place in his diary: "I got up at five this morning and walked to the waterfront and back," which would be twenty-four miles round trip over a rough trail that they had hacked out. He doesn't mention the fact that on his way back he packed all of the things that he needed possibly for the next two or three weeks. They packed cookstoves on their backs; they packed everything that you need in your home, and that's the only way they could pack it — there were no horses — other than the river itself for canoes. Certainly, you could get it up to the river bank, but in a lot of cases you still had to pack it a long ways.

It's the [Bella Coola] valley that runs east and west, and the part that they settled would be from salt water to twenty-four to twenty-five miles up the valley. And [the Bella Coola River is] quite a large river, lush growth; down on the valley floor itself, huge timber — fir, cedar, hemlock — interspersed with miles of devil's club and under-

Two of the best broadax men in the Bella Coola colony, Andrew Svisdahl and Mathias Hammer, probably in the winter of 1894–95. Photograph by Iver Fougner, courtesy Provincial Archives of British Columbia / 95374

brush. Then along the river, a thick growth of willow and alder and birch and that sort of thing. There just wasn't anything easy about it. It wasn't these sylvan paths that you hear about going through the forest of *Evangeline* by any means at all. It was tough going.

MILO FOUGNER: The Indian people, they were a very important factor in the life of the colony. I think, perhaps, that both sides discovered integration and segregation wasn't so important per se as mutual trust — mutual admiration, if you like — for one another's good points and mutual understanding. When I was a boy, you respected the Indian people to the point where you would never intrude on one of their affairs unless you were asked, unless you were invited, and you considered it an honour if you were. By the same token, our affairs were the same.

Now, integration says that these barriers should all be cut down, but I'm not prepared to agree that the situation is any better now than it was when I was a boy. In fact, I feel that there was more respect, possibly, between us in those days than there is now.

TED LEVELTON: For a monetary consideration, naturally, they were always willing to take your freight up [river]. They hauled freight all the way to Hagensborg in canoes. These fellows that lived a way up there, say half a dozen of them, would sort of club together and come down and buy maybe a ton and a half of provisions — the heavy stuff like flour, sugar and this kind of stuff. And they'd get the Indians, and they'd take it up for five dollars. Two men would take that canoe all the way to Hagensborg and unload the stuff there and then come home again, which saved those fellows a tremendous lot of hard backbreaking work. They'd pole it. Two or three men can take one of those spoon canoes up places that you would swear that nothing but a very powerful motor could drive a vessel up through.

MILO FOUGNER: We grew up with the Indian kids, of course, and could speak with them, and I suppose we heard more of the imagery of the different dances and what it meant and that sort of thing, and knew the different costumes.

When my dad was Indian agent, he had a field matron at Kitimat send in her annual requisition for drugs, and amongst it was a barrel of Epsom salts, which is one hundred pounds of Epsom salts. So my dad wrote to her and he said he'd received her requisition and passed it on, but he said, "What are you going to do with one hundred pounds of Epsom salts, move the village?"

ANNIE LEVELTON: The Indians were surprisingly very good to us. They could have resented us pretty badly but they were awfully good to us. And we were good to them. The settlers, I will say this, were fine men, and never once did we ever hear of any scandal with them, bachelors and all. They never went near the village. They were polite to the Indians and the Indians were polite to them, and they understood each other.

You'd go down to the wharf and hear one fellow say, "How many fish did you catch?" and he'd be speaking Norsky. "I got so many fish," and the other fellow would say something in Chinook, and that was fine.

Although the scenery and climate of the valley may have reminded settlers of parts of Norway, one element of the natural life of the area was new to nearly all of them — the grizzly bear.

ANNIE LEVELTON: I saw a bear and never even knew it was a bear when I was a little girl. I didn't know that it was a bear until I saw a picture of one in later years. I thought it was a big dog I'd seen.

Mr. Bakken arrived one morning down at the cabin and he was laughing, he was nearly in hysterics. And Mother said, "What in the world is so funny?" "Well," he said, "I did a funnier thing today than I ever did in my life," he said. He was coming from his home — he lived about four miles up the line, I guess — and he had to cross what we call the Snootli bridge and as he came along on this side down the hill, a big grizzly meandered right out on the road right ahead of him.

The grizzly was so close to him that he didn't really know what it was at first, I guess, and the grizzly just stopped and looked at him. And he just couldn't think of a thing to say, so he tipped his hat and said, "Good morning!"

TED LEVELTON: A very close friend of ours, Karls Christopherson, he was a bachelor, but he used to stay at our place a lot and he was very comical sort of guy. He was a great man with kids. He would tell us some of the most hair-raising yarns. I'm sure that none of them were true, but boy, he had us spellbound. We'd just sit there with our ears strained right out to make sure we didn't miss anything when he started telling some of these yarns.

He, with several other guys, had been up to what is known as the Salloomt Valley, which runs off the main valley here about twelve miles up. And they'd been prospecting in there and found a very likely looking prospect. And they had this analyzed, and it analyzed very well, and they decided to develop this thing.

Anyway, this one Christopherson, with several other guys, had been up there doing some work. They built a cabin and made a pretty good road in there. And he was coming out again with a big pack of blankets and personal clothing, and he had a frying pan in one hand and a kettle in the other. And he was walking along the trail — this was in early summer — and all of a sudden, a big old grizzly pops right out of the bush, right out in front of him, got up on her hind legs and started roaring and coming towards him. Well, here he was with his big pack on his back and he couldn't get rid of that in a hurry and he figured it was no use running, so he thought the only way is to go right at her and see if he could bluff her out. So he started beating this frying pan and his kettle together and kept walking towards her. And he finally bluffed her! She started backing off, and she backed off and backed off, and she finally got up and beat it. And he said he could feel the cold sweat running down the back of his neck all the time he was doing this. But, he said, when he finally realized what he was doing, the kettle was absolutely flat and the frying pan was all dented up, but he said, "I think it saved my life. I fully expected that old girl would have gone for me, because she had a couple of cubs there."

I can remember we had some terrific winters. The first couple of winters we were here, we had terrific snowfalls. The people up the valley had a hard time because they had to break a road for twelve miles in the snow.

I can remember a good many times those fellows would come down from Hagensborg, twelve miles up, and they'd come down here

The Bella Coola colonists in a rare moment of leisure. Photograph by Iver Fougner, courtesy Provincial Archives of British Columbia / 95349

to Clayton's and get, oh, sixty pounds worth of provisions. They'd put that on their backs and they'd start back up again and they'd get it back up to our place at nine or ten o'clock at night, absolutely pooped out. They were just barely able to drag their feet behind them. They stayed at our place overnight.

ANNIE LEVELTON: My mother was one of the most generous women in the world. She always had the coffeepot on, and it made no difference if they were black, red or white, she fed them all.

TED LEVELTON: I can remember, oh, six or eight or ten of these fellows coming in a bunch. They had no blankets with them, and it meant that we had to put some bedding on the floor, and they'd flake out in a row on the floor.

We slept upstairs. This house was only about seven feet high on the wall, but they'd put some joists in and then they'd laid some boards along the top, about eight feet wide. It was just a very small room up in there, but that's where all us kids slept. Whenever any youngsters came in, we'd flake out like sardines in a can, you see, along these boards. I can remember looking down over the edge — they had a board set up on edge at the side of this floor so you wouldn't fall off it

— looking down and seeing this row of fellows' faces in the early morning light. You'd see them all lying there with their noses in the air, some snoring away to high heavens, and other fellows with a great big bunch of whiskers on. We used to get a big bang out of watching the different facial expressions you'd see down below — some fellow, you know, snoring away in good style!

Although some of the original colonists had left the valley soon after their arrival, newcomers continued to arrive, and by the end of 1896, the colony had 158 members. The men earned some money working on the construction of a wagon road from the waterfront up the valley. Land for farming was gradually cleared and cabins built. A church congregation assembled, and a choir was formed. A post office, a store and a library were established. Gardens provided a variety of vegetables, the streams were a source of salmon, and there were deer and geese.

In 1896 the colonists did very well fishing at Rivers Inlet. In Torliev Viken's words, "the men returned with money in their pockets and courage in their hearts to return to clearing land."

MILO FOUGNER: The Reverend Saugstad was the first to die of the colonists. He had great plans, he had organized so many things: a salmon cannery, sawmills and he also planned a river steamer to bring supplies up and down the river.

He foresaw the farming, of course, and dairying as being the big thing, putting in the creameries and exporting the products of the creameries and also farm products of various kinds. Regular meetings were held and then annual colony meetings, and they had committees of all types for administering the colony. It would have been interesting, and I suppose that has been said many times, as to just what would have happened if they had continued under his strong leadership.

No Paradise, No Utopia: Danes at Cape Scott

Edited by Gordon Fish

The settlers at Cape Scott came with the same high hopes and determination that characterized the colonists at Bella Coola. However, in place of the methodical survey carried out before the Bella Coola Valley was chosen for settlement, the discovery of Cape Scott as a suitable site for a settlement came about more by accident than design.

In some notes based on the recollections of early settlers, Bernard Dane tells of the "accidental" discovery:

> The "Founder" of the first White settlement at Cape Scott . . . was one Rasmus Hansen, whom, in company with another Dane had been fishing halibut out of Seattle on the then newly discovered Fishing Banks on the North-end of Vancouver Island about the year 1894.
>
> One of those cruises, he sought shelter in Goose Bay [Hansen Bay], which is about halfway between Cape Scott and San Josef Bay on the West side of the Island, and explored the long lagoon [Hansen Lagoon] that emptied into the bay in quest of Ducks or Geese. At the head of this lagoon he found a great stretch of Tide Meadow through which ran two nice streams, which, at the time, were full of Salmon.
>
> At that period there were very "hard times" in the States and many people were seeking "pastures new," especially in the milder climate of the West Coast. Advantage had been taken of this and two Norwegian settlements had been started, one at Bella Coola and one at Quatsino.
>
> Rasmus Hansen conceived the idea that the head of this lagoon would be a very desireable spot to start a Danish settlement, and in the year following wrote a number of articles in the Danish Weekly Papers published in Cedar Falls, Iowa, and Omaha, Nebraska. He received many interested enquiries, which prompted him to get in touch with the Provincial Government, and with the help of Colonel Baker (the Minister of Lands), an agreement was reached whereby the four Westernmost Townships in the Cape Scott area were reserved for a Danish settlement.
>
> — BERNARD DANE, "Cape Scott"

The correspondence was handled by a group of Danes at Enumclaw, Washington.

LESTER PETERSON: People came out then with the knowledge that they were going to work. It was going to be no paradise, no utopia, but there was going to be a certain degree of freedom and a certain degree of local autonomy.

I think it was much the same as many others — Hansen probably dreamed of a little bit more freedom from working on a halibut boat, in the same way as my father later on dreamed of a little more freedom to get out of an iron mine. So it was not with the thought that you'd avoid work, but with the thought that you might have a little of your own freedom. And it was possible to form a colony which could be very much like the modern municipality, in which you'd have your own local laws in a framework of federal and provincial laws.

Before leaving Enumclaw, the organizers of the colony formed a "provisional company" and elected a board of directors, who were responsible for any further contact with the British Columbia government and laid out the rules for joining the colony. The basic requirement for people who wanted to join was the payment of fifty dollars to a fund "which shall be used for means of communication, a co-operative store, and other enterprises for the growth and improvement of the colony."

LESTER PETERSON: In 1896, two men went to the cape. One stayed the winter, [N. C.] Nelson, and reported to his group the next spring that this was satisfactory and in March [19] 1897, the group went up on the *Willapa*. The women and children went up on the *Willapa* and they were accompanied by Ernest Cleveland, the government surveyor, who was to lay out the area. And some of the men went up on a small schooner, the *Floyborg*.

JOHANNE HARESTAD: My mother and father, Mary and Carl Rasmussen, went to Cape Scott as pioneers in 1897 from Rossholt, Wisconsin. They later left Cape Scott and went back to their home in Wisconsin, and they were there for some years and then decided to come back again. My father was a steam engineer and, when they first came as pioneers, he brought in a little sawmill, hoping to saw lumber for homes for the settlers, but eventually went broke because the people needed lumber but they had no money to pay him for it.

Although a number of the first settlers left before the spring of 1898, the population rose as newcomers continued to arrive.

PETRA AMSDEN: I arrived at Cape Scott with my parents in 1899. My father was Bertold Christian Benson Bekker. I was four years old. We came on the *Willapa,* and the day that we arrived, the minister [Jens Jensen Mylund], who had been engaged to be a member of the settlement, was leaving. The church could not pay his salary.

There was no wharf and they came out in a large boat — I think they called them dories — which were rowed by a man standing up. All the supplies for the settlement were brought ashore in that way.

There was a house near the store, and we were able to live in that house for a very short time. I remember Mother's first washday. She was surrounded by Indians. There were three or four women sitting cross-legged on the floor watching her. She gave them some soap, which pleased them very much.

Unlike the settlers at Bella Coola, the Cape Scott colonists appear to have had little contact with the Indians. The closest Indian village was the Kwakiutl village of Nahwitti on Hope Island.

PETRA AMSDEN: After that, we stayed in a two-roomed log house near the lagoon, and there was a stream flowing past the house. One room held our furniture that we'd brought up, and the other room we had to sleep and cook. And the following year, our house was built. It was built with the help of settlers. Father built so much, and the others got together and the women did the cooking, and it was what you call a bee — a housing bee.

My father wanted a farm. He wanted to carve a sort of country estate out of the forest. He started to carve out a farm and till the soil in a densely forested district. The soil was very good, but all the trees had to be removed. He had a crosscut saw, a double-bit ax, a stump puller — a small one — and steel cable, I suppose it was, and a gun. He had about four or five guns of different types. That was about all his tools. And his knowledge of cultivating the soil, and he was a very good husbandman.

We had no horses up there when we arrived, though they bought a horse later on, and a mule. But they were not very successful, because the horse's hooves are not suited to muddy and miry places. We had a steer that did all our pulling and all our heavy work. He had been a rather ferocious beast, but they cut off his horns and put a ring in his nose, and the poor fellow was fairly tame after that. He never lost his ferocious attitude, but he became almost a pet with my sister and myself.

We had no carts with wheels, but if you explore through the woods you will find that the red cedar puts out a side shoot, and when you cut that off at the trunk you get something that looks like a ski runner or a sleigh runner. Well, you look till you find two that matched, and then they were smoothed down so that you had two sleigh runners. Then they put a sled on top of that, and everything that was brought down from the store — heavy things like sugar and meal and flour and oats and anything that was heavy — was dragged and transported that way.

When we eventually were able to harvest the fields, it was timothy hay that grew there — wild timothy hay, which was very good as cattle food. But, of course, it must be harvested at such a time that it didn't drop its seed, because if it was harvested and dried and the seed had dropped, then, of course, most of the nourishment disappeared.

Theo and Johanne Frederiksen of Cape Scott with a dead cougar.
Courtesy Ellen Mellstrom

Every year I remember Father saying that he had never yet lost a harvest, and he did not lose a harvest up at Cape Scott. It was the drying of the hay that was difficult, because Cape Scott is a very wet district.

We always had a garden — strawberries, raspberries and red currants, white currants, black currants, and Father planted apple trees. But large fruit trees were not satisfactory. It was my job to pick one quart of berries every day, and that was terrible because I was afraid of the forest and I soon picked every bush that was near the house, so then I walked a mile and a half to two miles down to the store and picked it on the beach, because then I was near the beach and wasn't afraid. But as the years went by, I lost my fear. There were blue huckleberries and red huckleberries, and we could get cranberries in the marshes.

Father shot deer and geese and ducks. We had pintails, canvasbacks, butterballs and mallards. Then there were mud hens. They had to be very careful because they became rancid and fishy. The waterfowl were all right when they arrived, but if they stayed too long on the mud flats, they got a bad flavour. Also, there were wild grouse in the woods, and they were good, too. We had to live on what Father could shoot; otherwise, we had our hens and our cattle and so on and we killed a pig every year. We never ran short of supplies, not really. They ran short of tobacco once, the men did. You never forget that; oh, that was terrible.

After we moved into our own home, I eventually went to school. I guess there were eight or nine children. I can't be certain because they came and went. Reading, writing and arithmetic were taught well, and after a while Mr. Christensen decided to give us French and German as well. I can still remember a little bit of German, but I don't think any German would be able to recognize it. Father taught me to swear in German, just to tease my mother.

Mr. Christensen was a charming man. He was a very fine mathematician, but his joy was literature. His favourite author was Joseph Conrad, and his favourite expression was, "Joseph Conrad did not describe a storm, he created one within the pages." And he taught me all the love of literature, history and geography that I imbibed afterwards, which has been a joy all my life.

Father was an educated man. He spoke four languages and a smattering of Greek. He taught me the names of plants and flowers in Latin. Father, although a minister's son, was not very religious, but the principles of religion and the guidelines for living were all there and must be obeyed. I think perhaps the first was truthfulness.

Away from the Outside World: Finns at Sointula

Edited by Gordon Fish

The colonies at Bella Coola and Cape Scott were established largely in response to specific economic conditions in North America. To a certain extent, the same is true for the Finnish colony on Malcolm Island, conceived by a group of Finnish miners already in British Columbia. However, unlike the other colonies, this one would be utopian.

A considerable number of Finns had worked on the construction of the Canadian Pacific Railway, and when that work was completed, some of them found work in the coal mines in the Nanaimo area of Vancouver Island. Work in the mines was dangerous, and there were frequent accidents. Wages were low, and any attempt by the miners to improve their situation was firmly resisted by the mine owner, James Dunsmuir. When the North Wellington mines were exhausted, Dunsmuir opened new mines at Extension and then at Ladysmith. The miners had to move their homes each time if they wanted to keep their jobs. With very little work to be found elsewhere in the area, they had no choice but to move. Living conditions in the mining towns were, in many ways, as bad as working conditions in the mines.

Teodor Tanner (right) and August Oberg (left) at Sointula, circa 1904. The community sawmill is in the background. Courtesy Sally Peterson

WAYNE HOMER (paraphrasing the history of Sointula written in Finnish by Matti Halminen in 1936): Dunsmuir was a slave driver who gave his employees a harsh time and is said to have introduced bootleggers and company beer outlets to ply the disgruntled workers with booze to keep them quiet. It was under these disgusting working conditions that the first Finnish Brotherhood of Temperance Societies was born in Nanaimo. This new revolt against drunkenness and associated vices spread rapidly across Canada and into the United States. It was from this unbearable harassment and miserable working conditions in the coal mines that the idea of establishing a collective workers commune under socialist principles was born.

KAISA RIKSMAN: They had heard of something similar in France. A man named Fourier had had a colony, like a Shangri-la or something. So these people asked the B.C. government for land to which they could move as a group. And then they wrote to Australia to Mr. Kurikka and asked him to come to be the leader of this group. He wrote back and said that he was very ill and he was in hospital and he didn't have a penny to his name; but if they would send him money, he would certainly come. Which he did.

Matti Kurikka was well known in Finland as an author and a playwright. As editor-in-chief of the Helsinki newspaper *Työmies* (The Worker), he wrote articles on a wide range of subjects, among them socialism, class struggle, the value and dignity of physical labour, the status of women in the community and the need for universal suffrage. Kurikka had left Finland in protest against the political situation there, but his attempt to establish a Finnish community in Australia was a failure. He arrived in Nanaimo in August 1900.

KAISA RIKSMAN: When these people asked the government for land, the Land Office threw a lot of maps at them and said, "Take your choice." And they picked Malcolm Island, because it was by the sea and seemed like the only place where they could have farms, because their idea was to make their living through farming.

Malcolm Island is located at the northern end of Johnstone Strait, between northern Vancouver Island and the mainland of British Columbia. About fifteen miles (23 km) long and roughly two and a half miles (4 km) wide, it was heavily forested with cedar, spruce, fir and hemlock.

> *The first members of the Colony to go to Malcolm Island left Nanaimo on December 6, 1901. They travelled in a sailboat owned and captained by Johan Mikkelson. Theodore Tanner was elected leader of the group. The others were Kalle Hendrickson, Otto Ross and Malakias Kytomaa. Mostly they sailed, but sometimes there was no wind and they rowed. After passing through Seymour Narrows a shotgun went off accidently in the boat and Mikkelson's hand was hurt. The others administered what first aid they could and got him finally to Alert Bay. He was sent to Nanaimo on the first steamer. He lost only his thumb although at first the doctors thought his arm would have to be amputated. The others reached Malcolm Island on December 15, and anchored at Rough Bay.*
>
> — AILI ANDERSON, *History of Sointula*

KAISA RIKSMAN: It just happened to be during a big storm. In fact, it was such a big storm that there hasn't been any like it since. It blew all the trees down on Haddington Island nearby, and these men had to take shelter in some big tank that some outfit had left. So they didn't think too much of it at the time, but anyway, it didn't scare them enough not to come back. They went back and reported that they found the island favourable, and two more men came who were the builders, the carpenters, and they built the log cabin that's in Rough Bay. They built it, and of course a sauna was the next one.

There were seven altogether, and one, Mr. Wilander, brought his wife along, so she was the first woman. They were the only people here when I arrived; I was twenty-two then. I came from Finland along with this other lady. Our husbands were here in Sointula already. They had heard about Sointula from Mr. Kurikka when he went on his lecture tours. He and Mr. Salmi came here, and then I and Mrs. Salmi and our four children came to Sointula together.

We arrived on June 3, 1902. We arrived here late at night. It was pitch black, of course, and all the bay was covered with these big kelps — these great big snakes in the water with these great big heads on them. The boat tied up to some sort of a slip, and we had to walk along these logs to the shore where this little shack was.

In this log cabin there were five double bunks for all these families. Hay was piled on these bunks for a mattress, and my husband and I and the two children got one of these bunks for our own.

The first meeting to decide on how to proceed and just what they were to do was held in June of 1902. And they held a three-day celebration at that time, where they had meetings and had plays and sang.

They were going to share everything. Everyone would be working for the common good. No one owned anything separately and individually. They planned to farm and log, and all the proceeds would be divided equally.

I think the main idea was to have a free society. Especially, they emphasized that women should have equal rights with men. At that time women had no property rights, they had no rights whatsoever in wages, so this was one thing that was applied here. The women had a dollar a day wages, as the men did, and they had a right to speak at meetings and they had a right to vote. And they had to work. Everyone had to work.

Another thing they wanted was a society where there would be no government church. There would be no liquor vending, and no women should have to sell themselves, whatever that would mean. They could have religion, but no one would be forcing any particular religion, and they could believe as they wished.

The company was to look after all the children — all the expenses, clothing, food and schooling. No one would be charged extra for children. The idea was that later on the children would be the workers and they would look after the elders. All the women went to work in the kitchen or laundry or wherever they were needed, and they had a nursery where their children were sent. They could be left there overnight, but most of the women took their children home in the evening.

That summer the colonists officially named the settlement Sointula — "the place of harmony." There were now over a hundred people in the colony, and the future seemed promising, despite the lack of money to buy essential equipment and supplies.

KAISA RIKSMAN: Each family was supposed to pay two hundred dollars, but that's where the trouble really began. A lot of people arrived and they didn't have the two hundred dollars, so the colony didn't have the money it expected to have. But they didn't turn anyone away, so everything they bought was mortgaged.

The main industry was going to be farming, but they found that it just woudn't do. This area wasn't meant for farming, and it meant so much work clearing land that they would all starve before they got started. So they turned to logging and fishing.

They weren't really farmers. The people that came here were expert tradesmen in their own line — tailors and blacksmiths and whatever was necessary — and they were educated. They were not ignorant people by any means. Mr. Makela, he was a very well educated man. He had gone through university in Finland and he was translating English books into Finnish. And they had a doctor [Dr. Oswald Beckman] here, too.

When they saw that they couldn't farm, they had to turn to logging to make a living. And then to make homes for people to live in, they had to build a sawmill. That was the first thing that was built, and then a blacksmith's shop.

RICHARD MICHELSON: I was born in Wellington, B. C., in 1894. My father's name was Takkomaki and my mother's name was Pauna. I was registered under the name Takkomaki, but my father changed his name a little bit afterwards. He came to Sointula in 1902, more or less to get out of slavery in the mines. He used to work in the mines in Wellington and Extension.

For the first couple of nights we stayed in a log house until the tents were raised for the different families. We lived in the tents until the sawmill got around to making lumber for building houses for different families.

When we got here, we didn't get any money. There were no wages paid to anybody as far as I can understand. Everybody was registered for a dollar a day for the time they worked. Everybody worked, including all the women; some of them were in the laundry, some in the cookhouse and some of them looked after the children. I remember my mother worked in the laundry.

They had a mill and a foundry. They used to make their forms and melt their iron, and they made different parts for machinery. They made charcoal, and I guess it's quite a business to make charcoal, because you have to have a watchman day and night. There was one man, a tailor by trade, and they set him to watch the charcoal. He didn't like being put into a job like that, but you had to do whatever was necessary at the time.

I worked as a whistle punk for a logging operation. There were two of us youngsters, and one would take the morning shift and the other one would take the afternoon shift. We were about eight years old. The camp was down at Pulteney Point at that time. The colony had [steam] donkeys down there and bunkhouses. They had their scouts going around looking where they could get the logs out easiest.

ARVO TYNJALA: They opened up dairy places. Of course, there wasn't any open ground here, but they had to feed their cows. They had to go elsewhere for the feed and they went as far as the head of Knight Inlet and the head of Kingcome Inlet to get their grass on the river flats.

Nobody had any private property, or anything like that. It was all one community under a sort of co-operative. It was just like one household, you know — everyone was together. They dined together, worked together and tried to make things go the best they knew how.

RICHARD MICHELSON: I think about once a week they had. a general meeting. As youngsters, we used to go to the meetings but we didn't know much about what was going on. I remember one time I went there and I fell asleep against the table. I woke up in the middle of the night and the meeting was all over, and the only one around was a watchman. He didn't wake me up, but when I woke up, well, I just got up and walked home.

A housing shortage caused a great deal of concern. There simply were not enough houses being built to accommodate all the colonists. Living in a tent had been acceptable during the summer, but with the onset of winter, the crowding and discomfort gave rise to complaints and prompted some people to leave. An attempt was made to alleviate the problem, but the result only made things worse.

ARVO TYNJALA: In 1902 a kind of apartment house was being built. The first two storeys were divided into apartments, and on the third storey there was the meeting hall. On the twenty-ninth day of January, 1903, that thing burned down. It was built out of rough, wet lumber — straight green stuff that was newly from the woods. You know how it dries; there were big cracks in the walls and there must have been an awful draft in there.

KAISA RIKSMAN: They didn't have any definite knowledge as to how it started, but they surmised that it had started from where the heating system pipes had been extended with a wooden flue. They didn't have enough money to buy more pipes, so they decided that would do.

When the fire started, most of the people were at a meeting upstairs, so that's one of the reasons that so many people were burnt to death.

I had two children at that time, and the youngest was fretful that evening, so I wasn't able to go to the meeting. I went to bed early, but I was still awake when I heard someone crying that there was a fire. I jumped out of bed and looked around to see what I would take, and then realized that I could only take the children. So I took one under each arm and I went out.

I decided to go out the front entrance, which was one floor lower. And when I got there, there was so much draft the smoke was going through the doorway, along the top of the door and rising up to the top of the ceiling, so that it was all clear, and I was able to get out with no discomfort at all.

Many other people were jumping out of windows because they were afraid to go through the front entrance, because of the kerosene barrel that was stored right by the door, and they expected it to explode.

Eleven people died in the fire — eight children and three adults.

Word was got to Vancouver, and people sent clothing and food from there. Of course, travel was so slow it took quite a while to get word down there, and again for the boat to come up with supplies.

ARVO TYNJALA: That was a big disaster — just about the finish. It would have been worse yet, but we got quite a bit of help from the outside, from Vancouver. People collected and sent clothing and all kinds of help.

Work was quickly begun on the construction of houses for all families with children, but in the aftermath of the fire there was increasing dissension in the colony as people discussed the possible causes of the fire. There were even stories of the fire being started deliberately to hide evidence of the embezzlement of colony funds. Nothing ever came of such stories, but the disaster left bitter division in the colony.

Worse yet, the economic situation was not improving. Logging was not profitable, because timber prices were low and operating costs were high. Low prices for salmon meant low incomes for fishermen. Because of the long distances between Malcolm Island and possible markets, the output of the brick factory was used mainly on the island, and while the foundry and the blacksmith shop were of great value to the colony, they did not bring in much income. Only the sawmill showed a profit, and late in 1903 construction of a new mill began. Nevertheless, the population totalled 238 at the end of the year, up from 193 twelve months earlier, and there was renewed hope in the future.

This hope was dashed by another setback.

> *Kurikka was in Vancouver at the time when North Vancouver notices about bridge building contracts over Capilano and Seymour rivers were in the papers. On the advice of a certain Finnish businessman from Seattle, Kurikka placed a $3,000 offer for the contract in the name of the Kalevan Kansa Colonization Co. Ltd., and $150 down to hold it. This sum would be lost if the colony didn't take the contract.*
>
> *Many long discussions were held at meetings in Sointula over this, and new estimates made. The general feeling was that it would be wiser to withdraw the offer and lose the $150 than to go ahead. But Kurikka talked them into it. He envisioned better and larger contracts with Vancouver later, once they got in on the building of the city. He insisted that the colony's financial situation was such that it forced them into taking on the contract. All the timbers and lumber needed could be taken from Malcolm Island. That would help so much it would surely turn out a profitable undertaking. The contract was signed.*
>
> *As the work progressed and Kurikka realized the big mistake made in the estimate of the cost he urged the men to go on strike but no one would listen to him any more.*
>
> — AILI ANDERSON

This episode was followed by yet another controversy, this time about Kurikka's views on love and marriage, which he had expressed in articles in *Aika*. When the bridge builders returned to Sointula late in 1904, a special meeting was held to discuss the matter. Many people were concerned about the idea of "free love" seemingly implied in Kurikka's articles. Although there was no suggestion "free love" was practised in the colony, there were fears that outsiders would form a misleading impression from the articles. This, plus the bridge fiasco, seriously divided the colony on the issue of Kurikka's leadership, and Kurikka's old partner, Makela, was now part of the opposition.

AINO HALMINEN: Kurikka was a socialist to a certain extent, but he wasn't quite the man that Mr. Makela was. He figured that he was just a little bit above the others, to tell you the truth. Whereas Makela considered himself just an ordinary man, same as all the rest of the people there.

KAISA RIKSMAN: Makela was very educated. He had gone to university and knew something about law, and in every way he was — what would you say — a wise man.

ARVO TYNJALA: He was really the building force. Kurikka was more of a lecturer, a spokesman. There was quite a difference in their ideas, too.

The meeting resulted in Kurikka's resignation from the colony. Accompanied by nearly half of the colonists, he moved to Webster's Corners in the Fraser Valley, where they tried to form another utopia. Later he went back to Finland, but returned to the United States once more and eventually died in New York in 1915. The remaining colonists tried to continue at Sointula, but were unable to overcome the problems caused by a lack of manpower and the burden of debt.

Toil and Peaceful Life: Doukhobors in the Kootenays

Edited by Majorie Maloff and Peter Ogloff

To understand and appreciate these narratives as they were told by elderly Doukhobors, one should know something about their history and faith.

It was in 1651 that a patriarch of the Russian Orthodox Church, Nikon, introduced reforms in the rites of the church. Those who didn't accept the reforms became known as "Old Believers" and were savagely persecuted. The schism made people question their own beliefs, and there arose many freethinkers and dozens of sects. There is no evidence of a direct connection between the schism and the Doukhobors, except that it was in those years there appeared people who simply called themselves Christians, and whom in 1785 Archbishop Ambrosius called the

Waiting to leave for Canada. Doukhobors at the port of Batum, Russia, in December 1898. Courtesy Provincial Archives of British Columbia (Tarasoff Collection) / 47020

"Doukhobors," that is, "Spirit Wrestlers." He meant to convey that these people wrestled against the Holy Spirit of the Orthodox Church. Accepting the name, the Doukhobors gave it a different meaning, saying: "We do not wrestle against the Holy Spirit, but being pacifist, wrestle against injustice not by the power of carnal weapons, but by the power of the spirit of love and goodness."

Throughout the eighteenth century they were persecuted for their refusal to attend the Russian Orthodox Church and to serve in the army. In 1897 the Doukhobors managed to submit to the Dowager Empress of Russia a petition requesting permission either to settle somewhere together in the Russian hinterland or to emigrate. The latter request was granted in March of 1898.

Many friends took an active part in looking for a suitable country (which was found to be Canada) and organizing, together with the Doukhobors themselves, the emigration and settlement, as well as the negotiations with the Canadian authorities.

The main item in the negotiations was religious freedom, especially the exemption from military service. Other items discussed were the registration of marriages and exemption from compulsory education. An item which later on became of utmost significance to the Doukhobors and their relation with the government, the taking of an oath of allegiance, somehow was not discussed. Perhaps under the term "religious freedom," the Doukhobors assumed the freedom not to take the oath of allegiance, as the taking of it is contrary to their religious beliefs.

About 7500 Doukhobors came to Canada in 1899 and settled in Saskatchewan, where they were allotted homesteads in block, their nearest town being Yorkton. With the most primitive tools, a lack of work horses and barely enough food to keep body and soul together, they began their struggle for survival.

Everything seemed to have been going well in their life until the autumn of 1906, when the government decreed that the Doukhobors should take the oath of allegiance if they wanted to own the land on which they had settled. Following their religious beliefs, the Doukhobors refused to take the oath. The government took over most of the land and sold it to newcomers, and the Doukhobors were again forced to move somewhere else. Land was bought in British Columbia, and in May of 1908 a group of men and women came to the Kootenays and began clearing land for their first settlement at Ootischenia, where they began building their uniquely styled villages, an example of which is preserved as the Doukhobor Village Museum near Castlegar.

ALEKSEI IVANOVICH MAKORTOFF (born 22 April 1891): We came to Canada; in the beginning, there wasn't anything anywhere, wilderness. We settled where at that time the village of Petrovka was.

I recall that I drove the oxen, ploughed. You would walk alongside and urge them on, and an older man held the plough. And you're supposed to drive them forward, turn them wherever.

In our village there were almost three hundred people. Homes were built communally. One would be built, a family moves in, say Makortoff's or whoever; another one is built, third one, and so on in a row.

We were already real workers. I remember we hauled lumber on the oxen from Tambovka. In Tambovka there was a sawmill. And beyond Tambovka there was this forest, tamarack. Either tamarack or pine. And so I would take straw on the oxen for the engine. Then, when some was sawed, we boys hauled the boards home from Tambovka on the oxen. Tambovka was about seven miles from us. We would haul a great deal home. And so this was our work, the boys at home.

When we got a bit older, seventeen or eighteen years of age, girls, friends of the same age, and Sundays, in the summertime, we had a flat field there and so we would go out and play either softball or "Whom do you grieve for?" For "Whom do you grieve for?" there would be a group of boys and girls standing in a circle. They start. One boy would step away from the group and call out: "I'm grieving! I'm grieving!" The group asks: "For whom?" And then he's supposed to name her. Then she starts running around this circle, and he's supposed to catch her before she gets back to her place. And so this was your girl, then, if you caught her. The girls were so fast then. These finish running, another begins, and so this was the game. Or

Doukhobors working the land at South Colony near Yorkton, Saskatchewan, in 1899. Courtesy Provincial Archives of British Columbia (Tarasoff Collection) / 86677

playing softball. Not only young girls, even married men and young ladies, Sundays. Oh my, but it was nice then. It was warm. Everyone had their own games: women had theirs, girls had theirs, children also had their own of some sort.

And in the winter, we had in Petrovka a river and it would freeze over, and all the young boys and girls would be out skating. Although there weren't any skates then, but simply on your shoes. The snow would be cleared from an area about twenty feet long so the ice would be clean, and then you would take a run at it and slide on the ice. And so on, one after another. All day long. Not only all day; night would find you still on the river.

In the summer we swam. The river, although it wasn't very wide, but it was deep in places. Stone Creek. It was very rocky.

When we had settled, the Kamsack road had not been built yet. That I remember, how the CPR put it through. And so we, boys that worked on the oxen at home, got the idea, three of us friends: "What is this, at home, at home, let's go get a job." And the elders aren't giving their permission, Father, Mother. "You're too young to go anywhere." "No, we're going." It just so happened that this road was going through, and all the Doukhobor men were working on that project. We said, "Let's go. Look, all the older men are there and we'll be there with them." And so it was, the three of us were hired as well.

So we were there. We worked for a very short time, and the job finished. So now this camp is moving far north. A new road was being built there. The "extra gang" is needed there. So now the older men all quit. "It's far and to go all the way there, no," and so they quit. But the three of us were stubborn. "What for? We just left home and to go back, it will be embarrassing. We're going." We worked there for a long time, until the winter cold, then the "extra gang" couldn't continue.

On the railroad, you know, there is the tamping. The ties are laid down the width of the railroad. Then some sand is dumped, and you walk along with shovels, one from that side, one from this side. In this way the sand is packed under ties. And it will be tamped in full. And so you walk down the line. The "extra gang" consisted of hundreds of workers. And coming behind, they would be laying the rails down on these ties. All the way along. As soon as the rails are laid down, then on each tie two spikes are placed. Particularly for young boys this was an easy job. So you walk along, drop two spikes on this end and two on the other end. And then next they come with hammers and drive in these spikes beside the rails as they should be. There was that work. And then comes yet another group, jack. It would happen that a tie is too high or too low, and so they line them up so they'd be even. You pump the jack and it lifts it, whatever amount. And the foreman, as if, follows and lays on the rail and looks with one eye to make sure they're even. Or he'll shout, "Raise it," or "Lower it," in some places. There's a water boy walking around with a pail, whoever wants a drink walks up. I don't remember what the wages were. I think they were a dollar a day.

We came to British Columbia. For three years we lived in Perry's Siding, and then we moved to Ootischenia to Kanigan's sawmill. That's what it was called, Kanigan's mill. Hrisha Kanigan was the manager of the entire mill. I first happened to get the job of stacking lumber. Two of us, Vasya S. and I. He was on top and I would pass it up, and so this was our job. The mill didn't saw too many, and yet it would saw five, ten thousand, and each one has to be lifted up. The lumber was big, thick beams. And so we did that for a while, and then a planer was obtained for this sawmill. From the saw and to the planer, for planing. Timofei S. brought this planer. And this planer was huge, for planing the bigger lumber in particular, either beams or girders. The planer was set up, but to operate it? He says, "I won't operate it. I will only look after it." So Hrisha tried this and that. "Aleksei, take it upon yourself to work it." I tried. It went well. I worked on the planer for quite some time, a year or two, until there was that big changeover.

Well, this big planer was taken from here to that other mill. My work came to an end. So then this planer was taken to another place and set up. But then who? One would give it a try, and the planer is big, the lumber heavy. After one day of work: "I can't," and quits.

Another. And so they went through several like this. Then: "But who worked on it there in Ootischenia?" Well, someone mentioned that such and such, some Makortoff. So here comes one fellow. "Are you Makortoff?" "Yes." "Was it you that worked on the planer at the mill for Kanigan's?" "I did." "Well, in that case you are needed." Well, what to do, so I went.

And it was already fall, winter. Well, in the winter, you know how it is, either rain or snow, the timber is wet, frozen in the mornings, and it so happened that we had to plane beams. And so you put it in the planer and it's icy, the rollers turn but don't pull it. And so you have to push it then. And so together, Samarodin and I. It was such torment. Then you take another beam and pound with it like with a hammer, hammering it in there. And so it will start pulling it, pulling it. Until the wood unthaws, then it's all right, but in the mornings particularly. Oh, it was such agony. Well, I lasted out the winter. Then I quit. I said: "I'm going, the log floats, they'll pay more there."

And so I went to this log float. Slocan City and then from Slocan City seven miles up the mountain. The camp was there. On the river there are made these gates. They are kept closed for the entire summer. The water is accumulated by this dam and so much would collect, like a sea. When the gates are opened, the logs go through the gates, and the water drives them down the river. And this river goes downhill. There, in the same manner, are another set of gates. Then the gates are opened, and the water goes through, and the logs are let through. It drives them and gets them to this place; here the gates are closed also, and the logs collect here, and the water as well. And from this place is made a flume, three feet or wider, a trough going downhill. Then you open these gates and let the logs through one by one into this flume. They go down to the big river then. This flume will gather the logs from all areas of the river. Ten, twenty people with hooks, and you walk along the shore and wherever one catches, you push it off. In places one, two or three and a whole pile will accumulate. Then you have to poke at them to get them moving. The first gates would be opened, letting the logs through, and you are assigned a length to watch. When one catches, you release it.

It's not a good idea to climb on top of these piles. Feodor drowned then. And I was working with him. The logs started moving, and one stopped, another stopped. Well, now they have to be prodded. And he jumped up on them and loosened the front one. They started moving, the logs. You move quickly, you walk and keep an eye out where you can jump to them in time. Each person looks for a place for himself. He climbed up, the logs started floating, and he couldn't jump off and fell through. And here are the logs and they came together. Well, let it be waist deep, but what can you do then, and here they are one after another and pushed him down, and he went under, drowned. And so even on the big river, one or two, and a whole mountain of logs will accumulate. Then you had a boat there.

McKuen, the foreman, appointed me much of the time to run the
boat. So the camp is moving and you're following behind on the boat,
just in case; perhaps someone has climbed up somewhere and wasn't
in time, and so the boat was for this purpose. Or maybe you'd get to
where, and the logs are way over there, and you can't get to them on
foot, the water will carry you away, so you go up to them on the boat.
Then you stand and guide them one by one into the flume.

And so there were two of us, Vasyl K. and I. And from nowhere
appeared a stump, floated down with the logs. So now it has to be let
through as well. So we let it through, and there was this bridge there,
used for crossing when necessary; it floated under the bridge and
came to a stop, this stump, got caught. So from this side, we poked it,
prodded it, no. You'd walk around to that side, can't see where it's
caught. So we poked it, pushed it, no. Then I said to him, "Well,
Vasyl, I'm going to crawl over this stump under the bridge." I just
climbed on it like that, on this stump, and it appears I must have
pressed it down somewhere or overbalanced it, and it started floating.
And I with it. Luckily, it went ahead of me. I stayed behind and I
wasn't floating frontwards, but backwards. And there, for about five
or ten feet, the river ran evenly, slowly, and then there was a sharp
decline, and I came very near to this drop-off; and as I was floating
backwards, I grabbed on to the sides, on to the boards, and held on,
didn't go any further. My hat floated away. Oh, just barely, barely. If
it had been in time to get me to the drop, then I couldn't have held
on. Then this flume declines sharply there. They just fly down it. And
there the big river was partitioned off, this boom, two logs across the
entire river. And every morning prior to letting the logs through, you
have to go down and check, in case the flume, a board knocked out,
otherwise they will do a lot of damage, the logs just fly. And so you go
through and check everything, all right, everything's fine. And then
you have to walk across the whole river on the boom to make sure
they haven't untied or broken apart anywhere. Otherwise, the logs
can float away then. And I don't know what it was, either you get
accustomed to it, you have no fear of anything. Well, you try and walk
across the entire width of the river, wow!

ANUTA PAVLOVNA POPOFF (20 March 1888): There were five of us children. A bench
would be placed for us, and on the bench a bowl, and we would stand
on our knees around the bowl and eat so quietly; if anyone just starts
turning up his nose, Grandfather will show his belt. "When you are
eating, be still. You must be quiet." And we would just glance back at
Grandfather so that he wouldn't give someone the belt, for the lash
would always be hanging on the wall. And he: "Make sure you don't
upset the bowl. If anyone is going to tease or anything, I will use the
belt on you." That's how they disciplined us, the small children.

And we already knew some prayers. I was their oldest one there.
As we would stand on our knees, we would be told to recite, whoever

had learned a prayer. I would begin first, next to me my sister, there, a brother. I would be told: "And you make sure that he doesn't make a mistake, some word. Correct him." Every day in the morning, before breakfast. When we finish eating, then we say a prayer of thanks. Not everyone, the little ones, they weren't able to yet, but Grandfather had already taught us. So then we would say grace before we would sit down, and the prayer of thanks when we finish eating. And then we go outdoors to walk around there and play. While Mother or an aunt clear away the dishes, we play outside.

When we left for Canada, I had turned ten, into my eleventh year. Here, there was a different system. While Peter Lordly was in Siberia, each family had their meals separately. But when Peter Lordly came, then we ate together.

When I turned thirteen, then I was already appointed to herd cows. Then the cows were tended so they wouldn't get into the wheat and trample it. Then girls of that age would watch them. We would change off, the boys. We girls would take our turn by a week each, and then the boys would start.

Children were given the job of weeding the wheat. There in Saskatchewan in the wheat, the grain fields, there was a lot of colza, it has a yellow bloom. And until we got bigger, we would weed and then we would go, Mother and all the sisters worked together.

We worked with our mothers. We didn't misbehave so that young girls would run off somewhere and do mischief. We conducted ourselves with our mothers. We children would all go along until my sister was to get married, then she wasn't here with Mother; otherwise, we all worked. If a girl would be even a little disobedient, go off somewhere, to the river to swim, she would be spanked. Naughtiness was not tolerated. You would swim when everyone had unharnessed the horses for a rest. Children didn't run around wherever they pleased. Each was given his own work to do. And then we started raking the wheat. The men mowed it by hand, and we raked it. Everything was done in order.

There was a big kitchen, and as we came from work and approached it, we'd start singing a hymn of some sort. As we came up to the kitchen, we were greeted. We finish singing the hymn, then exchange greetings. The cooks invite us: "Please be invited to the table for dinner." We go into the kitchen and sit down. Those who can sing, a group, all sit in one row. By the time the cooks sets out the bowls of borscht, we'll sing a hymn and sometimes we'll sing two, depending on how the cook finishes. She asks that we may now say grace. And so we say grace at the table. So the first course is served, we finish. By the time the second course is brought, we will sing another hymn. Such was the custom. . . .

And then to marry. They found our partner, not we. But the parents. I didn't know that I will marry that one, but the one that Mother and Father shall allow me, that is the one I will marry.

Doukhobor workers at a communal meal at Brilliant, B. C., in the 1920s.
Courtesy Provincial Archives of British Columbia (Tarasoff Collection)
/ 47080

It was considered sinful to work on Sunday. It was said: "Whoever shall work on Sunday shall not earn enough for one meal." He will be paid back for it. During the week, something will happen that he won't work for two days. On Sundays we went to prayer meetings. After the meeting then you could go visit whomever you wanted, some relative perhaps. I was ten years old and I would want to sleep in at least on Sundays. Mother would come, wake me: "Get up, we'll be leaving for the meeting right away." She would just go away, and I would close my eyes again. And one time she just grabbed me by my hair: "So this is the way to wake you. I came and told you, and again you shut your eyes? You get up and fast, because everyone is going to the meeting right now." It was just starting to get light. There were no clocks there. The roosters woke you yet. All the old people there knew. When the first roosters would crow, it was midnight; and when the second ones would crow, it was four o'clock. The parents are already all getting up.

If it's a weekday, they all get up and go to cut the hay, thresh.

There, the threshing was done on the ground, on a threshing floor. Where the threshing is to be done, they will roll the ground; it will be like ice and slippery. This was called a threshing floor, and here the wheat, oats, the threshing goes on on this floor. Father and my older sister would go and bring a load of wheat to thresh, and in the meantime mother is preparing breakfast. They have breakfast and quickly go again. By the time the sun is up, they will have brought a couple of loads of wheat from the field to the threshing floor. Then the rest that have finished breakfast here hitch up the horses, and there were rollers. I already sit and drive the horses, ride, threshing. You just have to steer with the reins; it goes around and around. I was twelve and I could already harness and unharness the horses. We begin threshing. There, once the threshing begins, from four in the morning and until ten at night, they're on the threshing floor, hurrying to finish, because there, once the fall rains start, in Russia, then you may only be able to finish threshing in the winter. Then, when the threshing is over, Father and Mother begin winnowing. Made for us is a type of pusher. By the time they winnow the wheat, we will have already pushed all the chaff into the chaff shed. . . . And the small boys, as soon as one is able to get around on his own, they start training him to horses, harness them, and then plough. That was the boys' work, but our work was here with Mother. And when they would start cutting the hay, we'd be there.

As soon as it's nearing lunchtime, we'd run home, and there Grandmother has already prepared something for lunch, and we'd bring it then. They wouldn't go home for lunch. You hurried then as much as possible, because by the time you go home and finish with lunch, so Grandmother would make yogurt and bread, and we'd bring it. They would finish eating, and we'd take all the dishes back.

By the time I was twelve, I was already working on the mowing machine. Father bought a machine to mow the hay and a pair of oxen, and I would hitch these oxen to the mower. Father made harnesses for them. I'd sit on the mower and go. Well, the oxen were quiet, except when they'd want a drink. There, in Prince Albert, we had marshes in places, bushes and water there. No matter how hard you hold them back with the reins, you can't hold them. They'll drag you into the water, mower and all. They will have their drink and then come out. . . .

We had to saw wood for the winter. Haul wood. I actually lay down my saw and got married. We children worked right from the time we were little.

PIONEER LIVES AND TIMES

When pioneers tell their stories about their lives and times, some common themes are evident — hardship, backbreaking work and a sense of humour. But the stories also reveal a striking diversity in the experiences of those who settled in different regions of the province: the sea coast, islands, mountain valleys and interior plains. And, like every frontier, British Columbia in those early days had its tough individualists and eccentric characters, whose true pioneering spirit made them local legends even in their own time.

Ranches on the Open Range

Edited by David Mitchell and Dennis Duffy

Father Charles Pandosy, a Catholic missionary of the Oblate order, arrived in the Okanagan in 1859 and established the first permanent white settlement at Okanagan Mission. In addition to conducting missionary work among the Indians of the region, Pandosy encouraged white settlers to come to the Okanagan to farm and ranch.

The period before 1890 was one during which white settlers in the Okanagan Valley acquired huge tracts of land. The reasons for these acquisitions can be summed up in a single word: cattle. In 1890, while there were no more than four hundred white settlers in the Okanagan, over twenty thousand head of cattle grazed freely over the valley's ranges. Cattle ranching was almost the sole source of income for settlers in the region and it expanded rapidly under ideal conditions. The cattle ranchers were a determined and resourceful breed of settler. Their strong-willed and flamboyant personalities helped shape the valley and contributed to the development of a society characterized for many years by its friendliness, self-reliance and social freedom.

One of the first cattle ranchers in the Okanagan Valley was Tom Ellis. Soon after arriving in the region, he established a ranch at the present site of Penticton. Later, Ellis was believed by many to be the largest landowner in British Columbia and became widely known as "The Cattle King of the Okanagan." His daughter recalls:

KATHLEEN ELLIS: He came from Ireland in 1865 on May twenty-fifth. He was the eldest son, and there were seventeen of them at home, and I think he felt he had to do something. I think it was a very popular idea in those days to immigrate to Canada. He came here with the idea of raising cattle. He said that when he arrived and saw the place, he didn't think very much of it. But he was told that this was a very good place to raise cattle, because there were plenty of places to grow feed. So he said he'd try it for a few years.

I think he had grazing rights on about thirty thousand acres. Now that doesn't mean that he owned the land necessarily. When people say he owned land from the border to Vernon, I don't think that's quite correct. [When Ellis retired in 1906, his ranch had increased in size from a modest farm to a preserve of forty thousand acres (4000 ha). In addition, he held grazing rights on tens of thousands of acres of government-owned range lands.]

He spoke often about the Indians and he said he didn't have any trouble with them. He was very friendly with them. He tried to improve their ways, and they really had a great respect for him. Not that he was overly friendly with them or anything. He said that you had to hold your own with them, so they would respect you. They worked for him, and Mother used to have the Indian women in the house.

LEN HAYMAN: After Ellis got married, he built a church. His children used to go over there and play on the organ. When Reverend Green got there, he sent for the bishop to come and consecrate the church organ — his daughters couldn't just go and play any secular music in the church, you know. Ellis heard that he'd done this and he got very cross. He got a hold of Reverend Green and said, "Who told you to send away and get the bishop to consecrate the church organ? When I want it consecrated, I'll do it myself!"

Ellis and other cattle ranchers in the valley left their huge estates unfenced, so that their cattle could range freely. This contributed to the valley's special character and caused some interesting predicaments for newcomers unaccustomed to the ways of the Okanagan.

BOB GAMMAN: That country was infested with cattle. I hated the sight of the things, because they were very wild; they were very curious. If you were on horseback or in a buggy, they wouldn't look at you. But on foot, they were dynamite!

Well, I was getting a long [survey] shot from the engineer, and a bunch of cattle came after me, and I was frozen stiff with fear. I didn't know what to do. But luckily — very luckily this was — a cowboy came over to me at full gallop and said: "Don't run, my boy. Don't run or you'll get killed. They'll stampede you and squash you. Lie on the ground flat; let them smell you. They won't touch you, they won't hurt you, they'll smell you with curiosity."

Rancher Val Haynes. Courtesy R. N. Atkinson Museum (White Family Collection), Penticton, B. C.

He saved my life. Otherwise, I'd have been trampled to death, I'm sure. Well, I wasn't aware of these sorts of things. It was all new to me. That cowboy saved my life, there's no question about it. But it was a horrible sensation. I was scared mortally stiff. That was the worst experience I had by far in my life, I think.

Val Haynes, son of the pioneer judge, J. C. Haynes, was one of the first white children born in the Okanagan Valley. After working as a cattleman for Tom Ellis, who had purchased his father's holdings, he began ranching on his own. Haynes became well known throughout the region for his cattle, his fortitude and his generosity. His daughter, Alice Thompson, recalls:

ALICE THOMPSON: My father knew cattle; he grew up with cattle and that was his life. He was never too fond of horses, because there were thousands of horses in the Okanagan. Of course, he felt that the grass one horse eats could feed two cows.

He was always good to the unfortunate. He never thought himself any better than anyone else. In all the years my father managed the ranch he never ate separate from his hired men — he never called them hired men, he called them his cowboys — he always ate at the same table as the men that worked under him.

CARL McNAUGHTON: I was a good friend of Val Haynes. He always had a cheery word for me. When I was running the cattle sales up at Okanagan Falls, I would meet him there — although he was quite an independent person. He didn't use the sale ring as much as the other ranchers. He was a big enough rancher that he could ship direct in large quantities. His stock was considered the best, so he was always able to get top price without fooling around at an auction sale. His mind was always on cattle.

Val always wore his high hat and his handkerchief. As a cowboy, it was always a marvel to see how he rode and the things he did at his age. He was quite a heavy drinker, but I never in my life saw him offensive or unkind.

BOB GAMMAN: He used to tell me: "I know all my cattle by the look of their faces." He was a very, very tough man. All he ever wore was a silk shirt and a saddle blanket. He'd go anywhere, any time of the year, with nothing but a silk shirt on that hangs about his neck and his saddle blanket, and he'd camp out. Why he never froze to death, I'll never know, but he never did. He was a tough man.

ALICE THOMPSON: There is one incident that isn't too well known. I think it was about 1905, in Penticton. Father came in on horseback and, of course, spent the night drinking in the saloon. And it came getting towards dawn when he thought, well, he had to go to Summerland to gather cattle. So, he climbed on his horse and away he started out for Summerland.

Well, this was between Christmas and New Year's. And on his way he noticed these footprints, and they seemed to be staggering around in the snow. So he followed this one, and it went off on an angle, and he came to this coloured man. He learned later that there were five of them on their way to Summerland to serve the New Year's dinner. This man had frozen to death, and he saw he couldn't do anything for him so he kept on, and there were still more tracks. So he counted them and he came across another one that had been frozen. So he went on and he found either the third or fourth one, and he was sitting right at the foot of a tree. My father thought he was alive. He got off his horse, but he was stone dead. Well, he said, "There's another one around here someplace." So he climbed on his old horse and kicked the old horse in the belly and took off. And, sure enough, here he found the man, and he had just fallen again when my father jumped off his horse and ran to his side and picked him up. He saw that he was just about all in. So he took off his coat and his gloves and he pulled off his boots. He said that the man had little patent leather shoes and he took his shoes off him and put him on his horse and immediately rushed him to Summerland — they weren't too far away.

This coloured man was always grateful to my father for saving his life. And my father said he never could understand why they had succumbed to the cold, because he said that to him, you know, it was thawing. He would call it chinook weather. It wasn't really cold. But he said he guessed that they just weren't accustomed to the climate.

CARL McNAUGHTON: He was well respected. As far as I know, he got along very well with the Indians, and the Indians respected him. I can remember that at his funeral — Indians don't usually attend white people's funerals — but there was a delegation there, and they walked up to the grave before it was filled and acknowledged Val.

BOB GAMMAN: He was a fine man, open-minded and big-hearted. He'd give you anything he had in the world, oh yes. They all did in those days.

The O'Keefe Ranch, situated in the northern part of the valley, was once one of the largest ranches in the Okanagan region. Its founder, Cornelius O'Keefe, was also the first postmaster in the southern interior of British Columbia. Cornelius O'Keefe's son recalls the ranch:

TIERNEY O'KEEFE: The ranch certainly had to be self-sustaining due to the fact of the distances to any source of supply. At one time there was a flour mill on the ranch. I actually saw grain ground in the grinder. The flour mill was operated by water power through a turbine. It wasn't the only flour mill in the valley. In those days people were very, very handy with the tools they had and they did marvellous jobs. Today, we think we're pretty good, but to be honest, I don't think we're a patch on the old boys.

CHARLIE SHAW: O'Keefe was quite a cattleman. He was a very small Irishman. He was very generous in some ways and very miserly in other ways. In other words, he hung on to the nickels, but when he threw a party everyone was welcome and he had champagne — all you could drink. But he didn't do that too often. He was very miserly with his help. He was a stubborn little Irishman.

CATHERINE NEAVE: On Saturday, O'Keefe, who was a great driver, would say, "Hurry the horses through, boys, hurry the horses through. They're going to have a rest tomorrow." And on Monday it was, "Get the horses going, boys, put them through. They had a good rest yesterday."

One man asked what time they would get up in the morning to go to work, and O'Keefe said, "When the rooster crows." Well, roosters are rather unpredictable. One decided to crow about midnight. So the boys got the men up, and they started for the woods. They drove for hours before the daylight came. That rooster wasn't around for very many more breakfasts.

CHARLIE SHAW: Oh, I remember Mr. O'Keefe. The ranchers depended on rain for their cattle, you know. There was no such thing as irrigation then. He came down the street one day, and I said, "Good morning, Mr. O'Keefe." We young fellows were brought up right — we always said "Mr." to older people. He was just looking up, and it was sprinkling rain, you see. It had been a dry spell for about three weeks. And he said, "Good morning." And then he looked up and he says, "Thousands of dollars! Thousands of dollars! Thousands of dollars!"

No ranch contributed more to the development of the Okanagan than the Coldstream. Situated at the north end of Okanagan Lake, it was first established as the Vernon Ranch by Forbes and Charles Vernon. But its fame really began when the Vernon brothers sold the property in 1891 to the Earl of Aberdeen — later the governor general of Canada. Aberdeen had first travelled to the Okanagan in 1890 when he purchased the Guisachan Ranch, near the present site of Kelowna. He became enthused by the prospects for the future development of the valley and after acquiring the Vernon Ranch, which he renamed Coldstream, he initiated significant new developments. Aberdeen actively encouraged settlement in the Okanagan Valley and, in addition to raising cattle, he built an elaborate irrigation system and planted the first fruit orchards in the region intended for commercial purposes.

EFFIE McGUIRE: Oh, the Coldstream Ranch was a lovely place in the early days. It was a central place for everybody to come. It was very nice.

TOMMY WILMOT: It was just the most wonderful country in the world for boys. All the Coldstream ranges were wide open, with cattle running. Our house was just down below all this range country. And I would run away from home if I'd see the cowboys starting to move cattle; I'd seize a pony and away I'd go, cow-punching.

Lady Aberdeen's brother, Coutts Marjoribanks, became the first manager of the Coldstream Ranch. He is remembered as one of the more colourful personalities of the era.

W. A. MIDDLETON: The most famous character at the Coldstream Ranch, as far as I was concerned anyway, was Lady Aberdeen's brother, the Honourable Coutts Marjoribanks. He was as full of life and vigour as a young fella. Riding horses, breaking in horses and herding up cattle — he was just in his glory. As I recall, he was quite a gay blade. If you ever met Marjoribanks, I think you wouldn't forget him in a hurry. He was a big man, stout. When I first saw him, he was dressed up in flowery chaps, an Indian jacket with fringes on the sleeves, gauntlet gloves with Indian beadwork, a big sombrero or cowboy hat, big red handkerchief around his neck, and riding boots and spurs. I thought he was something wonderful.

One of the stories that I still remember them talking about is that he rode into Vernon one day, and he had quite a good-sized blue roan saddle horse, and, of course, he had his western saddle and was all fixed up. And he rode into the Kalamalka bar, right through the door; he didn't get off his horse at all, he just rode right into the barroom and ordered drinks for the crowd — which I understand was quite customary in those times; you never drank alone, you ordered everyone in sight to join in.

Grow Fruit and Grow Rich

Edited by David Mitchell and Dennis Duffy

The idea of growing fruit in the Okanagan Valley was not a new one, even at the turn of the century. Apple trees had been planted by Father Pandosy at Okanagan Mission as early as 1863, and small private orchards were bearing fruit on ranches scattered throughout the valley.

But the greatest impetus to the development of an Okanagan fruit industry came with Lord Aberdeen's purchase of the Coldstream Ranch in 1891. Lord Aberdeen's intention was to encourage development in the area by subdividing part of the ranch for sale in ten- to forty-acre (4-ha to 10-ha) lots. Once this had been done and the land irrigated, the Coldstream became the site of the first commercial orchard in the Okanagan.

Aberdeen's purchases of the Coldstream and Guisachan ranches were arranged by G. G. Mackay of the Okanagan Land and Development Company. Mackay was a pioneer of land development in the Vernon area.

The increased availability of land, coupled with the inception of CPR train and steamboat service in the valley in 1893, set the stage for a real estate boom. Numerous land companies came into being, buying up, developing and promoting the fruit lands. The Land and Agricultural Company of Canada, a Belgian syndicate, purchased several properties — including the O'Keefe Ranch — and published advertisements with the legend: "Grow fruit in Vernon and grow rich!"

The optimism and rapid growth that characterized those years reached an apex in the first decade of the twentieth century. The man largely responsible was a visionary land promoter named John Moore Robinson. He came to B. C. from Manitoba in search of a gold mine and discovered another form of potential wealth literally growing in the trees. The early days of Peachland are recalled by Robinson's nephew, and by one of his daughters.

WILLIAM ROBINSON: Well, he'd read about California. They were in the orange business down there, and there were small orchards that they were irrigating, and small lots, you see. He thought if they could do that down there, they could do it in the Okanagan in a small way, for peaches and apples and pears and that kind of thing. That is where the idea came from.

He bought land, named it Peachland, and said he was going back to the prairies and was going to bring a trainload of people out to settle in Peachland. He went back, and the next spring they came out with a carload of people and that started Peachland, settled it. They put an irrigation system in and they started planting trees, peach trees and so on.

GWEN ROBINSON HAYMAN: Of course, when the people up the valley heard what he was going to do, "Oh," they said, "that man is. . . ." They'd tell the people on the boats coming down that my dad was crazy, thinking he

*Real estate man H. P. "Breezy" Lee of Vernon had 30 000 of these post
cards printed and sent them to prospective customers in Alberta.
Courtesy Vernon Museum and Archives, Vernon, B. C.*

could cut up the ranches and run in the orchards. Oh, they just made
fun of him and everything. And the next year they were doing the
same thing.

He was so thrilled with seeing peaches and fruit being able to be
raised in Canada. And it upset him so much that there were so many
Canadian people going down to California, you know. He thought
that they should remain in Canada, that we couldn't afford to lose
our good Canadian citizens.

PADDY ACLAND: He founded, first of all, Peachland, and called it Peachland. That
attracted a man that was sitting in thirty below zero, you can imagine.

With "The Canadian California" as its slogan, the town of Peachland proved to be
a financial success — although its growth was limited by the hills that surrounded it
and crowded it along the lakeshore.

PADDY ACLAND: Well, Peachland, basically, was a row of houses along the lake. They
were building houses on the hillside, all the way up. They were beginning to put up little houses there and beginning to plant orchards.
The joke was that somebody was going along the road by the lake,
and a man fell flat on his back in front of him. He got up and said,
"This is a hell of a bloody orchard I've bought; this is the third time
this morning I've fallen out of it." And I can well believe it, because it
was going up like that.

The bench lands surrounding Trout Creek, some fifteen miles (23 km) to the south, seemed suitable for a similar but more extensive development. Robinson chose this as the site of his next conquest. The acquisition and development of the property required considerable capital investment, and Robinson wisely sought financial backing from a number of prominent eastern financiers and business-men.

HARRY CORBITT: Of course, his outstanding feat, I would say, was in Summerland. He moved to Summerland, after he got through with Peachland, and did the same thing there: bought up water rights and pre-emptions. Then he went to Montreal. There wasn't enough money around Winnipeg then. And the first person he interviewed was Sir Thomas Shaughnessy, who afterwards was Lord Shaughnessy. He was the president of the CPR. When Robinson left his office, he'd sold him twenty acres in Summerland and made him president of the Summerland Development Company.

DOROTHY ROBINSON (another of Robinson's daughters): There was Sir Thomas Shaughnessy, C. H. Hosmer — two names I remember — and they liked his story. A group of these men put up the money to start Summerland. Sir Edmund Osler, too, was one, and Van Allen, I think. They all acquired orchards in Summerland. But at the end they were very, very pleased with the deal, because I know the family silverware came from the gift they gave my father in appreciation of his success in Summerland, and what their money had done to build up under his care.

HARRY CORBITT: Well, after getting four or five outstanding personalities from Montreal, he went back to the prairies, and they just rushed in to buy land. That was the beginning of Summerland.

PADDY ACLAND: He came down and he founded Summerland with this gorgeous lake, and the sun was beating down on you, and all you've got to do is. . . . "I'm going to give you ten acres and in very few years you'll be making one thousand dollars or five thousand dollars a year off it, just as simple as that." He got them in by the gallons.

DOROTHY ROBINSON: I think most of the Summerland people originally came from Manitoba. Summerland, he always claimed, was a hand-picked com-munity, because there were such fine people that started in Summer-land. I think you can see that in Summerland today.

Directly across Okanagan Lake from Summerland was Nine-Mile Point, where Tom Ellis's cattle grazed. The land surrounding it was acquired by J. M. Robinson as the site of yet another development — the town of Naramata.

DOROTHY ROBINSON: All I know is that he used to look across the lake; and in a beautiful valley like this, with such lovely climate, he didn't think that just one man and a lot of cows should live there. He didn't like that idea. He thought that people should live on the land and should enjoy the climate and the beautiful valley. He used to sit on his veranda in Summerland and look across the lake at this beautiful

Picking fruit in the Okanagan. Courtesy Kelowna Centennial Museum, Kelowna, B. C.

property, where just a few cows grazed. So he bought it and started Naramata. Oh, it was a terrific little village, lovely village. At least, as far as I'm concerned, it was just wonderful. It used to be all trees, you know; all wooded and beautiful trees. But the difficulty is, unless you loved trees, the first thing people would do is cut them down.

BOB GAMMAN: Well, when I got to Naramata, it was in the early spring and most of the people here then were young men who were building houses for people and putting up shacks and so forth. Then settlers came in. Most of the land that was sold here was never seen by the owners. They bought the land off the map, had it cleared, planted and kept it for a while and sold it to somebody. And those same lots would turn over three or four times. It was surprising the number of people that bought land here that had been handled before by four different people.

The one commodity most vital to the success of the orchards — and most awkward to obtain — was a steady supply of water. It could be found in the lakes and streams hidden away in the hills, but the difficulty lay in bringing it down to the dry benches where the orchards were being developed.

RONALD HELMER: The Okanagan had a good many irrigation troubles. In the early days, the price of water was very low. As acreages increased, they became higher and higher, and eventually, there wasn't enough water during the irrigation season to supply all the orchards. Then began the work of building dams, enlarging the flumes and ditches, and which all cost a lot of money. As this went along, years came and more dams were needed.

H. C. S. COLLETT: I think it would be better to take one instance because they apply, pretty much, to all of them.

The first movement was to find an area in the hills where there was a creek running through with sufficient supply of water to dam up for a reservoir. That was the first thing. The South Kelowna Land Company developed that area up at McCulloch [southeast of Kelowna]. The water came down through the natural course of Hydraulic Creek, the headwaters of which had been dammed up. There's a deep canyon there, and it came down through a siphon and up on the other side into a concrete canal. From Hydraulic Creek to Canyon Creek, it crossed the canyon of Canyon Creek, through another siphon up on the other side, and was distributed to the lots from the main canal by pipelines. The water was distributed throughout the irrigation season — the irrigation season is May, June, July, August and possibly part of September. The allowance per acre was three acre-feet per acre for the season. An "acre-foot" is twelve inches of water over one acre. The allowance was based on three acre-feet per acre; although certain types of land did not require that much, some required even more. But it was distributed over the land through a system of flumes and pipelines, and administered by the water bailiffs. They did the turning on and off.

HARRY ALDRED: The water meetings were a source of interest. They were somewhat heated, I would say. As a boy I used to go fishing on the lake in the evening, and they'd be having a water meeting in Doctor Irving's veranda. I learned a lot about life, because I'd sit there and hear somebody shouting out at the top of his lungs: "But you lying old bastard, you know that isn't true!" And that gives you an idea of what went on. There was a lot of that; it was quite amusing, although they used to get pretty heated about it.

RONALD HELMER: One story I remember: up in the Vernon district was an old man who had a little piece of land. He was very poor, and he irrigated, and sold his little crops in the different stores. But he had a neighbour who was always stealing his water. He complained about him to the authorities, but he could get no redress from this neighbour stealing his water. Well, one day he went out and he found this man stealing his water, and he shot him.

A case of murder came up, and all the big people in the district went to back this old man in his defence. They said that he'd been in trouble with this man; he'd complained here and complained to the Water Branch and to the police, to his friends and everybody, and could get no redress. And so the only thing he thought of was — to save his own troubles — he would shoot this man; the man would be dead, and he would be hung. Well, the judge very wisely gave him a suspended sentence and told him to be a good citizen thereafter.

Packing Along the Telegraph Trail

Edited by Allen Specht

Hazelton's situation at the head of navigation and in a basin where several large rivers converge made it the natural supply centre for the interior. It began as a transfer point for supplies coming off the canoes and loaded onto packhorses destined for the Omineca mines. This function continued for later mining activity all over the interior and downriver to Lorne Creek and other spots. In 1880 the Hudson's Bay Company built a post in the town and used the river route and train system to link up its inland posts with Port Simpson. When the Yukon Telegraph Company completed its line in 1901, Hazelton became the supply depot for the linesmen's cabins.

WIGGS O'NEILL: The boat would pull into the landing and put the gangplank out and the foot plank out. The passengers would start to disembark and go to their hotels. There would be practically the whole town of Hazelton on the bank, see all the people coming off and so on and so forth. And all the dogs would be down there, too. Hazelton was quite a dog town. And the air was full of howls, because when that whistle blew, why the dogs howled. A landing in front of the Hudson's Bay and one in front of what they call Cunningham's store (he had a store in Hazelton, too). They had warehouses. Freight was all stored in the warehouses and distributed to the different consignees. There'd always be packtrains going up the Skeena and up toward Babine or in the Bulkley Valley. There was no roads at the time, just trails. The packtrains would be at their bivouacs or wherever they were waiting. Most of the freight on the boat was for respective stores at Hazelton. And they really sold the stuff to consignees who took it away on packtrains.

H. H. LITTLE: You see, Hazelton, as the head of transportation, was the gateway to all that country. We had packers. Charleson and Barrett were the first ones. They had the contract for supplying the Yukon telegraph as far as Sixth Cabin. They had one train of mules and one train of cayuses, and at that time there was a lot of packing into the Omineca. I've seen them pack big links of pipe for sluicing purposes. Big stoves. It was quite a sight to see some of the things that were packed on those horses. Some of them were big and could take a good load, but most of them were not so big. There was one there'd take about a four hundred-pound load, I think — the biggest one that I remember.

Sperry Cline spent most of the early decades of the century in Hazelton. Later in life he took an interest in preserving and writing about British Columbia history. This account of British Columbia's most famous packer is a reading rather than a spontaneous narrative.

A packtrain on the trail in winter. Courtesy Provincial Archives of British Columbia / 94318

Jean Caux, better known as Cataline (centre, hatless), loading his packtrain at Harvey Bailey's for a trip to Babine Lake in 1897. Courtesy Provincial Archives of British Columbia / 8760

SPERRY CLINE: When I first came to British Columbia, just after the turn of the century, Jean Caux, better known as Cataline, was still an important figure in the commercial life of central and northern B. C.; in fact, a large portion of the province relied on Cataline's packtrains for their continued existence. No settlement was too remote and no mineral discovery too inaccessible for him to undertake to supply it. I heard many stories of his efforts told by pioneers. A placer strike would be made on some distant stream, and when word of the discovery reached the outside a gold rush would start. Men carrying a limited supply of necessities on their backs would trust to Cataline to follow with cargoes of food and other supplies to the new diggings, and he never failed them. On two occasions the greater part of his pack animals died from hunger and other causes, but the supplies always got through, once on the backs of Indian women whom he pressed into service. As the years passed it became inconceivable that he would ever fail in fulfilling a freight contract, and he never did.

He was a striking figure; a Buffalo Bill head of hair, a Napoleon the Third imperial beard, broad shouldered, barrel chested, and tapering from the waist down to the narrow hips and thin shanks of men who spend a lifetime on horseback. His apparel seldom varied; a broad-brimmed sombrero, a silk handkerchief around his neck, a frock coat (in later years it was a mystery where he obtained them), heavy woollen trousers and a rather dainty pair of riding boots. In summer, to protect his hands from mosquitoes, he wore buckskin gauntlets but discarded them as soon as the mosquito season was over.

It was almost impossible to carry on a conversation with him. He had originally spoken a sort of French-Spanish dialect of the Pyrenees, but over his long association with different races he had acquired a few words of every Indian tongue from Mexico to the sixtieth degree of latitude, some Chinese from the packers of that race and a few words from every European with whom he had come into contact. To further complicate matters, he spoke very rapidly and in a kind of oral shorthand, any word of more than two syllables being abbreviated.

I never learned his exact age, but it must have been just a little short of the century mark at the time of his death. During all these years he had lived hard, worked hard and drank hard. Nearly everyone that ever knew him has told the story of "Cataline's Hair Tonic." He drank brandy if it was available, but, if not, other hard liquor would be substituted. Whenever he took a drink some of the liquor would be poured into his hand then rubbed on his head. There was always a great deal of speculation as to the reason. Some attributed his wonderful growth of hair, which he retained until he died, to this treatment. One day when he was in a good mood, I asked his reason. His answer was that if you put a little of every drink outside, you would not have a hangover next morning.

He had absolutely no business ability and always relied on the other fellow. Every spring he would get credit from the bank or the Hudson's Bay Company and leave it to the mining company or whoever he was packing for to reimburse his creditors. This resulted in him finding himself destitute in his extreme old age, and it was because of this that I became so well acquainted with him.

When old age forced Cataline to retire he was living in Hazelton, where I was the provincial constable in charge of that detachment. In those days there was no easy government money, no old-age pension and no welfare organization, and it was largely up to the constable to look after the destitute in his district. In fact, everything that was too hot or unwholesome for other departments to handle was added to his duties.

When forced to quit, his business was sold to George Biernes, who at that time had a ranch at Mission Point across the Bulkley River from Hazelton. Biernes supplied him with a cabin on the ranch, where he lived quite happily on the small allowance that we were able to obtain for him. He spent his time wandering among the ranch stock and he made frequent visits to the village. He never grew old in spirit and always enjoyed the company of younger people, most of whom he met in the barrooms.

In Search of Silver and Gold

Edited by Peter Chapman

Shortly before the turn of the century, the advancing American mining frontier transformed the Lardeau-Duncan river valleys from a seldom-travelled and mostly uninhabited wilderness into a bustling mining camp. The transformation began in the 1880s, when prospectors first reached the northern end of Kootenay Lake in search of silver and gold.

Early reports from prospectors were disappointing, and the rugged and trackless country remained on the periphery of mining activity until the fall of 1892, when encouraging news of mineral deposits along the Duncan River drew the attention of prospectors. In the spring of 1893, before the snow was off the ground, hundreds of prospectors were in the field.

Railway construction along the Lardeau River stimulated prospecting activity, and in 1903 a rich gold strike was made a short distance from the rail line near Poplar Creek. As a result, hundreds of people streamed into the valley, riding the newly completed railroad directly to the centre of activity.

GEORGE HANNA: I remember my mother telling me about the gold rush up in the Lardeau. There was such a remarkable amount of gold up there that they ran an excursion from Kaslo. The people expected the whole Lardeau was solid gold. They never did find where all this gold was up there. My dad was tied up in that with a lawsuit about staking claims. They were protecting it with guns, and my dad was very bold. He walked in and staked it anyway. He wasn't inhibited by the threat of somebody going to shoot, because he knew they weren't going to shoot. In this country the law was too strict.

The initial rich gold strike near Poplar Creek was not repeated by the masses of prospectors who rushed to the scene, and attention returned to Ferguson, where the new railway to Gerrard was having a dramatic effect. Cheaper transportation costs and the hope that soon the railroad would be extended along the shores of Trout Lake and up into the heart of the mining country encouraged mine owners, who placed orders for heavy equipment. Plans were laid to replace the packhorse and the sledge hammer with the aerial tramway and the piston drill. Five miles (8 km) above Ferguson, a concentrating mill was constructed and tramways were built to the Nettie L and Silver Cup mines. The ore was loaded into buckets and lowered on a cable supported along the way with towers to the bottom of the hill. At the concentrator the ore was reduced to high grade concentrates, which were then shipped in ore wagons to Trout Lake, placed on a barge and shipped south to the railroad. This was the optimistic scene in Ferguson in 1903.

ETHEL GARRETT WHITE: My father ran the Nettie L for a while, then he prospected and leased different mining properties. My dad was born in Iowa. He worked in the Black Hills, then came up to Boise, Idaho, and ended up here. He was at Ferguson in 1902.

My father ran the Nettie L before he went to the Silver Cup. The men kept quitting. They'd say they didn't like the cook, and he kept trying to get a new cook. Finally, he realized they just wanted to get down to town and get drunk. So he went up to Revelstoke and got the best cook in the country. He called all the men in and said, "Now, I have the best cook that's available in the country, and anyone who doesn't like her cooking can come and draw their time, because I'm not getting another cook." It wasn't long before the whole crew came in and drew their time. So he went out to Revelstoke and got a new crew. It wasn't long 'til some of those were drifting back and wanted work, and he said, "No, I still have the same cook, and you didn't like her cooking before, you won't like it now."

The optimism of 1904 faded the following year when the Five Mile concentrating plant closed. In the meantime, the Argenta Mine near the head of Kootenay Lake had just finished construction of a wagon road built on pilings through the Hamill Creek canyon. The wagon road connected the mine with the waterfront at Argenta and allowed machinery to be brought in and a carload of ore to be shipped out. But growing evidence suggested that the development was being carried out to exploit the company's shareholders rather than the ore in the mine. Chris Hanson recalls his father's experiences at the Argenta Mine.

CHRIS HANSON: Jens Christian Hanson came into this country from Spokane in 1896. He worked for a while in Rossland and then came up into the Lardeau country. He heard about the gold rush up there and, of course, he was a prospector. Dad was born in Copenhagen, Denmark. When he was twenty-one years old, he sailed for Greenland to the cryolite mines to learn mining. From there he went to Philadelphia, and from Philadelphia he went to Minnesota. He worked around at farming for a while, then he worked through to the Black Hills in Montana where there was a bad strike, so he pulled out. He went to the Coeur d'Alene. Then he heard about the Kootenays.

He worked up around Trout Lake in the mines, but only the Nettie L worked over the winter months. He didn't care too much for that, so he came down to Sandon for a couple of years. He was working at the Lucky Jim at Zincton, and it closed down, so he and a friend took a contract to drive a tunnel on the Argenta Mines.

I was born in the hospital in Kaslo in 1905, and I was about ten days old when we took the boat up to Argenta. My mother lived at the compressor plant and Dad walked up to the mine and down every day. It took twenty-five minutes to walk from the compressor plant up to the mine. Charlie Dandel boarded with Mother and Dad. The manager, Mr. Gardy, lived at Nelson, but he never showed up. My father worked up there for nearly a year. When they finished their tunnel, Dad stayed on as a watchman. He got in pretty nearly a year

*Readying for a blast in an Argenta mine on Hamill Creek, probably in
1909. Courtesy Provincial Archives of British Columbia / 55351*

as watchman, but it was a little crooked the way they handled the
money. The money was sent out to a lawyer in Rossland to pay them,
and the lawyer got playing around with the manager, and they spent
the money, and Dad and Mr. Dandel didn't get paid. So they filed a
lien on the property, and after a year Charlie Dandel got half the
property and Dad got the other half.

Around the turn of the century, there were three levels working at
the mine, and there must have been twenty to twenty-five men
employed. A carload of ore was shipped from the Argenta Mine to a
smelter in St. Louis, Missouri, but there is no track of how much it
ran in regards to silver and copper. Algot Johnson told me, "That
came from halfway between two levels. That's where the rich ore is."
Some good ore was found in the number one tunnel, but the foreman told the workers to take all the waste and pile it in there. They
were jibbing with one another, trying to get control. It was a common
occurrence through the Lardeau that partners would try to beat each
other. Some staked mines and did a lot of promoting and didn't have
anything to promote. They mined the public.

Andy Daney, a Rough and Ready Man

Edited by Peter Chapman

Prospecting in the Lardeau-Duncan was difficult. Railroads and stern-wheelers brought prospectors to the northern and southern ends of the valleys, but from there the going was arduous. Packhorse trails passed along the narrow valleys and clung to steep mountainsides as they ascended to the high country, where most of the prospecting was done. The trail from Upper Arrow Lake to Trout Lake passed over an easy grade and caused no difficulty, but once the shores of Trout Lake were reached, the trails climbed steadily upwards into the mountains. From Trout Lake City, one trail rose to the northeast along Lardeau Creek and led to Ferguson. Most prospecting took place in the vicinity of Ferguson.

Strings of horses laden with mining supplies wound their way out of Ferguson to the various mineral claims. The dangerous work of packing demanded much skill and great strength. One packer, "Andy" Seldon Morton Daney, became a legend in his own time. He is recalled by his daughter-in-law.

EDNA DANEY: Andy Daney was rough and ready. He came in here from Telluride, Colorado, in 1895. At the time there was only a pack trail to Ferguson, and there was one hotel. He got a job at the Broadview Mine, packing, northwest of Ferguson. That's how he started to work here. Then he started to go packing for himself. He bought a horse and set up business. He married Evelyn Jowett in Trout Lake in 1900 and had a house built in Ferguson up on the hill; it was quite the house in those days. Oh, it was nothing for Andy Daney to lift up a hundred-pound sack and throw it on a horse and have it tied on.

FRANK ABEY: Andy Daney used to ride a big black horse called Steamboat. That horse weighed fifteen hundred pounds. He was the only man that ever did ride that horse. I was only a young fellow. When his teams would leave Ferguson, he would get on his horse and ride to Trout Lake, and about the time the first wagon came into Trout Lake he would always be there to help unload; and when the last team was loaded and started out for Ferguson, he would head out for Ferguson and be there when they came in. Being a young fellow, I admired him so. He was more than human.

Although most prospectors who scoured the Lardeau-Duncan were Americans, a great deal of British capital flowed into the region. Some of the ventures were inspired more out of enthusiasm than sound economic thinking.

GEORGE PALETHORPE: There was a very conspicuous mountain called the Badshot. There was quite a lot of English money around there in the early days

"Andy" Seldon Daney on his horse Steamboat, Ferguson, B. C., 1910. The black horse would let only one man ride him, and that was Andy. Courtesy Edna Daney

when it was first struck. Some prospector sold an Englishman with money a claim on the Badshot Mountain. He bought it and was in the bar inquiring how he was going to get the ore out of there. One old-timer spoke up, "The only g.d. way to get that g.d. ore off that g.d. hill is a g.d. packtrain of g.d. bald eagles."

By 1905, the boom was over. But despite the collapse of the mining boom, some people remained dedicated to their prospects. Most mineral claims were worked on a small scale, and their owners laboured without the aid of compressors or tramways. High-grade ore was put in sacks and packed down the mountains, just as it was done before the turn of the century. This meant plenty of work for packers like Andy Daney and his employees.

GEORGE PALETHORPE: I was working in the old Eureka mine up on Eagle Creek. The foreman there was an old friend of Daney's. Daney asked him if he knew a young fellow who would be willing to learn the packing game. He said, "I thought of you, what do you think of it?" Three fifty a day and board. Oh, that was big money. You worked every day of the month. June to November. Then sometimes there was winter work, rawhiding ore.

The first night I got into Ferguson, it was after dark. An old-timer asked me, "Where you from, kid?"

I said, "Nelson."

"Oh, down in the flat country, eh? How's things in the flat country?" I wondered what kind of country I had got into. Well, the next day going up the north fork, I saw it.

I was working on Andy Daney's packtrain for two years. We packed supplies to the mines and ore down to Ferguson. From there it was hauled to Trout Lake. The longest trip they had was one called the Old Gold. The horses would only stand a round trip once in a while. It was too heavy. After they had a carload of ore, I took a mule train over to the mine and stayed there. Made two trips a day over the summit and dumped it over on the Lardeau side. The mine was on the Duncan slope. Heavy snow country. The mine crew had to shovel the pass out for us the first of July one year.

It was struck by three old-timers: Cy, Hemlock and Hughie Brown. When they made their first trip in here, there hadn't been a single stick cut on the townsite of Ferguson. They were the first men in here, I guess. They had a good lead, but not too much ore. The receding glacier exposed a good body of ore, and that's what they were working on.

The Triune Mine was shipping. I did a lot of packing there. Triune Basin was a tough place; the mine was up in the sidehill. A baby tram brought the ore down to the basin, and horses came up, dumped the stuff there, loaded up with ore and went down. Everything had to go up on horses to that place, mine timbers as well as regular supplies. It was bare rock and ice and snow.

Andy Daney was raised in Colorado, apparently very similar countries: stood on edge, straight up and down. I guess that's why he made it so good. The story was that he came in one summer with nothing and in the fall owned a big outfit. He was an expert. He was about the straightest man I ever had anything to do with.

He was very powerful. I saw Daney sleigh-hauling ore and the sacks were frozen. He jumped on them and they didn't break apart. He picked two of them up and threw them on the wagon. Four hundred pounds. His standard for loading packhorses was a horse a minute.

He was chain lightning in his movements. One day I was in one of his shacks looking for some repair material and here was an old Colt .45. Of course, kidlike, I had to pull it out and take a look at it. In walked Daney. His eyes were fiery. I said, "Andy, I heard about this fanning the hammer on these old pistols, but how in the hell did they do it?" The fire died down. He went to work and explained to me. He said, "I know how it's done, but I couldn't do it myself." And he demonstrated. His hand was just a blur, he was so fast. He said he couldn't do it. That was Andy.

Whatever the Weather: Red-Shirt Bill and the Royal Mail

Edited by Imbert Orchard

M ail days were great occasions for people to meet and gossip as they stood or sat around waiting for the mail to be sorted. Letters were their only link with the family and friends they had left behind. The newspapers were their windows to the outside world, then, as now, the world of politics, wars and other disasters. When someone was unable to pick up mail for himself, a neighbour would likely do it for him, then send it round with one of the children. But for many years the Atchelitz and Sardis district had its own rural delivery.

HORATIO "RAISH" WEBB: Mr. Miller, the postmaster at Sumas, would put all our mail in a sack and give it to an Indian we had engaged, who would go from house to house, each party picking out their own mail. We paid him so much a year. He [the Indian] was the father-in-law of Billy Ballou, the mail carrier of the famous days in the gold rush.

Billy Ballou was the first. He carried the mail on his back from the head of navigation to the Cariboo mines, and presumably all the way from New Westminster in the wintertime. Then Frank Barnard took over, and the moment the Cariboo Road was passable, he was running a stage line, meeting the boats at Yale and taking passengers, mail and express on into the interior. Barnard's Express Company had the mail contract for years, and when the steamboats couldn't run, he had to engage a carrier to bring both mail and express, and passengers, too, if there were any, up from New Westminster any way he could. The man who had the job for many years was a relic of the gold-rush days, a memorable character by the name of Bill Bristol. Some of the valley people drove team for him when the mail had to go by land from post to post, men like Reuben Nowell, Henry Kipp and Raish Webb. Bristol lived on what came to be known as Bristol Island, a few miles downriver from Hope; and in his later years he was a good friend of young Martin Starret, who grew up on a stump ranch just across a slough from Bristol's farm.

MARTIN STARRET: He was probably in his late sixties in the early '90s when I first remember seeing him. Being a neighbour of mine, living only half a mile or so away, I saw quite a bit of him. He was a typical eastern Yank. He spoke with a drawl. He was a loudmouth and profane. I know a lot of these profane men that are whirlwinds, and he was one. He wasn't an overly large man at all; I suppose he'd stand five-foot ten. And he was barrel chested and had a rather hooked nose and a very kindly eye, and was very jocular in his manner unless he was perplexed. I never knew him to panic.

He left his hair generally long and he had a beard. He'd trim it once in a while. He wore a slouch hat and he never tried to be neat. He'd have overalls and he wouldn't have any suspenders as a rule. He wouldn't know where he'd left his belt; he'd have it tied with baling rope. He never worried what people thought of him. What he wanted was results. But there was nothing exceptional about what he could do as far as his strength was concerned. It was the stamina that counted with him, his remarkable "stay-with-it." In after years he walked from Princeton right over to Hope in a day. My father told me any gait he'd start out with in the morning, why, he'd keep that up till long after dark. As my father expressed it, "It would tire any other man to walk with him, just seesaw, seesaw, all day long."

This Bill Bristol, he was born in Syracuse, New York, and he'd come around the Horn in a windjammer. He got off at San Francisco, or 'Frisco as he used to call it, and he worked in the mines there in '49. He must have hung around there quite a while, because he came up here in 1858, and as far as I know he didn't get any further than, I guess it was, Sailor Bar or American Bar above Hope here.

At that time, like after the Cariboo Road was completed to Barkerville from Yale, he got the job from the Barnard Express for carrying mail and express between Westminster and Yale. It was only in the season when the boats wouldn't run, like in the fall and early spring

Bill Bristol, nicknamed "Red-Shirt Bill," carried the mail from New Westminster to Yale. Courtesy Provincial Archives of British Columbia / 5018

— all winter too, of course, when the water was shallow, a steamboat drawing eighteen inches of water and very often unable to make it over these riffles. And when that happened Mr. Bristol would have to carry the mail.

When the weather was good in the early fall, he'd use a rowboat. Then, when the winter came, he'd use nothing but a dugout cedar canoe with a shovel nose to go over the ice. There was ice running in the water — icebergs. Maybe some of them would be twenty feet across, and maybe six inches to a foot thick. Well, he'd get the old canoe on top of some of them, and then he'd back up and get in between them, and push around with poles and paddles. He had to line it outside with sheet metal or tin, so as the ice wouldn't cut the canoe. It was just an ordinary Indian-built shovel-nosed canoe. I suppose it would be two feet to two and a half feet wide, and maybe five fathoms long; that would be thirty feet. And there were thwarts, of course, in it; they weren't seats. They were there to keep it wide, and sometimes they were just little round poles. Well, the first thing a passenger would do, he would want to sit on them, and then Mr. Bristol would have to explain to them, "You sit on the bottom. You sit right down there on your behinder and stay there!" He said the passengers often objected to the rough food they were eating. Mr. Bristol's mainstay was dried salmon. Granny Rabbit said one dried salmon would last him six days.

He employed nothing but an Indian crew to work with him, as he could, I suppose, not exactly bully them, but encourage them to a greater extent than he could any white people he might employ. Another thing, an Indian wasn't afraid to jump out into the water and wade, and if it was shallow, he didn't object to getting his feet wet. When it came to paddling, the Indian, having wielded a paddle for years and years, first on one side of a canoe and then on the other, the left was almost the same as the right. In guiding these craft up stream, there was no such thing as feathering it or hitching it at the stern in order to direct the craft on its course. From the time he left Westminster to Yale, every motion was to propel it ahead, as time seemed to be a principal element.

He told me that going downstream was the most tiresome. "You're practically in one position all the time," he said. "Paddle, paddle, paddle, one side and then the other side." Sometimes we would use a boat and long before we got down to New Westminster I could just imagine I was sitting on pins and needles.

"When I landed there, I'd always grab my paddle, because somebody might pick it up and use it. So I'd carry the paddle with me and the locksack. I was known down there as Red-Shirt Bill."

Well, the way it was told me by a gentleman named Bob Hume, Bill Bristol, in stepping out of the canoe after he landed, would never let go of the paddle. He'd carry it up town with his mail sacks on one shoulder. He said he'd have the paddle as protection against the Indian dogs that would come to bite him. He looked so queer coming up the beach in this red shirt and hunched over with those mail packs, they all wanted to bite him.

He told me that during the last few years of carrying the mail, this Old Yale Road was built, and he was able to drive a team from Yale to Westminster. But before that it was all river work.

Raish Webb was involved in at least one of these land journeys. It was during the winter of 1882; Bill Bristol left New Westminster by steamer with the mail bags, as usual, on a Thursday morning. But a cold wind got up, and by the time they were opposite Fort Langley, the river was frozen so hard they had to tie up to the bank. Not till Saturday was the ice actually hard enough for Bill to cross to the fort with the mail bags and a passenger, a Mr. Green, who was going to work on the CPR survey above Yale.

RAISH WEBB: On arrival at Langley the only team they could get was an ox team, with which he went as far as Langley Prairie where he struck the trunk road to Hope. There, he got a team of horses and sleigh from Innes brothers, who were large farmers; they took him as far as Mr. York's, Upper Sumas, where he secured another team and sleigh, just stopping long enough to eat. He telegraphed me to meet him with the team and sleigh at Chilliwack at six P.M.; I did so, for there was big pay at this work. The last team he used were not shod, and the horses got footsore coming around Sumas Lake, which made him two hours late. I took the Chilliwack mail down to the post office at the Landing, whilst Bristol and Green ate their suppers. About nine P.M. we started for Hope, with nearly a foot of snow on the ground; Henry Kipp had gone to Hope that morning with his team and sleigh to meet the down-coming mail from the upper country, in response to a telegram he had received from Bonner's [Barnard's] Express at Yale. More snow fell after Mr. Kipp left, so there was no track left.

We got to Popkum about eleven o'clock. Waking up Mr. and Mrs. William Knight, we unhitched our horses and fed them. Mrs. Knight, like her dear mother, soon prepared our supper with a smile. We stopped until a little after midnight to give our horses a rest.

The next twelve miles (19 km), to Jones's place on the Ohamil reserve, took them nearly eight hours. The first big obstacle was a bridge, which had been cleared of snow by the wind; but no sooner had the three of them pushed and dragged the runners over that, than the sleigh sank through the snow into a deep rut and turned over. So everything had to be unlashed and unloaded, and expecting the rut continued up the steep slope ahead of them, they, and the passenger, too, toted the sacks of mail and express up to the top of the hill.

RAISH WEBB: After loading at the top of the hill we started off feeling sure our worst trouble was over as we had about four miles of heavy timber to pass through, but our troubles were waiting us. A large fir tree had fallen across the road from the side of the mountain. We had to

BARNARD'S

Express Line Stages

CARRYING H. M. MAILS,

Will make

Regular Weekly Trips from Barkerville,

Arriving in Yale on Thursdays, in time to connect with the steamer "Onward" for New Westminster, and with the H. B. Co.'s steamer "Enterprise,"

ARRIVING IN VICTORIA ON SATURDAYS.

The California steamers leave Victoria on the 7th and 22d of each month.

ap27 3m   F. J. BARNARD.

An ad for Barnard's Express from the Cariboo Sentinel, *4 May 1872. Courtesy Provincial Archives of British Columbia / 89894*

unload everything, putting it over the tree, take our horses off, lift the sleigh over, then separate our horses and take them around the root end of the tree; in less than four miles we did this five times. We got to Jones's about eight A.M. All we had to give us light was a candle. We all enjoyed breakfast. Mrs. Jones was of Indian blood, but had been educated in a school where she was taught cooking; her house was always very clean. We stopped there about two hours, then started for Hope. By the time we got halfway to Hope we met the mail coming down with Mr. Kipp. Mr. S. Tingley of the Bonner's [Barnard's] Express was with him. Bristol went back with them, Mr. Green and myself going on to Hope where there was a man awaiting to take it on to Yale. Mr. Green told me afterwards that they charged him forty dollars for that trip.

When the trains started running, Bill Bristol retired to his land, and Barnard's Express gave him a gold watch, "in remembrance of his long and faithful service." But whenever the trains were delayed by slides and washouts, as happened quite frequently to begin with, people would realize how much they missed the old chap who had brought them their mail so regularly, whatever the weather. By then he had other things to do, like clearing his land and farming it, and walking great distances over mountain trails. He died in the early winter of 1909, retaining to the end his dry sense of humour.

"Wa-a-all, doctor," said this inveterate traveller, "I think I'll be goin' on a lo-o-ong trip today."

Free and Fearless: Children of the Backwoods

Edited by Imbert Orchard and Derek Reimer

Bert William was four years old when his family started homesteading in the hill country east of the Langley prairie. They lived on what is still known as the Brown Road (240th Street), but it was then little more than a trail through the primeval forest. Here and there a settler was struggling to let in the sunlight and get a few acres on which to grow crops. Otherwise, it was a world where humans were vastly outnumbered by bear, cougar and deer.

BERT WILLIAMS: Somebody was going to shoot a dog. Dad was like me, he liked animals, and he brought this bitch home, and it wasn't long before she had pups. Dad had made a hole under the house where the dog could go in, and she had her pups there. So this night my grandmother had come over and had supper with us, and one of these homesteaders — Tom Graham, it was — called in. They used to call in to see if they could fetch anything from the store — mail or anything. They'd walk down to Murrayville; that was four miles from our place, and they had a mile or two miles to walk home. Tom had called in and brought something for Mother, and of course Mother made him stop and have supper. And Grandma was going, and I wanted to go home with her. Just as we got outside, there was a terrible noise. If you ever heard a panther scream, it's like a baby crying — terrible. He was just a few yards away. I remember Grandmother calling into the back door, "Emily," she says, "come here. There's something making a noise like an old country fox, only worse."

This fellow came out and he said, "Oh, that's a panther." He had to go another mile through that bush, but Mother wouldn't let him go. So she took my sister and grandmother across to her place, and Tom slept with myself and my baby brother, and there wasn't much room. Well, this panther made a hole under the house big enough for him to get in. But as soon as he'd go to come in, the dog would nab him, and he'd back away. Then he'd be at it again, and he kept that up till daylight. And in the morning the sill was covered with blood. She'd fought him off.

Our hunters were the Murray brothers, John and Bill Murray from Murrayville. They had their own .44–.40 rifles, Winchesters. That was the highest-powered gun in the country at that time — well, almost. They used to have these hunts to hunt these wildcats. So we were sent off down to tell them about it. As they were coming up with the hounds — of course we were with them — the hounds took the

A family of settlers in the Fraser Valley. Courtesy Chilliwack Museum and Historical Society (William Dusterhoeft Collection) / P982.20.140

scent. He'd gone right out the Brown Road and into the swamp where Hill Top is, on the highway going towards Aldergrove. (We used to pick cranberries there every fall.) Well, they went in there and they got him and brought him out. And his fur was all chewed up from this dog. He was a big fellow. He measured nine-foot six from his tip to his tail.

The homesteaders that had teams used to look after other homesteaders. They were real gentlemen, most of them. I remember one fellow by the name of Archie Beaton. He rode a little horse, and if he was going to Westminster, he'd go around to these homesteaders to see whether they wanted anything from town. If they had any money they'd give him their money and their note, and he'd bring it and leave it at the end of the road; and there it would stay until you fetched it. Nobody would ever touch it; your name was on it, and that's all that mattered, them days.

I remember this night we were to go out to see whether Archie had got back. Sure enough, here was the stuff at the end of the road in this box. I think we were short of matches or something, I forget what; but anyway, we got it and were coming home. Of course, it was

only a trail through the bush; and as we were coming along, something was following us. We'd stop, then go on for a piece; then we'd
step off to the side, and we'd see eyes shining. He followed us right
down to the gate. We were telling Dad about it, but nobody seemed to
care, you know, because they never tackled anybody. A little while
after, oh, did he start howling. Of course, that was another trip down
to the boys to tell them there was a panther around. And they got it
away down the Salmon River this time. They always used to get them.

There was two kinds of wildcats: a big one and a little one. Everything had to be shut up — verminproof. Well, the first garden we had,
Grandmother and Mother and my older sister, they were out, digging
it up. I was supposed to be picking up something, you know, helping.
My grandfather was a smart old codger; he'd smuggled a crate of
chickens all the way across the continent on a colonist car: plymouth
rock hens and a rooster. Well, these chickens were picking around on
the clearing, and there was a big log there up off the ground a little,
and all of a sudden something come up over this log, and it had one of
these hens. Grandmother, she was right there; I can see this old black
dress, yet, that the ladies used to wear them days right down to the
ground. As he went under this log, she put her hands on it and jumped
over, right on top of him, and he went right through the front of her
dress — a great big fellow. You could hear him going down through
the bushes. He left the hen, but it was a fright. Well, gather it up — it
wasn't badly hurt; the crop was ripped — take it to the house, sew it all
up and doctor it. And the hen was all right.

Martin Starret was born in Hope on 17 July 1888. His brother, Will, was two years
older, and his two sisters, Birdie and Eleanor, were younger. When the provincial
government changed hands, his father lost his job as road superintendent and had
to eke out a living as a stump rancher. He had two or three horses and a cow, pigs,
ducks and chickens. He shipped apples, plums, pears and cherries to Vancouver,
and when money was low he had to get a temporary job somewhere. Martin was an
active, inquisitive child. His father called him "Mowich," which is the Chinook word
for a deer. It suggests a youngster who is always on the move, light of foot, quick
and intelligent.

In the summertime Martin's father liked to go prospecting in the mountains
around. As Martin said: "He was very optimistic, as most prospectors are inclined
to be; otherwise, they'd be no good in the world." One summer, after haying was
done, he took Martin and another boy along with him. Martin had just turned
nine.

MARTIN STARRET: Up behind Flood Mountain there is a creek that is now called
Wardle Creek. We went up there and we camped away up in the
divide, and the rock rabbits whistled all night long. We didn't take
any blankets that time, so when the fire'd go down we'd have to kick it
together. And we said we'd never go camping again without blankets
if we could help it.

Martin Starret as a young man. Courtesy Karl J. Wiggins (Ethel V. Starret estate)

Later that summer they tackled Silver Peak, a large mountain due south of the ranch. Galena was discovered there in 1868 not far below the summit, and was worked for six years; in fact, the Eureka Mine, as they called it, was the first hardrock mine in British Columbia. The ore had to be brought down by packhorse and shipped all the way around the Horn to Swansea to be melted. The young Martin was typically alert to everything he encountered on that trip and, what is more, he remembered it in considerable detail seventy years later— even to his sensory reactions.

MARTIN STARRET: We started one day after dinner. All morning we were putting packs together. I suppose I had, oh, fifteen pounds, and friend Fred — he was twelve — he must have had around thirty pounds. He carried the tent and a slab of bacon, or something. My father carried the prospecting pick and shovel, the ax and the blankets. I think he carried all the blankets and a lot of other things. I remember carrying the tea pail in my hand.

It was a warm day, and the hayfield changing to woods was an entirely different smell. You could smell the moss and the tang in the air from the fir or the hemlock; they all smelled a little different to me in those days. There was huckleberry bushes growing along the way, and my friend and I would grab a handful of them, eat them and run a little bit to catch up. My father would smoke his pipe once in a while and let a stream of smoke out behind. But he'd never grab at the huckleberries; I guess he thought that was all foolishness.

When we got over on the edge of Silver Creek, most of the time we were following this old Eureka pack trail that the mules had packed ore down years before. And we didn't talk much, because we'd have to talk loud to each other for the sound of the creek. Then again, the breeze that came from the creek smelled different from the woods; and it changed from this cascara or barberry tree and dogwood to more alder and birch and maple. And as we proceeded up the mountain, why, there was no more maple and then no more birch, and just cedar in the low places. As we would change to these different types of timber along the trail, it would be a little different scent, and you'd realize you were getting in a kind of another room, like. The cedar always had a pronounced smell, and then the balsam. I don't remember seeing balsam before, but my father picked a balsam tree for the bed. He said that by sleeping on balsam brush, you wouldn't catch cold so readily as if you slept on some other conifer bush. A lot of old prospectors say the same thing: the smell of this balsam brush will keep the cold away a long time if you are cold at night.

The first fire — not that time so much as the time before — the smell of the campfire smoke was quite different from cooking over a stove; and I soon learned that different kinds of wood gave different kinds of odour in the smoke. And I found out right there, the first trip with my father in the mountains, that there was nothing so appetizing in the morning as the smell of nice coffee. We had coffee that first trip, but we didn't have it the second trip; we only had tea. Coffee was too strong for we boys, he thought. All we had was bacon and beans and bannock and tea, and we boys put lots of sugar in the tea so it wouldn't taste so strong to us. My father didn't mind a bit.

The next day the trail became a series of switchbacks. Trees had grown up on it or fallen across it, and it was quite steep, but the blazes were still visible on the tree trunks. When they got up to the mine, they found the log cabin still standing, so they slept in the old bunks. They found a bellows and anvil, some eight-pound sledge hammers, as well as drills and dynamite caps. The galena vein had given out due to a fault in the mountain, and people had come up in recent years to see if they could find where it went. Martin's father had the same idea, because some days later he and Martin, just the two of them, made a trip around to the other side of the mountain, looking for the Eureka's lost lead — to no avail, of course.

MARTIN STARRET: This prospecting, I've done it! Gee whiz! I learned that it's no good for a poor man, especially a man like me that is getting on in years. A prospector is a class of man all by himself. If he has no optimism, he is no good as a prospector. He has got to figure it out: "Well, she's just around the corner, and I got her." But I was never that kind. I used the other grey matter. "Look, there's smarter men than me never made it. Why should I go and try it." That's the way I figured it out, and my father came to the same conclusion, too, in after years.

The Payne brothers, Charles and Gerald, came to the Gulf Islands from England in the mid-1880s. They were followed by their four siblings: Katie Bradley-Dyne and Hubert, Harold and Isabel Payne. Through Gerald and Harold's daughters, Dorothy and Dora, we have a lively record of this remarkable family.

When they emigrated, the Paynes were an upper-class English family, complete with nurses and nannies, tutors and cooks, English magazines and an income from home. But like many other similar families in British Columbia, they were unable to maintain their English way of life in the new country. Isolated on a coastal island, away from the social institutions of England, the family became partly English and partly North American. The children combined a British precociousness with an extraordinary undisciplined freedom. As one of them put it: "We really were most peculiar children."

DOROTHY PAYNE RICHARDSON: We had far more freedom in many ways. I don't think always that the relations approved of how much freedom we did have — to do what we wanted and do rather dangerous things for children of our age. But, at the same time, we had to mind our manners; we certainly had to watch our table manners and we never slammed a door without hearing about it. But we were allowed to do all sorts of things that other children weren't.

My brother, for instance, had a shotgun when he was just the same height as the shotgun. We had guns, we had boats. We were allowed to use tools. When we went log salvaging, my brother and I rented a big logging-jack from our uncle, and peavies — all kinds of things. And we used to take off for a whole day if we felt like it. Nobody would say: "Where are you going?" or "When are you going to be back?" We'd just go off. It might be by boat, it might be by land — but more often by boat — and if we didn't come back for two meals in a row, somebody would come and look for us, perhaps, but very rarely. We all did it. I know my youngest sister at the age of eight was allowed to have an air rifle, and she became quite a good shot. In fact, she's a better shot than any of us now.

DORA PAYNE: We all learned to row by the time we were four years old. I remember the water over on our side of the island was very cold, and we were considered very backward because we didn't learn to swim until we were eight, but that didn't prevent us going out on the water. As soon as we could swim, we could use the launch — we had a small launch — and that was the only thing that really spurred us on to stand that awfully cold water, because we did get tired of rowing.

My brother and I used to spend hours making rafts. And we used to trade apples with the Indians for old, leaky canoes which we used to patch up with tar, and then we'd put a sail in them. We were on the water almost as much, I would say, as we were on land, because we used to play on the beach, we used to fish, we used to row. On all our picnics we went on the water; every time we wanted to get mail we went by water. We just didn't have any fear of the water at all.

Of course, Dad would let us. He never told us not to do anything because it was dangerous. My brother and I — he was twelve and I was ten — used to salvage logs out in the Gulf of Georgia in January. That was the month there were bad storms, and the booms used to break up. We'd take the small launch and we'd go out in the gulf and we'd corral these logs and wrestle them down the beach and pull them by hand through Boat Passage where the tide was running fast and get back long after dark. Dad never told us we couldn't. I remember one month we each made forty dollars, which in those days was a fortune. But I may say, much to our fury, Dad made us put it in the bank, which, to us, was just the same as throwing it away; we'd never see it again.

The life was very different, I think, from the life other children led. Our amusements were different, because they were mostly connected with the water. Of course, we didn't go to school; we had governesses. Only we had lessons from about nine o'clock till one o'clock, and after lunch we were supposed to go for a walk — in winter. It was about a mile out to the gulf side; we'd walk out to the gulf side and then we'd find a nice big tree with pitch running down the bark and we would set a match to it and watch the tree burn. We burned down more trees! But finally we had to stop that, we were making the place look perfectly awful.

Greenhorns, Mudpups and Remittance Men

Edited by David Mitchell and Dennis Duffy

O f all the social groups that composed Okanagan society during the pioneer period, the young Englishmen were the most distinctive. The valley was an isolated frontier shaped largely by the energies of its youthful settlers. Many were hardworking and determined; others were detached and transient observers with little stake in the development of the region. All, however, contributed to a casual and unrestrained style of living. The young Englishmen were regarded as somewhat curious by many early Okanagan residents, but they helped give the valley a particular English character that readily distinguished it from the American frontier. The greenhorns, mudpups, remittance men and others are fondly remembered by pioneers of the era.

BOB GAMMAN: The country was full of the queerest people you ever met in your life. They all had a history behind them, you know — they all had a history. They were wealthy boys and remittance men, lots of them, but they'd all had experience. They'd hunted in Africa. They'd been to India. Why they ever came to Canada, I don't know. But they were real men, they really were.

PADDY ACLAND: It's quite true that the fellows that came out from England in those days — when I say England, I mean Great Britain, because there were Scotchmen and Irishmen and Welshmen — they were entirely different from people that came out later. They came out as a challenge. They came out from a point of view of adventure.

The bulk of the young Englishmen didn't know what the hell they were coming out to in the first place. They just imagined a sort of beautiful halo around everything. I guess I was one. I didn't think anything of getting up at three o'clock in the morning and riding twenty miles to play the fool with some friend somewhere else. The fact of making money never entered my head. When I ran out of money, I had to go earn some, that was all. I was one of thousands doing just that.

DOROTHEA WALKER: My husband was educated for the church. He was studying theology, and Greek and Latin and all the classics. Nothing practical. He was at Oxford and he wasn't working; he was much too keen about cricket and football and things, so they took him from school and they had a tutor for him for a year, but even then he wasn't working. He was still playing cricket and still playing football. And at nineteen he kicked over the traces and told his father he was not going to be forced into the church. "Well," his father said, "it'll have to be the colonies." They didn't know anybody, except they had a lot of relations out in India, but they were all in the army. That wasn't any use; training to be a parson was no good for that. And so, the result was he was sent out here as a pupil to learn farming at five hundred dollars a year. He arrived in September in a tweed norfolk coat and knickerbockers, you know, and woollen stockings and a tweed cap.

PADDY ACLAND: You know what mudpups are? Well, mudpups came out in those days. The parents paid a farmer, we'll say five hundred dollars, to give him work for the first year. And he was what they called "a pupil." Well, after he'd worked for about two months, then the farmer began paying him five or ten dollars a month back for it, according to how good he was. Well now, it seems a bit unfair; but at the same time, it wasn't altogether as unfair as you think, because some of these fellows could smash up machinery so quickly, or ruin a horse so easily, that the farmer did run a risk.

BOB GAMMAN: I wanted to be a farmer, of course. I had a year on a farm and I was green as grass. But my boss was a real gentleman. He never got mad with me. I had runaways and goodness knows what and smashed up things. But he'd never touch a thing when I was in a jam. He'd tell me what to do; he never touched a thing, and I learned an awful lot, I really did. I got so I was really efficient. In a very short time I was driving four-horse teams and what have you. These farmers don't bother whether you're green or not. They say: "Here, take the team and go." They do. It's surprising how I avoided accidents and things, you know.

PADDY ACLAND: I got a job with pick-and-shovel work, working for the Summerland Development Company. I picketed my horses out on the flat there, which is now a town. I was joined by another fellow, who was just about as green as I was. We used to ride about with imitation lariats, and so forth. In fact, the horses were the cause of both of us getting sacked from the Summerland Development Company, because we were continually losing the horses and not going to work; we had to go and look for them.

RONALD HELMER: As a horticulturist, I had no chance to get any work; I was unknown. So I had to do what every other young man coming out to Canada had to do: he had to make a reputation for himself as a worker. I was lucky, and I did. I took anything that was coming along. Miller, the manager of the Coldstream Hotel, had promised me if he ever heard any jobs going that he would let me know. On a Sunday, Miller sent down a young boy to the church when I came out. I was in my best Sunday clothes, and I went up to the hotel and asked Charlie Young if he wanted any help. Well, he looked me over, sized me up and he said no; he had all the men he wanted. Well, I thought it was funny, because Miller told me he wanted men. So, I went home. I got in my overalls and old "cow-breakfast" hat — looked very tough — and landed in the hotel and asked Charlie if he wanted any help. "Yes," he said, "I do. You can come tomorrow morning at seven o'clock. And if you know two more men like you, bring them along."

HARRY ALDRED: I had an English accent, and it was a bad thing to have in those days. In fact, there were notices round I've seen: "Men Wanted: No Englishmen Need Apply."

CHARLIE SHAW: Of course, in those days there were so many Englishmen who got a cheque every month or so; they were called remittance men. And they really truly were. The family gave them so much a month, or so much a year, to stay away from home. They were really ostracized, you see. Sort of black sheep of the family.

BOB GAMMAN: Kelowna was a rendezvous for remittance men by the hundreds, and they spent left, right and centre. They used to buy horses and play polo and tennis, and they used to raise particular hell. But they were good chaps, you know. They were just fools. That's all they were, fools. They had no sense of money. They'd run into bills and never pay them. They could have done, but they blew it as soon as they got it. They got fabulous amounts of money, remittances, in those day. They'd have three or four hundred dollars a month remittance. Good God, the manager of the Bank of Montreal wouldn't get four hundred dollars a month in those days, you see. And they blew it.

CHARLIE SHAW: There were a lot of remittance men here in those days. I don't know why. But, apparently, they wouldn't conform to the social customs of their family. They were rebellious against the old family traditions and customs. They refused to conform. They had ideas of their own and they wanted to live as they pleased. And, of course, that wouldn't suit the family, so he got so much a month to stay away from home. Well, they were truly remittance men, and you would be surprised at the number of those men; they were quite numerous in that day. In fact, all these little old towns had probably a dozen of these men at least that you knew of.

J. R. DENNISON: Somebody would get a remittance in, and they'd go off to town and buy a bottle of scotch and proceed to celebrate. And when that one was gone, they'd probably get another and keep this up for four or five or six days. They were always very generous and treated everybody in sight. So, of course, the money didn't last very long. And then they would steady down and have another period of about three months of normal living. Then, somebody else would get a remittance, and away they'd go again.

CHARLIE SHAW: None of them seemed to fit in. A few of them took up orchard work, but most of them just hung around and did nothing, waiting for their next remittance.

J. R. DENNISON: There is one observation I would like to make, and that is that an Englishman always seems to be doing things thoroughly. If he came out here and decided he was going to the dogs, he did it in a very thorough manner. Nobody could do it more thoroughly than he could.

CHARLIE SHAW: In those days, a man who would die wealthy in the old country would leave his sons an annuity — so much every six months or a year. It wasn't left in a lump sum. It wasn't really a remittance. But, of course, we classed them all as remittance men. Any man that got a cheque from the old country was called a remittance man — especially if he didn't do anything much here.

BOB GAMMAN: There was a man named Red Marshall and he was a remittance man. Well, he wrote to his family and said that he wanted to buy a ranch. They sent him the money to buy the ranch, but he never bought it. Well, the following year after this money had arrived and he wrote and told his parents that he'd got a ranch, his sister came out to see it. Well, what in the name of God was he going to do? He got in touch with the manager of the hotel where he'd been staying for years, I suppose, and told him the situation. He said, "Here, Marshall, I'll tell you what I'll do. You can come out and live on my ranch and claim it's yours, and I'll be your foreman." His sister came out and was perfectly satisfied that he'd got a beautiful ranch. She went home quite contented. He never owned a stick!

PADDY ACLAND: The English youngsters were not wedded at all to the orchards. They were real adventurous; they wanted to go out trapping and they wanted to go prospecting. When the winter came, of course, then everything shut down. Now, the Englishmen used to do this: say there were three young Englishmen, and one of them had a house. The three of them would go and live there together because it was cheaper. Probably it was cheaper, too, because one of them had money and the other two didn't. But they were good-natured and helped each other out.

DOROTHEA WALKER: My brother-in-law had an income from the day he was born. Then, when he came out here to farm, his father bought him a farm and all the stock and all the implements. Everything. His real income wasn't big, but he made that farm pay as soon as he learned to do a little farming. And the country was full of nice young men like that.

VIOLET BLANKLEY: There were a lot of bachelors that came out from England — remittance men. A lot of them came out and they bought ten acres of young orchards. I think they wrote and told their friends and there were several of them that came out. I had four proposals of marriage when I had only been here a short time.

DOROTHEA WALKER: The proposals just went like nobody's business at a dance, or if you were out riding or something. But you didn't take a lot of them seriously, because you knew perfectly well these men couldn't buy beans and bacon during the winter.

JOHN WILSON: Most of us Englishmen, we went to the Anglican Church on Sundays in the hopes of getting asked out to dinner for a good square meal. And it never failed. That was part of the week's entertainment. They always looked after the bachelors, the married folk did.

RONALD HELMER: When I got to the Coldstream Hotel, it was practically full of men who were unemployed. And I asked old Mr. Miller if he didn't lose all his money on these people because they had no money; he was giving them credit. But when these men went out and worked, they paid their hotel bills. Now, I asked him, "Don't you lose money on this?" And he told me that in all the time he had been in that hotel he had only lost on one case. And all the hotels were the same way. In those days people could be trusted.

CHARLIE SHAW: There was an Englishman I knew in Vernon. . . . He always wore a short beard, well trimmed. He was very English in his way. The funny part was, he'd go in his old tweed suit to a formal function and he was accepted because everyone around knew of this wager he'd made and why he was wearing these old clothes. It was a bet made in the old country. He was boasting, it seems, about the suit he had bought. And he made the bet with someone in the old country — they must have taken his word for it that he would play the game and he wouldn't cheat. Oh, that would be terrible, to cheat! There would be no fun in winning the wager if he had cheated, you see. He had to wear that suit every day for twenty-five years. He had to wear it every day, all day. No one in Vernon ever saw him in anything else. I think there was something like ten thousand pounds on it or something, so it was well worth while. But I don't think it was the money; it was that stubborn English idea of winning the wager, you see. And he finally won the wager, all right. He was quite a character. We figured he was a remittance man.

Due to the preponderance of English immigrants among the population, many of the valley's recreational and social activities had a distinctive English character — although the particulars were often altered to suit the country.

DOROTHEA WALKER: We had an awfully good time here, you know. People didn't work so hard as they do now. Plenty of private dances and riding parties. My two hobbies had been gardening and riding, and I had never missed a paper chase or a coyote hunt or a gymkhana. Every person had two horses because they were cheap to keep and the roads were vile. And no young person would ride in a buggy if they could sit on a horse.

We had coyote hunting, and it was just as good as hunting in England. Just as difficult. They met at least once a week, and it was always at my father's place at his stables, for the reason that there was a crossing across a creek. And we used to cross the creek and up on the benches, and in those days all the benches belonged to the Roman Catholic Church. And the fences there were all those great high log fences, about four high, enormous logs. The hunt, of course, just laid down two of the logs and left two, so the people who had good horses could get over, and the people who couldn't take the jump could darn well go home. I always had two good saddle horses — and one particular fine one, a real type of English hunter, sixteen-hands high, she stood. And she'd take any fence, so I could follow to the end of the hunt always.

You may wonder about the hunting dogs we had. One man brought out two of his foxhounds from the old country from his father's estate. He brought them out with great pride and at great expense. But they took to sheep killing, so that was the end of the real foxhounds. But the dogs we used were deerhounds, and they were very good. Now, the ride we took would be over the benches and, of course, if we found a coyote, we'd follow the coyote; but if we didn't find one, the ride would be over the benches and over the Sawmill Creek. And then onto what is now Dilworth Mountain and right up to the end of that big mountain, almost on the lake out of Kelowna, called Knox Mountain.

We nearly always stopped to finish off with afternoon tea on a place on the Brent Estate. And we had with us one man who had a real English horn, and he used to toot this horn violently to announce we were coming to tea. And very often we'd go to some neighbour for supper and turn back the rugs and dance until four o'clock in the morning. And nearly always after those dances, I'd get on a horse again and off for a ride in the morning instead of going to bed. When you're young, you can stand that.

Playing polo at Kelown, B. C. Courtesy Kelowna Centennial Museum, Kelowna, B. C.

In those days everybody was properly groomed. I mean, there was no such thing as the shabby way they ride today with a pair of overalls and a slouchy hat. You rode in well-tailored riding habits, proper bowler hats, with proper riding boots. I always rode sidesaddle; so did all the other women. After you were sixteen it would have been indecent to ride astride.

And then the paper chases — I was always one of the lucky ones who had a good horse. And Paddy Acland and I were often the hares, you see; some fine jumps we had.

PADDY ACLAND: All the younger people, both Canadian and Englishmen, they got along awfully well together. They had their own tennis clubs and they had a cricket club, and in the fall of the year they used to have these paper chases, which were a lot of fun. It was all done on horseback, you see. You'd send out two hares, and then you'd give them a ten-minute start and you'd go after them. When they eventually finished, they finished up at somebody's house, and you had a large tea party. And after you'd got tired of women's company, which you had to do in those days, you went off into somebody else's house where they had more whisky than tea to drink, and that's where they stayed for the rest of the evening.

TOMMY WILMOT: We used to play polo on Sunday morning and rush back home and tie the ponies in the creek. It was real cold water; we used to tie them on a rope tight across the creek, in case they'd been hit, you know, on the legs, because the cold water would fix them up. We'd go in and have a bite of lunch, rush up and let the ponies go, change our clothes, and go down to the country club and play tennis all afternoon. I played rugby, football, cricket and polo, all in the same week.

The Squire of Saltspring Island

Edited by Derek Reimer

Henry Wright Bullock was the epitome of British formality and conservatism on the Gulf Islands. He was the "squire" of the islands with his imperious manner, three hundred−acre country estate and liveried servants. Bullock obtained his servants from orphanages and apparently felt that it was his duty to give the less advantaged a start (and a place) in society.

Mr. Bullock arrived on Saltspring in 1892 and titillated and terrorized the residents from that time on. His parties, picnics and soirées were important social events. He was scandalized by the casual dressing habits of the islanders and never tired of instructing them in matters of style and taste. Despite his overbearing manner, he seems to have been well regarded by all who knew him.

MRS. M. K. CUNNINGHAM: Mr. Bullock had an estate. There were two lakes there, and he used to have a nice driving path where he could ride his horses and so on. He had a large acreage there and he put in dozens and dozens of trees — two or three dozen of one variety. It quite intrigued me that he had so many of one kind. He had nut trees as well as apples and he had a very nice tennis court.

I suppose he must have had money in England, or it must have been left to him, because he had plenty and he really spent it. He supported the church very well and kept it going for many years when they were rather slack. He was what they used to call in the old days a squire. He drove around and enjoyed tea parties and a social life with the people. He didn't work; he just really enjoyed life.

He was a wonderful character who entertained a lot. I remember in my younger days, when I was first married, how I was invited out to many of his dinner parties. He used to have seven-course dinners with everything — soup and grapefruit, and soup and fish, and it wouldn't just be a little skimpy piece. He'd have a great big piece of halibut that would fill a huge platter for just my husband and myself.

Henry Wright Bullock, known as "The Squire of Saltspring Island,"
probably in the 1890s. Courtesy Harold J. Page (Bea Hamilton estate)
and Provincial Archives of British Columbia / 90847

Then he'd have a huge roast, a fourteen-pound roast of beef, and there would only be three or four cuts taken out of it. As each course came, the previous one was taken out into the kitchen.

He had several boys that worked for him: one would work in the house, one would wait at the table, one did the cooking, one drove his car, and then there'd be the gardening — all the different things to do. He got these boys from the Protestant Orphans' Home in Victoria and he trained them all.

These boys would have all their friends in, and they'd sit around the kitchen table at Mr. Bullock's and they would consume each of these courses as they came out from the dining table. There were seven courses, anyway. When you got round to the dessert, there would be three or four beautiful desserts — fancy jellies and trifles and different things, and a lot of whipped cream. Mr. Bullock always insisted that you put a spoonful of sherry in your oxtail soup, or whatever you were having. He had various different things for the men to drink and a box of chocolates for the ladies and coffee in the drawing room. He really entertained.

WILLIAM PALMER: He lived with himself, in a sense. He used to have his meals in the dining room, and we had ours in the kitchen. But he would come out and have a cup of tea with us in the kitchen, you know what I mean.

He was quite sociable, really, but he used to have this old-country style. He told me that when he was a younger man he used to have two sittings and he'd go through the dinner with each of them. "Of course," he said, "I can't do that now that I'm older."

He still lived in the olden days and he dressed in the older style, a long black frock coat and a top hat in black silk. He still wore this type of costume right until the time he died. He used to drive around wearing this in his car. Previous to that his boys used to drive him around with a horse and buggy.

Where ladies' dress was concerned, he liked to see them with very, very thin waists; eighteen-inch waists, I think, he used to like particularly. You don't see those sort of things today. Anyway, he liked that and high heels and gloves and veils and earrings — you know, really dressed nicely, according to his taste. He wasn't shy at telling the ladies how they should look. In fact, he would often like to visit you just so that he could talk about how a person should look.

MABEL DAVIS: We used to go to his dances before the First World War. He would send out those very formal invitations, RSVP. We'd have to wear our proper evening dresses and our evening gloves and our evening fans. Sometimes he'd give dinner parties or luncheon parties. They were just something.

He had a beautiful house, before it was burned, with a great huge hallway and wide stairs up to the top, then branching off. On one side of this hallway was a great huge drawing room, which was cleared out for the dance, and the other side was a dining room, with a great, long, long table, where he used to give these dinner parties.

He had his "Buttons" waiting on him. You should have seen him. He was a nice boy and very slim with his buttons down each side. He'd stand behind Mr. Bullock's chair. We'd be there, and some of my brothers. We'd try to make him laugh. Poor boy — what agony it was! Sometimes he'd try to laugh, but couldn't be allowed to, you know. Those wretched brothers — they'd do all they could to start him laughing.

But Mr. Bullock was a fine old gentleman. He had his fads. He used to tell us how he liked to see the girls dress. They had to have eighteen-inch waists. Well, I couldn't get below twenty-two. And he wanted high-heeled shoes five inches high, which was very high in those days. He liked them to have earrings and a veil. Oh yes, gloves! He used to give us gloves every now and again. Oh, he was awfully good! Then afterwards, when we were grown up, he had the younger girls and used to do the same for them.

And his silk hat! Oh yes, his silk hat. One day Mr. Bullock came and asked Mrs. Wilson if she would allow him to supply Eton suits and silk hats for her two younger boys, so that they could wear them to church. So she finally got persuaded that it would be all right, so they wore these Eton suits and silk hats to church. Then one day the boys opposite, who were considered quite a bit lower down on the scale, came dressed the same. She was so horrified that I think she sent the Eton suits and hats back to Mr. Bullock.

WILLIAM PALMER: My mother worked for Mr. Bullock. After she left, he had one boy to cook and the other boy to do the housework, and he had that for years. Well, then, in the Depression some of these boys were out of work and they came back. At one time he had four of them there. He used to find them work outside keeping up the grounds around the house. The boys came from the Protestant Orphans' Home in Victoria. As far as I can remember, he had about fourteen of them in succession.

There used to be a cane in his desk, and I felt it more than once! But I can tell you an amusing incident about it. One evening I was sitting around in the kitchen and I noticed a rust spot on the hotwater boiler, which I started to scratch, and before I knew what happened, out shot the water. Of course, Mr. Bullock was called. I can see Mother jumping up and down now as she said: "Mr. Bullock, take him and take that stick to him." He said, "I don't think I should. That might have happened when we were out, and the place might have been flooded." You know, I was just elated, because the hot water was between Mother and myself; and Mr. Bullock was on the same side, but he wouldn't take the stick to me. But he was very strict and he used to make us boys toe the line.

MRS. M. K. CUNNINGHAM: Yes, he was a very wonderful old chap. He was like Santa Claus to a great many people. He was very kind. He used to bring these boys out and give them this wonderful home and everything they wanted. He even bought cars for them. They had their own musical instruments, had their own orchestra, and they were really happy. When they left there, or if they grew up and wanted to start on their own, he would give them a piece of land and a house, or help them to build a house or something. He got three or four of them started in places of their own, so he was really a generous man.

WILLIAM PALMER: But he was a very kind-hearted man, and you had to put up with his eccentricities. He was very, very good to me. He gave me a start.

Dream Isle: Fred Tibbs and His Castle

Edited by Bob Bossin

Y ou can no longer see Tibbs's castle from Tofino. It is still standing, but in the sixty years since his death the forest has grown up around it until all three storeys have completely disappeared. To the unpractised eye, the woods on the little island are indistinguishable from the virgin timber of the surrounding mountains. Most people around Tofino call it Castle Island. Only a few old-timers still speak of Tibbs Island; on the chart it is Arnet Island. Tibbs himself called it Dream Isle and painted the name in meticulous letters on a large rock. Since the war, it has been pretty much uninhabited, the property of absentee owners from Vancouver and the United States, each profiting from its purchase and sale without ever stepping off a boat onto the island.

In Tofino, Castle Island is said to be haunted, though this information is always passed on with a grain of salt. Still, there is no question that the place has been unlucky — witness Tibbs's death, and Leach's, and Mrs. O.'s baby's. There was also the crab fisherman who went mad, and the scandal involving Mr. A.'s daughter. For their part, the Clayoquots are said to have shunned the island, labelling it *cultus* (Chinook for worthless or bad).

ALMA ARNET SLOMAN: He must have come about 1910 or '11. People wanted to get a road here, so they wanted more settlers, and sent these brochures to England advertising the West Coast. Most of the Englishmen went to Vargas, but Tibbs was at Long Beach. I think he worked up at the hatchery. He was a short man with a round face and curly hair. And he was a perfect gentleman. He wore a jacket whenever he wasn't working.

BILL SHARP: When he first came here, he came to Long Beach. Then he sold that property. Everybody thought he was crazy, but I guess he got five thousand dollars for it, which was a lot of money in those days. So he was just passing his time on that island. I used to see him working all the time. I'd row over, and we'd talk about, oh gosh, clearing land. that's about all you did in those days is talk about what you're going to clear and how you're going to do it and how you're going to take this stump out or that other thing. Then I'd row back.

ALMA SLOMAN: He was so determined. My father said to him that he should leave some trees for protection against the storms, but he just went ahead. He said he wanted to make a bicycle track.

TRYGVE ARNET: He always seemed to have money. He was always ordering stuff, buying all that lumber for the castle. Oh yes, I think he got quite a bit of money from England. I guess he was a bad boy and they shipped him out to Canada.

Tibbs Island in the 1920s. The 100-foot spruce that Tibbs built a ladder up is in the centre. To the left is the tower of his wooden castle. Courtesy Provincial Archives of British Columbia / 92588

FRANCES TIBBS DOMAN (a niece of Fred Tibbs): Fred was self-supporting! He wouldn't take any money from you. He certainly was not a black sheep; he was a very white sheep, I should say.

CONSTANCE TIBBS (a niece of Fred Tibbs): The family were oil brokers in the City of London, from way back in the 1700s. My great-great-grandfather was freeman of the City of London and master of the Tallow Chandlers Livery Company. But somebody swindled him out of his money, and he lost it. On his mother's side, Fred was related to Robert Browning, the poet. His eldest brother was a lieutenant-colonel in the army, and he married the great-great-great-granddaughter of the Earl of Leicester. That was Uncle William.

FRANCES DOMAN: Name-dropper.

CONSTANCE TIBBS: You could say they were well-to-do middle-class people — Lower Church of England, very Victorian, a very religious household. They had a few maids, a housemaid and a cook. Then, when Father was sixteen — he was a little older than Fred — they lost practically all the money because of a slump or something like that, but before that they were quite well off. Fred went to Bancroft School — that was a well-known grammar school — and then he took farm training and came to Canada.

FRANCES DOMAN: He worked his way across doing all sorts of things, loading himself onto coal trucks, I suppose.

CHRISTOPHER DOMAN (son of Mrs. Doman): He worked on the railway.

FRANCES DOMAN: Finally, he bought this little island off Tofino and he must have spent most of his time knocking down trees. He worked a fever. I don't think anyone in the family ever thought he was eccentric.

CHRISTOPHER DOMAN: Of course, all the family were nuts anyway. One of the uncles went for a walk one afternoon and came back three years later and asked if dinner was ready.

CONSTANCE TIBBS: Uncle William.

CRISTOPHER DOMAN: Fred was no different than the rest of us.

TRYGVE ARNET: Now, right in the middle of his island there was a great big spruce tree. Well, he topped it a hundred feet up. He went up through the limbs and as he came down he chopped the limbs off. We could see the difference every day. We were wondering what he was going to do. Eventually, he started to build a ladder.

KARL ARNET: He built the rungs right on the tree and then a framework of two-by-fours going up and pieces of shiplap every so far apart, so you couldn't fall out. It went right up to the fork of the tree, and then he put framework right up to the top of that. He built a seat up there. You could turn around and sit there. I was up there a couple of times. It was quite nice; you could see all over the islands.

I think maybe he sat up there and played his bugle or his cornet a few times. They say he took the gramophone up there, but I think that's far-fetched.

DAPHNE GIBSON: He used to play "Come to the Cookhouse Door, Boys" every morning at eight o'clock.

DOROTHY ABRAHAM: He had the most beautiful collection of records. The gramophone was his constant companion, wasn't it?

TED ABRAHAM: I suppose it was.

DOROTHY ABRAHAM: He used to play it up his tree. I wouldn't have gone up the tree for anything. Did you go up the tree?

TED ABRAHAM: I might have done.

DOROTHY ABRAHAM: I bet you did. You always loved doing things like that.

WINNIE DIXSON: He had his tree and he was building this funny old castle place. I don't know what he did that for.

KARL ARNET: The castle was never all finished. He just had a ladder going up to the second floor, and another ladder going up to the tower. He had his bed up there. The tower was only about ten feet square. When he went overseas, he put big shutters over the windows and he painted the girls on that. He did a very good job of it, too.

KEN GIBSON: Looking at it from the west, it was just like a castle in England. The well was below the window, the rose trellises were out farther and the love seat was off on the side. That was the picture he created.

TRYGVE ARNET: And right in front of the house, he flattened the face of a big rock and he painted "Dream Isle" across it in great big letters. Beautiful painting.

KEN GIBSON: The only thing missing was a princess in the tower, so he painted a beautiful picture of this princess and put her in the window that faces to the west over the top of his garden. The one he painted — that would be Buckle's great-aunt Olive.

LILLIAN GARRARD: Yes, Olive was beautiful then. Oh, yes. She's beautiful now.

VERA MARSHALL: I understand that people gossiped about Cousin Fred and said that he was slightly out of his mind. He certainly wasn't. He was bright as a button. I have an idea he wrote poetry. I have no reason for saying that, but he was that type of person — not mystical, but he was the sort of person a poet would be.

You knew he was disfigured. It wasn't pretty. It was on the left side; the hole went right up through here and out the other end of that part of his face. Everybody thought it was a war wound. It wasn't. I think one day when he was in his teens he was riding his horse, and the horse threw him and then kicked him in the face.

After we realized he was sensitive about it, we never mentioned it. He didn't even like to be photographed, though he sat for them in good grace. He wasn't in the least flirtatious or anything like that. He wasn't that kind. He was too self-conscious. He was what you would call a loner. That was why he shut himself up on that island. He would climb up that tree — I think he called it "getting away from it all." He said he liked to be away up higher than everything and look at the stars and the sun and the scenery. I can quite understand his feelings, can't you?

FRANCES DOMAN: When he was a child, he fell on his mother's sewing machine, on the things that stick up, and he got a diseased bone. He had heaps of operations on this bone while he was in school.

CONSTANCE TIBBS: That would have been about 1890. Of course, surgery wasn't very good in those days.

FRANCES DOMAN: I remember he had these big holes, some on his neck, some on his face. They were like great dimples, only excessive. It embarrassed him terribly, so he wanted to get right away where he wasn't known. That was what my father said.

KARL ARNETT: He was really a hermit sort of a guy, though he had us over to the island sometimes. He'd make cocoa for everybody and light a fire. And then he'd play the gramophone.

ALMA SLOMAN: He would come over and say, "I want you young people to come on such and such a night and hear my new records." He loved music and he was a beautiful singer. He used to sing "A Perfect Day" and "When Irish Eyes Are Smiling." He came to the dances, too, but he wouldn't dance. If someone asked him to dance in a Paul Jones, he would move to the other side of the room or go outside. He used to

Fred Tibbs with Vera Marshall in 1919 or 1920. Courtesy Provincial Archives of British Columbia / F–3427

make up poetry and he would read it at gatherings or put it on the bulletin board at the store.

FRANCES DOMAN: Where did we put that lovely poem, the one that was in Fred's Bible? I think it's sweet. It reminds me of Hiawatha.

WHEN NOAH ENTERED THE ARK

by F. G. Tibbs

What a terrible noise there must have been.
What peculiar sights Noah must have seen.
When he hunted and captured his wild beast show
Seven of clean, of unclean two
Of every kind of beast he knew.
For when he entered the ark
The dogs were sure to bark.
The wolves would howl and the tigers growl
The lions roar and the rooks would caw
While mixed with this was the serpents hiss
The squeak of rats and the purr of cats
The buzz of bees and the chirp of fleas.

What time and what pains he must have spent
As to the right and left of the brutes he went.
For the cat would swear in the face of the bear
The wolf would leap at the helpless sheep
And the bulldog fight all the dogs in sight
And the buffalo toss at the frightened horse
And the serpent twine round the Roebuck's spine
The beetle nip at the rabbit's lip
The wasp sting pierce the Zebra fierce
And the Eagle peck at the Jackal's neck . . .

DOROTHY ABRAHAM: He led a very lonely sort of life, though he seemed happy.
TED ABRAHAM: He fell in love with two girls.
DOROTHY ABRAHAM: Well, he didn't really know them very well, did he?
TED ABRAHAM: No, he didn't.

EVELYN SULLIVAN: He wanted to marry Winnie Dixson, but her parents wouldn't let her marry anyone.

WINNIE DIXSON: Oh, he tried all of us, all the different girls. He'd come over and sit down and talk with Father and Mother. I took a book and went upstairs if there were too many young men around. I left Father and

Mother to talk to them. Father used to tell me about it — "That man who is coming here is no good as a husband." I didn't have much interest. I didn't have time. I had about three hundred chickens.

OLIVE GARRARD BROAD: He used to come to the house and chat with Mother about England.

ENID GARRARD ROSEBOROUGH: He was really coming to see Olive.

OLIVE BROAD: I thought it was Ethel.

ALMA SLOMAN: He was one of the very last to go to the war. Then he went without telling anyone. That's what they all did. I think the postmaster knew he was going and told me. He gave me his soldier picture. It was taken from the side because of his disfigurement.

VERA MARSHALL: When he came back from overseas, Cousin Freddy said he'd realized he'd done a very silly thing. That will that he'd made was a joke, a rather cruel joke. It was his overworked sense of humour. These girls he left his property to, they didn't get on! He thought this was really funny. When he came back, he came to us and he said, "I'm going to change my will." He asked Dad if he would go up there as witness, which Dad was agreeable to do; but before he could do that, Freddy died.

ALMA SLOMAN: It was a proper will. He made it before he went to the war. They all did. He left the house to Olive and the island to me. Olive didn't want anything to do with it, so my father arranged that I would buy her share. I didn't have the island very long. I sold it to Mr. Leach, but he was killed before he finished paying it off.

OLIVE BROAD: Alma and I were friends, and we were both underage.

ENID ROSEBOROUGH: They were both blondes.

OLIVE BROAD: My father and Alma's father settled everything to do with the will. And someone came up from the family, I think. I don't really remember the will. There have been so many since.

This is the will and testament of me, Frederick Gerald Tibbs, (farmer), presently residing in Tofino, B. C. . . . I give devise and bequeath unto Miss Alma Arnet (because she's the nicest girl I ever met and another reason she knows), Lot 1460, Tibbs Island, and everything thereon, excepting the house and ten feet of land on either side including the house site. The house and contents thereof, except the gramophone, go to Miss Olive Garrard, of Tofino, B. C. (because it was built for her) so long as she remains single. In case of her marrying, the house goes to Miss Alma Arnet if she is still single. If not the house is to be sold and proceeds . . . to be used solely and absolutely in the cause of Christ, either in feeding or clothing the destitute or needy or by donation to some society or persons teaching the pure teaching of Christ, for the winning of souls to him.

Written by myself at Tofino, B. C., this second day of July, nineteen hundred and seventeen.

F. G. *Tibbs*

TRYGVE ARNET: He had a gasboat, the *Agnes,* and the first of July he took a bunch of us up to the hatchery for a picnic. We spent a really wonderful day up there. Then on the fourth of July we happened to look over in the afternoon, and the Clayoquot Hotel was on fire. And boy, did she burn! And Tibbs, he went over. We saw him going across in his skiff to fight the fire. I think it was the next day it happened. I remember everything seemed to happen at once.

He had been blasting some of the rock on the island which he owned with some old powder and he had got badly powdered and had been quite ill from the effects. Then the hotel at Clayoquot caught fire and Tibbs with others, myself amongst the number, had been very energetic in helping to prevent the fire spreading to other buildings. That evening I saw him jump into his little skiff, or flat-bottomed boat, on which he had an outboard motor, to go home. Tibbs had been appointed to look after the lights in the harbour which required his attention every other day. The next morning early he started out to look after these lights.

FRANK GARRARD, *Memoirs*

TRYGVE ARNET: They were all coal oil lamps at that time, big flat wooden floats with tripods on them and the light on top of that. He'd take a new lamp out and put it up, and take the old one home and refuel it. Well, anyway, that morning he'd attended to the first one and he went out to the far one off Mission Point. He just pulled the prow of the skiff up over this wooden platform float. Well, evidently, there was a swell coming in from the ocean. While he was up doing the light, the skiff slipped off the float. You know, with the motion it gradually worked off and started to drift away. The tide was ebbing, and there was quite a little breeze blowing. So he hung all his clothes on the rattlings of this tripod where the light was, so that they would be dry. He figured on coming back and putting them on again. Anyway, he stripped off and went in after it. I think I would have stayed on the light if I had been him.

ALMA SLOMAN: They said he finished the lamp before he tried to get his boat. He was so determined, you see.

Seeing his skiff and engine got away from the buoy, Tibbs, who was a good swimmer, started swimming after it. But about that time an Indian in his launch, passing by and seeing a floating skiff with no-one in it, took it in tow and took it over to the Indian ranch about one and one half miles off. He would not have heard Tibbs shouting on account of the noise of his own engine, so Tibbs apparently turned round and swam towards the nearest beach.

FRANK GARRARD

KARL ARNET: The tide was flooding, and a little bit of a west wind was blowing up the channel. The wind took the skiff faster than he could swim, and he saw that. Then he swam for the spit there at Clayoquot, the big sandbar sticking out. He swam for that and he got to the rock a little ways out.

WINNIE DIXSON: There was a rock, and he was so exhausted. I know he tried to get some Indian women to bring a canoe. They were digging clams out on the spit. They said that he shouted to them, but they didn't know what he was saying. They didn't understand English, and he didn't talk the Indian language. What they should have done was to have gone back down and told the policeman, and he would have got a boat and gone up and picked him up, but he had to swim the last part, to the island.

BILL SHARP: Between the rock and the spit there's a big field of weed, and this is what more or less exhausted him. You see, the tide was fairly low, and the weed, well, it's like grass and it's long, six or seven feet. When it's high tide, it's underwater. But then, as the tide goes down, it starts laying on the top. He'd be trying to push himself through this weed, and it would pull him back all the time.

TRYGVE ARNET: The Japanese boats were going out fishing that day, and one of them happened to look over and he saw this man coming over the rock with no clothes on. He thought that was awful funny, a man walking over the rock with no clothes on. Then he saw him come down and get in the water again on the other side, so he thought, well, I'm going to go and get help. So he went up and called Clarence Dawley and got him out of bed and told him, "There's somebody over here with no clothes on; you better go up there, there's something wrong." So they went and walked to the end of the spit.

BILL SHARP: He made the spit all right. He crawled up on the sand and lay there, but it was early in the morning, and nobody even knew he was there.

> *J. Arnold Hannah,*
> *Barrister in Law, Solicitor,*
> *Notary Public,*
> *Port Alberni,*
> *July 9, 1921*

Re: F. G. Tibbs, deceased.

On the fifth day of July, 1921, the death of F. G. Tibbs, of Tofino, B. C. was reported to me. On making an inquiry I found that the deceased had started to swim from a light buoy to the shore; that he had reached shore in an exhausted condition and as a result of overexertion he there and then collapsed. Everything was done to revive him but without success.

Kindly send me some more voucher forms.

> *J. A. Hannah, Coroner*

Swiss Climbing Guides in the Rockies

Edited by Susan Leslie

The CPR was central in the development of mountaineering in Canada. It was the CPR that made the Canadian mountains known to European climbers: CPR brochures circulated in Europe described the Selkirks as "the Alps of North America," and the Rockies as "Fifty Switzerlands in One." CPR steamers and CPR trains brought climbers to the western mountains, where they stayed in CPR hotels.

However, there was one serious drawback to climbing in Canada. There were no professional guides living here, and in the nineteenth century only the bravest and most experienced climbers would venture on an alpine climb without a guide. After the first mountaineering fatality in Canada in 1896, British and American alpinists began to urge the CPR to provide guiding services. In 1899, two Swiss guides, Edward Feuz, Sr., and Christian Häsler, Sr., were brought to Canada by the railway and stationed at Glacier House. For the next fifty years, there were Swiss guides in the mountains of Canada.

Edward Feuz, Jr., came to Canada with his father in 1903. Until 1949, he worked as a guide for the CPR.

EDWARD FEUZ, JR.: My father was the chief guide at Interlaken [Switzerland]. There was an English gentleman named Clark living in town, and he called up my father. Clark had a letter from London, England, from the CPR [asking for guides to work in Canada]. So the next year, 1899, it was all arranged for my dad, with another man named Häsler [Christian Häsler, Sr.] to come to Canada. And they came to the Canadian Rockies, to Field and Glacier, and they stayed there the summer and climbed. Somehow the company liked it, and within two years or so, there was as many as eight guides come out.

I came out in 1903. I was nineteen. I was here as a porter, at the old Glacier House Hotel. We had the [Illecillewaet] glacier coming down right behind the hotel, almost into the trees. We had to go up there whenever people wanted to go, sometimes twice a day. We had to chop a few steps going up with the ice ax and rope the people on and go up with them.

I stayed two winters [at Glacier House] to learn English. Two long winters I put in there. They were horrible. So much snow, and the only live thing we had was the train, two trains a day, one from the east and one from the west, and they would stop half an hour to eat. In those days they had no dining cars through the mountains. So they stopped there to eat, and sometimes people were tired from riding on the train, and they would stop over.

After the two winters, I went home, I was twenty-one; I was then of age. You see, you can't be a guide until you get of age. I just had a

Ascending the Illecillewaet Glacier with the help of Swiss mountain guides, circa 1910. Photograph by J. H. A. Chapman, courtesy Provincial Archives of British Columbia / 88194

porter's licence. A porter's licence means you can go along with a party, but you must carry the rucksack. There's lots of guides that will carry only a few pounds, you see, and they have to hire a porter to carry the rope and the provisions. So I got my papers, I got my book, and then I came out here again.

We climbed with a lot of important people. My father climbed with Lord Minto [Gilbert John Elliot, fourth Earl of Minto, governor general of Canada, 1898–1904, and viceroy of India, 1905–1910]. And we climbed with an Indian prince up Mount Sir Donald. Both of us went with him to be sure he was safe. And I climbed with that big man, Amery — viceroy of India, you know. They named a big mountain after him on the Jasper highway. Mount Amery. [Leopold Charles Amery was colonial secretary from 1924–1929; from 1925 he was dominions secretary as well. Feuz appears to have confused Amery with Minto.]

Amery came out on political matters [in 1929]. He had to give a lecture in Edmonton, but in the meantime he wanted to climb these mountains. He was quite a climber in his young days; he was out with Mummery and all kinds of climbers. So I got orders from [CPR] headquarters in Montreal to be ready for Colonel Amery.

Amery was a lovely person, a small, little man, didn't talk very much, very nice to travel with. We were out a whole month together.

Mr. A. O. Wheeler, the organizer of the Canadian Alpine Club, was there, too. He was trying to be the boss like he always had. We were on the way to the mountain, and Wheeler wanted to camp — I don't know how far away. So I had a row with Mr. Wheeler. I said, "Do you have to climb the mountain with Colonel Amery, or do I have to climb the mountain with Colonel Amery? I'm going to camp where I want to camp." I had been there before and I knew exactly where to camp, you see. So we went up there and we climbed the mountain. But that's some story.

We started up three o'clock in the morning with the lantern on the Alexandra River. Going up through the trees, we could see the weather was threatening. The clouds were down and the weather was going to be bad. But I kept on going. I thought, "Well, we're still in the trees. If it comes on bad, we can still go back." So, I kept going, kept going. The weather didn't improve. We got above timber line, and I looked up at the mountain and I said, "Well, Colonel, it doesn't look to be a very nice day. I think we should go back. We should have a nice day going up there on the first ascent. You can't see very well, and it's not much pleasure."

But the colonel, he turned around and said, "Edward, yes, but we don't turn around in Switzerland when we climb the mountains, do we?" he said, in a nice English way. I said, "Yes, we don't turn around. We go there. But in Switzerland you see signs ahead of you all the time where you should climb the mountains. I've never been up this mountain before. I've got to find it first. It's a different thing, Colonel, but if you insist to go, I can stand as much as you, Colonel, so say yes or no." He said, "Let's go."

So I went. And do you know, it got so bad we finally had to crawl on top on our hands and knees. The snow came down so fast in your face it stuck right to the eyelashes, and you couldn't see more than ten or fifteen feet ahead. I said, "Well, we come to the top, Colonel." I made a stoneman. And the colonel was lying stomach down, out of the storm, to rest his face.

Down in the valley, it was all black. Off we went, down, down and down, slow in that storm. When you're up that high, you can't go very fast. You've got to make sure of your handholds and your footholds, so that nothing happens. But everything is slippery. We went down, and when we got into the first trees, it was pitch dark. So I took my little folding lantern that I always have and I shoved a candle in. I kept it at the back for the colonel, so he could see where he stepped in the trees. He was so tired, the poor chap, that he could hardly lift his feet any more. So we walked in the trees for an hour. I said, "Colonel, I think a good idea would be to stop here for the night and make a fire and then go home in the morning. You're tired and it's very slow going. We'll never get there tonight. We'll have to walk all night. I've been out lots of times in worse places than this — right up in the rocks and tied onto the rocks all night. Here, we can make a little fire and be comfortable.

Amery turned around and says, "Oh, no. We don't do that in Switzerland. We go right down to the hut." I said, "Yes, but in Switzerland, you have a trail to go right up to the hut. You can see your little trail where people walked before. Here, we have nothing. I can't see where I'm going, and you're so tired you can't move." "Oh, I think we'll go on, Edward," he says. I said, "All right, Colonel, we go on."

It wasn't fifteen minutes after, he says, "Edward, I think your idea is a splendid idea." "All right, Colonel. When we get down a little further and I hear some water, we'll stop there, and I'll make a fire and I'll make you a lovely cup of tea, and I'll make you comfortable and we'll stay there for the night." "Very nice," the colonel said.

So I went down there and started the fire quick. I made him a bough bed next to the fire with branches, and by that time the kettle was boiling, so I gave him a cup of nice tea. And before five minutes, he was snoring away. I had to wake him up to eat, and he ate and he went to sleep again. And then he had a great smile on him. As soon as it got a little daylight, I woke him up and said, "Colonel, a cup of tea, and we'll be started for home."

The next day was a rest day, and then we pulled out. We were going to climb Mount Bryce. We went up there and the weather started to get bad. So we camped at the ice field and it snowed a foot overnight. Climbing was doomed.

So the colonel said, "Edward, we can't do anything today. I'd like to have a bath. How can we arrange that?" "Oh," I said, "that's very easy, Colonel. We just make a hole in the ground. I've got a very nice tarpaulin, and we put that in the hole. I get the cook to make lots of hot water in the pails, and we put it in there, and you just slip out of your tent and jump into your pool and have a little bath right out there in the open, right amongst the snow." "Wonderful," he said. So we fixed it up for him and he had a wonderful bath.

The same evening, it started to clear up. I could see that something was bothering him. I said, "Anything wrong, Colonel?" "Well, you know, Edward, when we got onto my mountain it bothered me a little ... this bad weather we had and ..." "Do you think we weren't on top? Is that bothering you?" He says, "Yes, exactly. I was worried we weren't quite on the top." I said, "Well, we'll fix that. It's going to be a nice day tomorrow. Let's climb Mount Saskatchewan. It's right opposite your peak, just across the valley. It isn't a very hard climb. We better just go there, and I'll show you the stoneman. You saw me build the stoneman on top, didn't you?" He said, "Oh, yes."

So we went up Mount Saskatchewan, which is over eleven thousand feet, and it was a glorious day. And when we got to the top, I said, "Now, sit down here. Here is the glass. Look right across. You see your mountain now, Mount Amery, over there." He took the glass and smiled and said, "You're right, Edward. It's right on the very top."

For more than a decade, the CPR imported guides each season from Switzerland. Then in 1910, the railway announced its plans to create a permanent Swiss colony near Golden in British Columbia. Edelweiss, as the colony was named, would provide a reliable, local source of guides for the CPR's resort hotels. The company also hoped it would be a picturesque addition to the Canadian mountain land-scape: the site chosen for the guides' houses (the first phase of Edelweiss) was a hillside above Golden, in clear view of the main transcontinental rail line.

In 1912, the guides brought their families out to Canada, in the belief that there would be an "authentic" Swiss village for them to live in. What they found on their arrival in Golden dismayed them. Edelweiss was half-a-dozen frame buildings, scattered on a steep, wooded hillside. The addition of gables, balconies and fretted railings did not make these eccentric houses Swiss.

EDWARD FEUZ, JR.: The whole thing was a failure. The CPR sold the best land, the bottom land, for a song. And the Swiss village up there, the six houses they built for the guides, belong to my brother now. When the guides all left, the company felt that one of us Feuz boys should have that village. And Walter, my brother, was the youngest, and we thought he should take it.

The Swiss guides' business at the hotel struck bottom [after the Second World War] and they done away with the Swiss guides. But we Swiss guides got a wonderful record, I'll tell you. Climbing from 1899 to 1949, when I retired, we never had a real accident happen with any of the tourists we guided. That's one of the finest things here in the Canadian Rockies, that we never had a serious accident.

Expeditions to Mystery Mountain

Edited by Susan Leslie

*P*hyllis Munday was climbing in the North Shore mountains before the First World War. Her climbing career began with simple day-hikes on Grouse and Seymour, but Phyllis Munday went on to become one of the most accomplished and adventurous mountaineers in the province. She was the first Canadian woman to climb Mount Robson and, with her husband Don, made many first ascents in the Coast Range.

There had been reports of high peaks in the Coast Range since the mid-nineteenth century, but in the early 1920s their exact height and location were still unknown. The Mundays' interest in exploring the coastal mountains was confirmed one day in 1925 when, from Mount Arrowsmith on Vancouver Island,

Phyllis Munday with her daughter Edith, 1922. Photograph by Don Munday, courtesy Phyllis Munday

they saw a tall peak break out of the clouds over the mainland. They had only a brief glimpse before the clouds closed in again, but were convinced that they had seen a mountain over ten thousand feet (3000 m) high. Mystery Mountain was what the Mundays called the high mountain; but the Geographical Board finally settled on Mount Waddington, after the nineteenth-century entrepreneur who attempted to build a road from Bute Inlet to the goldfields of the Cariboo. At 13,177 feet (4016 m), Mount Waddington was found to be the highest mountain entirely in British Columbia.

Phyllis Munday recalls various incidents from their Waddington expeditions. The incidents are identified by date and location.

PHYLLIS MUNDAY: The best way into the Waddington area was by the coast, which meant that we went Union Steamship at first. But it left you thirty miles or so down Bute Inlet. We wanted to get to the head of the inlet

The Munday party at Mount Waddington in 1926. Courtesy Phyllis Munday

and we couldn't depend on fishermen or even the trappers up there, because they didn't always come to meet the Union Steamship boat. So we built a boat, a fourteen-foot open boat. We just put an outboard engine in, and all our supplies — packs, tent, food and everything — and we went up the coast and up to the head of Bute Inlet.

But on our first trip in 1926, the chap at the head of Bute, who was a trapper, had a little boat, and he put us off on the rocks just near the mouth of the Southgate River. We climbed up to a pass and climbed Mount Rodney, and it was from that we really saw the whole range of Waddington. We knew that this was the way to go in: there was the mountain and the Homathko Valley running right up to it. We didn't know a thing about the Franklin Valley in those days, you see. So we went back from that short trip and made plans to come in to the head of Bute.

Crossing Scar Creek, 1926

PHYLLIS MUNDAY: So it was from the head of Bute that we started off up the Homathko Valley on our second trip in 1926. It was all right going up, but coming back, we couldn't get across the glacier creeks. The logs that we had crossed on going up had all gone, so we had to go up valley and make new bridges to go across. Oh, those glacier creeks are wild — carrying a sixty-pound pack on your back on a log over a wild glacier creek, and the end of the log was just on the other shore, and the water was so swift it was shaking the log! Oh, and to stay on the log with your pack on your back and get across!

When we came back down to Scar Creek, the logs that we had crossed on before had all gone. We had to go up Scar for quite a way looking for a new crossing. I remember the boys all went on, while I was trying to make lunch out of practically nothing. There was very little left, and I was picking berries so that I could make some sort of dessert. When lunch was over and all was packed up again, I went up and I saw this creek — absolutely wild — bashing up against a great big rock. By this time Don and one of the boys had got one log across from our shore to this great big rock in the centre. And then Don got another log and carried it across on this one log, so that he could run it across to the other shore. How on earth he did it, I don't know. I didn't see that going on, because I was busy making lunch.

One of the chaps came up to me just as I got there. I had seen the creek and what they called a bridge, and my heart was just pounding, I have to admit. I guess my pack would be all of sixty-five or seventy pounds by that time; the boys' packs were the same.

Johnny [R. C. Johnson] put his hand on the strap of my pack and he said, "I'll take your pack across, Mrs. Munday." He always called me Mrs. Munday; nobody else did. I said, "Oh no, Johnny, I'll take it. Everybody has to take their own packs." He looked me straight in the eye and insisted. So I said, "Okay, Johnny," and I let him take it. I took a picture of him crossing on all fours with my pack on his back. Then I went over. That creek was so big and so wild and . . . well, there wouldn't have been a hope in the world, of course, if anybody had ever got into it.

Storm at Fury Gap, 1927

PHYLLIS MUNDAY: We never carried a camp higher than Fury Gap, because you can do Waddington from Fury Gap, which is 8500 feet. It's the gap where all the weather goes swishing through to the interior side of the mountain. It's very open; nothing in the way of shelter there at all. That time in 1927 when we had to turn back from the peak, we just had a bivouac at Fury Gap. We got practically to the base of the tower of Waddington, but this storm — we had seen it; it was behind us as we were coming up. The sky was getting more and more stormy as time went on, and Don and I were having private little talks to each other so my sister, Mrs. Betty McCallum, wouldn't notice it. Finally, he said that we had to turn back. I felt at that moment that perhaps we could have climbed a little further, although there wasn't much sense in it unless we were going to be able to make the tower.

Coming down, we could hear the thunder way off in the distance, just a little bit of grumbling going on. And by the time we got down off the worst part of the mountain, coming down to Fury Gap, it was dark and windy, and the thunder and lightning were both coming together. There was no snap of lightning and then the thunder: they were both coming together. We had trouble keeping our lights alight. It was just pouring down. And there were all these tongues of fire on the rocks and tongues of fire on our ice axes — like a blowtorch, almost, with sparks of fire coming off the tip of the ice ax. We couldn't throw the axes away because we needed them all across the glaciers. There was nowhere to leave them, and we couldn't stay there with all this going on. And the rocks, too, had all these tongues of fire coming out of them.

We went on down to Fury Gap and we picked up our frozen tarp and all the things that we'd left there — film boxes and a primus stove and so on — and we stuffed them into our packs. Then we went down the slope onto some shelves of rock — wet, of course, and cold as the dickens — and put a tarp on these rocks, and we three sat on them, and then just pulled the tarps over our heads like a lean-to, and we stayed there until it was light enough to come down the glacier. It was the only thing you could do.

An Accident on Spearman Peak, 1927

PHYLLIS MUNDAY: We never used a piton at all; we just climbed. We always seemed to find a route somewhere or other where we didn't seem to need a piton. I'd manage to find something, though sometimes they were pretty hairy handholds and footholds, especially on one lot when we were trying to get onto Waddington by a different route. It was just near Ice Valley, between Spearman Peak and Waddington.

They were just fingerholds, actually — just cracks, and not much more for your boots. A rock came from somewhere up above and managed to use my head for a target. For a minute, I thought I was going to black out. All of a sudden, luckily, it struck me: if I fall, I'll pull Don off — I can't fall. It's amazing. I didn't fall. I just hung on with these four little fingers on each hand until I'd sort of got the dizziness over. We had to come down, of course, because blood was beginning to ooze all over the place. We got down further, and there was a sloping rock with a great big lovely puddle of water in it, and I could lie there; and my sister sloshed off the blood.

The Mundays never succeeded in climbing Mount Waddington, but it was their exploration work that opened the area to subsequent successful expeditions. Each year from 1926 to 1934, Don Munday published reports of their Waddington journeys in the *Canadian Alpine Journal*. His accounts and sketch maps interested many climbers, and there were numerous attempts on Waddington before its main summit, the north tower, was finally climbed in 1936 by two Americans, Fritz Wiessner and William House.

FROM SETTLEMENTS TO CITIES

A s more and more people were attracted to British Columbia, settlements grew in number and in size. The growth of Victoria, which had begun as a fur trade post, received a boost when it became the supply centre for the Fraser River gold rush. On the mainland, Vancouver, which had begun as a sawmill, became the province's largest city as a result of its location: it was both an international port and the terminus of the Canadian Pacific Railway.

Victoria: A City of Mud and Dust

Edited by Janet Cauthers

B y 1890, Victoria residents anticipated that their city would soon become a major metropolis — the San Francisco of Canada. The provincial government, the Royal (after 1910, Canadian) Navy establishment, and an assortment of activities related to the forest industry, fishing, sealing, agriculture and commerce were the focus of a thriving urban life, still somewhat new, rough and unsophisticated, yet displaying features of the most refined and cultivated European society.

MAJ. ROGER MONTEITH: I can visualize Victoria back probably as far as 1890. It seemed to me that the city in those days all centred on Government Street; that was the only business street in town in those days — that is, the retail section.

Those old grocers' stores were so totally different. There were no glass cases in those days — showcases. There was nothing in the way of refrigeration; everything was put out openly. There'd be hams and bacon, and generally, barrels of English biscuits mixed, currants, raisins, huge cheeses and a variety of other things, including, as a rule, a coffee grinder where they ground your coffee as you wanted it. The consequence was those places had a most, you would call it, "enticing" odour to them of all these different provisions there. You

The Fell and Company grocery store at Fort and Broad streets, Victoria.
Courtesy Provincial Archives of British Columbia / 65649

were entitled to sample any of them — their biscuits or their raisins
and that sort of thing. Most of them, the family grocers, were what
you might call very free and easy. There was stuff scattered all over
the place and on the floors. You just simply shopped around for what
you wanted.

Then the butcher shops, they had no refrigeration. There was
Goodacre's on the corner of Johnson and Government Street, the
B. C. Market further up Government Street and Porter's. You'd see
entire carcasses of beef and hogs, lamb and sheep there. You'd go in
there and order the particular joint you want off the particular car-
cass. I might say that beef in those days, to the best of my recollection,
was about eight cents a pound.

WALTER ENGELHARDT: This is another thing. You know, at one time it wasn't always
what we have today — great sanitary conditions. All along Government Street, where there were butcher shops, they had no doors, just
grating — at least gates that pulled together at nighttime — and all
the meat was hanging up in the store. When the wind blew, all this
filth and dirt was blown up Government Street there, and clouds
[went] into the butcher shops and everything that was open — your
mouth even, too, if you had it open. Well, nobody paid any attention
to it.

There was a bunch of American women over here one day, [and]
there was a bunch of dogs running along the sidewalk in front of
these women. Every grocery store that they passed, they turned

The Lawrence Goodacre butcher shop on Government Street, Victoria.
Courtesy Provincial Archives of British Columbia / 57148

up their legs all over the potatoes and everything that was along there. The women said: "Good grief! Look at the dogs over there, and we have to eat that stuff!" God, they were in such a fury they wrote [letters to the editor, but] I said: "Well, what's all the fuss about?" Everybody was healthy and there wasn't ever any sickness at all!

MAJOR MONTEITH: The streets in those days were always quite a problem. The sidewalks, even on Government Street, were boards laid crossways. I've seen grass growing through them on Government Street, and the horses nibbling away at this grass growing. The consequence was that during the winter months in the rain, [the streets] were a sea of mud. There was always a small crew of city workmen scraping this mud into little mounds. You had to be very careful before they were carted away that you didn't wade through these about up to your knees. Then, come summer, there was then just a sea of dust. The watering carts used to go around and water up and down the main streets maybe twice a day, but that didn't always alleviate the dust, because in about half an hour it was all dried up again.

WALTER ENGELHARDT: They allowed the hacks to all stand in a row, one behind the other all the way down [Government Street]. Horses being there all day, it would get a lot of manure around, of course. And when it was dry like that and there was wind blowing, all kinds of dust that deep, everything was flying up and down.

MAJOR MONTEITH: It was very interesting to see the hack stands and the express cart stands along Government Street. There was very seldom a cabby in sight there; you had to go into the nearest pub to retrieve him. They put in hours of waiting for fares and they killed time by going to the nearest pub, of which there were many. Very often you'd have to go in and call for your cabby. But if you had some particular cabby that you wanted to engage, and he didn't happen to be the first in line — say, the second or third or fourth — you got an earful from the other cabbies who were ahead of him there. The same way with the drays, as we called them — horse-drawn vehicles for freighting. On Yates Street and on Wharf Street they just waited by the hour for fares, and you had to retrieve [the drivers] from the pubs.

It seemed to me there was a bar on every corner, and very often one between. Of course, it's got to be remembered that those were totally different days we lived in. If you'd meet somebody on the street that you knew, you'd stop and have a few words with him instead of just nodding and going by. Well, that very, very often led to a suggestion from one or the other: "Well, let's go and have a drink." There was nearly always a bar at your elbow, whether it was the Brown Jug or the Grotto or the Garrick's Head, and you would go in and have a drink. Drinks in those days were two for a quarter, I might say. [You could get] any drink you wanted, outside of something like champagne or some expensive drink — but any drink you wanted. And there was no such thing as a jigger on the bottles to measure your drink. You'd call for your brand of scotch or rye or whatever you wanted. The bottle was placed on the bar in front of you. You poured out what you want: one finger, two fingers, half a glassful. As I say, they ran two for a quarter, so your drinks didn't amount to very much.

Another custom was if two or three of you went in for a drink there, why, you nearly all bought a drink each. It was a usual thing to ask the bartender to have one with you. Well, he'd had quite a few, he'd explain, but he'd have a little drop of his own. He had a bottle of cold tea there, or else he'd take a cigar. Then, when you got through, the decent barkeepers would always reciprocate: "Well, now have one on me, boys."

Now then, I don't want you to think that we spent our lives in bars, but that was a great part of the life in those days — the bars.

ROBERT HISCOCKS: There was a well-known saying that on Johnson Street, from Government Street down or up — whichever way you want to go — if a man was drunk, he'd roll out of one and fall into another one.

Chinatown and the Chinese

Edited by Daphne Marlatt and Carole Itter

The past is as opaque to direct experience as the "otherness" of a foreign language or culture. And Vancouver, like the small town it has so recently been (some people would say it still is), has a history of turning a prejudiced eye on cultural values that are different from WASP values. Two race riots, mob attacks on the Chinese in 1887 and 1907, were symptomatic of a province-wide oriental prejudice that crested in 1942 with the evacuation of the Japanese to camps in the interior. Black residents we listened to referred to Strathcona as a black ghetto in the Thirties and Forties. Powell Street was certainly a Japanese ghetto before the war, as Chinatown was the city's first racially defined district almost from its incorporation in 1886. So there is this issue of separateness and walls to seeing. How do "we" see "them"? How do "they" see "us"? A district with as many different peoples living in it as Strathcona was bound to have some conflicting viewpoints, and these are evident in what people told us, not only about actual experiences of discrimination, but also about conceptions of the other groups, as well as conceptions about the rest of the city, the West End as opposed to the East End, mainstream culture as opposed to ethnic minority cultures.

Gordon (Won) Cumyow was born in Vancouver in the early 1900s. His father was born in Port Douglas about 1861 and was reputed to be the first Chinese person born in Canada.

GORDON (WON) CUMYOW: My grandfather had his business in Port Douglas. He supplied these fellows who went into the goldfields, and they took off from Port Douglas. They tramped and they went by mule, anything they could use. But most of them just tramped it. A lot of them went up to the goldfields by Fort Yale; the stern-wheelers used to go up as far as there.

My father was a self-made man, you know. He went to school whenever he had a chance and, as a matter of fact, he went and studied law, too. He articled with a lawyer here for years and years but he didn't have the educational background. But he was much more educated than most, because he went to school in New Westminster. After the gold petered out, my grandparents moved into New Westminster, because that was the trading centre. When he got old, like all the rest of the Chinese, my grandfather wanted to go back to China to die.

My father talked Chinook. His father, having opened a store in Port Douglas, a lot of Indians patronized him. So that's how my dad learned to speak Chinook. As a matter of fact, back when the Indians couldn't talk English and they talked Chinook, my dad used to interpret for them in police court. It must have been strange to see a

Chinese talk Chinook. The reporters used to tell me about it: "Your dad knows how to talk Chinook. He talks Indian."

My mother came from China. She came with some missionaries; one of the families brought her here. Of course, they were Chans, and she was, too. And they gave her an education in Chinese — oh, she could read and write and talk very fluently, but she couldn't speak English. My father was the first court interpreter; he understood English and Chinese. And as the Chinese came back from the goldfields and from the CPR construction, they all landed in New Westminster, and then they got into business, you see. Then when Vancouver started in, why, they moved to Vancouver. The police court was involved with the Chinese because they had their difficulties, you know, with white men. They were always the underdog anyhow.

My father sent us to school when we were six, and then made us go to Chinese school after that. That was killing, spending five or six hours in school and then, at half-past four, I'd have to come down to Chinatown and go to Chinese school until half-past seven, then go home and do my homework. We lived up in Grandview; my father didn't want us to get mixed up with certain elements in Chinatown. In those days, it was more or less of a bad influence down here, when the gaming houses were wide open and the police were raiding them, and opium was being smoked. My dad wanted to keep us away from that.

When I tried to study law, the law society figured that all they had to do was get together and just pass a resolution. It was very simple — if you haven't got a right to vote, you can't study law. Simple as that. And the pharmaceutical association, same way. But once the Chinese got the vote, that was nothing. I studied law for three years. When they couldn't article me, I quit. My lawyer told me, "Well, fight 'em. Get a writ of mandamus. Force 'em."

I said, "What am I spending good money for, fighting the powers that be?" I switched to banking and I worked as a bank clerk for five or six or seven years.

Chinese lottery used to thrive in Vancouver. They had about ten of them running. All these old men that couldn't work sold lottery tickets. It was a big business in Chinatown, three out of four old men you met were runners. Golly, the police had difficulty raiding them. There was a lottery every day on the hour, sometimes every three hours, or sometimes four times a day. They distributed the results. For instance, in the lottery draw at three, by three-thirty the results would be on the street. They used one of the regular lottery tickets and burned holes in the winning numbers, and they marked the time. So anybody, no matter what part of town they were in, when these tickets were distributed, would just look and know whether they had won any money or not. Besides, the runner would tell them because he got a commission on it.

After the war, when Oscar Orr became a magistrate, that's the time he handled all the lottery cases. He killed the lotteries, killed the whole shebang, because he wouldn't fine them; he put them in jail. Sometimes he'd fine them heavy and put them in jail too. And that killed it. The Chinese didn't want to go to jail. It got so that he didn't fine anybody; if a man was found guilty, he'd go to jail. Gave him three months in jail, or two months or thirty days. Sometimes he gave them ten days — well, that was bad enough, they didn't want to go to jail. The police had a lot of difficulty proving the case, because they had to get a stool pigeon to go out there and gather the evidence. They tried to make me a stool pigeon and I was the official court interpreter and I said, "Nothing doing. I'll interpret for you, but I won't prove anything for you." They said, "Well, you're not one of us."

I used to go to court every morning. Never missed. Always something there, some kind of scrap or something. Or a white man beat a Chinese up or something like that. It was always busy. But since the gambling became legalized in Chinatown, there's no more raids. So there's not so many cases in police court now, like there used to be. As time went on, the Chinese became a little more educated and started thinking in the white man's way of thinking. So he never got into so many scraps and he began to compromise, you know what I mean? For instance, the white man comes in, maybe has had a few drinks. The Chinese learned to compromise with him, to humour him. Not to say, "Get out of here, you're drunk," as that offends the man right away. If a little diplomacy is used, there wouldn't be any fight. I have certainly noticed a decline in these incidents over the years.

The Chinese are great gamblers, they'd stake their own life on a gambling table. The police didn't try to stop it completely, but they tried to control it, so they raided them periodically. In those days, they could gamble any kind of gambling they wanted, but they won't allow syndicate gambling now. For example, fan-tan is a syndicate organization. You have got to have capital behind it, to play anybody who wants to play. So, if they had a ten thousand dollar capital, they could meet anybody who wanted to play against them. But the bank doesn't rotate; the syndicate is always the banker. For example, in blackjack, if you get blackjack, you get the deck. Well, if you're a banker, you've got a better chance than the man who's playing. Whereas the other way, in syndicate banking, you cannot change the banker. About fifteen, twenty years ago, the city said they would license all the Chinese gaming houses. But they stipulate that you only can play certain games — any game that the bank rotates. But no fan-tan and no Chinese lottery.

I never accompanied the police on gambling raids but I've seen them raid. They made it hard for the police to get in, so they could destroy some of the evidence inside. I know one raid there, the cops came back and said, "We had a helluva time down there. We couldn't find the evidence!" You've got to find the dominoes. They said, "You were playing *um gow* or *pai gow,* now where's the dominoes?" You know where they hid it? Chinatown is all built with what's called a "V" joint, the walls are wood where one plank fits into another. And they just slid one of the boards out, threw all the dominoes in there and closed it up. Well, there's a whole wall there, maybe two hundred, three hundred planks which go right up to the ceiling. But finally, the cops spent almost a whole day there, they had the place locked front and back, and that's where they finally found it. The whole thing was to get the evidence. No dominoes? They couldn't prove their case.

The gaming house was set up like this. There was the gambling room and they'd put another partition in front of it. Then you've got to enter through a narrow corridor. And right above this companion-way, there's a mezzanine floor, a guy up there watching. There's an electric spring lock on both doors. And if you go in, he pushes a button and this front door opens and as soon as you get in, he closes it. He presses another button, and then he lets you inside the next door along the corridor. When the police came in, they would give a run or a push or a jump, or bring the battering ram or mallets or a hatchet or axes, anything. But the idea was that they couldn't swing anything in that narrow corridor — there's no space! There would probably be a little store in front selling fruit but the man behind the counter was a watchman too, and he gave the signal. But for an ordinary fellow like myself, when I went there, they let me in. This was the situation there because at that time they were fighting the police.

There weren't many highbinders in Vancouver. I wouldn't even call them highbinders, they weren't that organized. For example, in San Francisco the tongs were organized, everything was what the tong said. They had control of all the gambling, lottery, fan-tan, anything — you name it, they controlled it. Nobody could infringe on their territory down there. If there was an infringement, they eliminated him. That's where the hatchet men came in, the *fu tow jai.* There used to be a lot of killings down there [San Francisco], but there were very few killings here.

My dad used to sell opium, told me they used to sell it over the counter, anybody could buy it, it was legal then. This would probably be 1906, 1907. I went up to the county court one day, to the registrar, and this registrar showed me a xerox copy with my dad's signature on it. He had drawn up the contract that this company was organized to import opium from China and sell it retail.

I used to go down to the cannery at Steveston as a kid, worked with these guys and we called them "hopheads." They smoked opium. You've never seen anybody work like those guys, worked like crazy. As soon as they get up in the morning, they take a shot and in the afternoon, lunchtime, they go in and have another shot. So that'll last them three hours, four hours. That kept them going. When I was

Chinese vendors on Dupont Street (now East Pender Street), Vancouver, in 1904. Courtesy Vancouver Public Library / 6729

working as a kid down in the cannery there, it was illegal. I used to go in the opium joint, and they used to have a small room and they had beds all over the place. It was hermetically tight, there were no cracks or anything in it, because opium can be smelled from a long distance — it's a very strong pungent smell. There was about four or five fellows laying in bed there. And when they walked, they would walk very light, sort of semifloating.

At one time, servant girls were brought over from China as daughters, they got around immigration that way. They used to treat the servant girls very good, except in Victoria — they did abuse them. That's why the Methodist church started that girls' school to give the Chinese servant girls refuge, who'd been abused by their owners. It could be either one, the man would abuse her sexually or his wife would lick the daylights out of her. [The Methodists] taught them English and they taught them Chinese, gave them an education. And of course, they converted them to Christianity. The Methodists did a wonderful job in Victoria there, just cut slavery right out practically, knocked the bottom out.

In those days, Chinatown was more or less shoddy, there was no neon signs or anything like that. They had boardwalks, wooden sidewalks, and the street wasn't paved, just a hard surface. Mud, you know, when it rained, just plain mud. The Chinatown that I remember when I went to Chinese school after six or seven o'clock at night, they boarded up the windows because there were too many drunks around and they broke the windows. So they put up sheets of boards that screwed into place.

The Depression affected Chinatown. But the Chinese got organized amongst themselves. They said, "Those who have money will put it up to help the poor fellows who don't have any money." And the Chinese Benevolent Association, which was the spokesman for Chinatown, opened kitchens with the money to feed their own people. Most of them were single men. The merchants got by because they were in business. But the Chinese helped one another, they didn't call upon the white people at all.

The Chinese took over Powell Street after the Japanese were evacuated. The Chinese picked up all their property for nothing; the government just gave it away. A lot of Chinese got rich over it. Buildings that were worth twice the value, the government sold them for half, anything to get rid of them. Of course, when the war was over and everything started booming, the people who bought property down there became millionaires, see? That's what happened. It hasn't caused any bad feeling since the war, no. It was the government's fault, you can't blame the people for it.

Chasing Cows and Chickens in the City

Edited by Daphne Marlatt and Carole Itter

Elisa Martini Negrin was born in Vancouver in 1917. Her parents emigrated from northern Italy in 1913.

ELISA NEGRIN: There were six daughters born, and I can remember back to 1925, when we moved to Atlantic Street, and my dad couldn't stand to see empty lots and he said, "My goodness! We could do something about helping ourselves. We can plant a garden and we can . . ." We had chickens 'cause I can remember chickens all my life, and with chickens he expanded to goats so that we could have milk. That wasn't enough so he said, "We'd better get cows." That was quite a battle with City Hall, but he knew about sewerage and cement work and he told them just what could be done. He said, "You support my kids or I get a cow and support my own." He got his permit — even in those days you had to get a permit and, of course, city inspectors came to see that it was built properly. The barn was all from old ties off the Great Northern Railway and planks that were brought up from Stanley Park. We were very independent and made ourselves useful. Anyway, he got his barn built and he had four cows at that time — one, then two, and then two were fresh and two were expecting and then it always kept going like that. We had a few customers for milk, and Mother made cheese and butter, and we had all the cream we wanted. We didn't have money, but we had plenty of food.

When we came into our teens, I was a herdswoman, because there was no boys in the family. To herd the cows, we went down on what we called the Great Northern flats, which was really mucky clay. Boots and all or feet and all, we were in it as knee-deep as the cows were. Yes, and they used to come all the way up to the Grandview district and the roundhouse there; in fact, all the way up to Nanaimo Street. And that took a lot of running, I'm telling you! Sometimes there would be thirty or forty cows — there was my family's, the Piccolo's, the Zanata's and Big John's. There was only about half a dozen families in town that had cows, and there wasn't any English families that had them. In fact, there was a battle there, too, thinking there was going to be odour and this and that. Let's face it, the poor cows couldn't have a chance to have a job, and the people were ready to pick it up for the gardens. Nothing was ever wasted! No way. We had the cleanest streets in town. And never mind, people used manure for medicinal purposes, we had people with eczema coming — they believed the old housewives' tales that the morning dew that settled on it was to nurse wounds and they believed it was a cure. Oh yes, they came from all over — these were the British people, the Russians and the Ukrainians who were great on that, but we didn't know the potions. They even picked these mushrooms, puffballs, and picking up this liquid, the dew, they made a potion or something to use for sores.

We kept all the boulevards nice and neat, cutting the grass for hay. Our truck drivers were the young fellows, our own friends, and they thought it was just great to be able to sit down and picnic with us and that's the way it was done — a lot of singing, a lot of fun, a lot of teasing, a lot of fooling around. It was summertime, that was a holiday for them. And maybe you'd hear Dad say a few cuss words at them — horsing around at night and the haystack would go over and he'd want to know who the son-of-a-gun was, eh? We'd start at six o'clock in the morning and we'd go on until eight or nine at night, until it got dark. You had to cut it and then it was just left there, and

Norma, sister of Elisa Martini Negrin, in the backyard of the Martini home on Atlantic Street, Vancouver, circa 1927. Courtesy Elisa Martini Negrin

then we'd go back and forth two and three times a day. Where Nanaimo Street is and where Raymur is and Atlantic Street, now that was all done by foot, all on foot.

The city pound would be picking the cows up, always on the alert, but when they found out it was our livelihood, they knew there was no point, and they knew the girls were trying to get them because my other sisters were out with me, too. Once the cows went astray, the first thing *before* you went after the cow, you had to go home and get somebody to come and help you, eh? Especially when you were up in the Nanaimo Street area; it was almost bush area and a lot of grazing land, and if kids saw a cow, "My goodness, a cow!" you know, and instead of staying clear of it, they wanted to go close and scare the cow, and away it would run in different directions again.

I think it was after 1936 when everyone thought they'd had enough of it, and then the restrictions from City Hall came in. After all, it *wasn't* farming country — we were in the city, let's face it!

The Barnum and Bailey circus, now that was in '26 or '27, with the big top. That was the boom, that's when the Italians made themselves rich. Dad recruited different Italians and they had to lay out all the sawdust, and on the flats it was all water, eh? They worked hard and that was good money then. Plus, Americans, they're used to liquor for their crews, so they said, "Well, where do we go?" The Italians all had their beer, they had their wine. It was moonshine too, because it was open house to everybody and there were no restrictions 'cause it was primitive, those early years. This was when — I don't know if they call it bootlegging or what — but it was manufactured all over the place. And that kept the circus men happy, and that set a lot of families on their feet. It was maddening to all the British subjects to see all these "immigrant children" as they called us, going in free. We *worked* for them. We figured we did our part to make them happy, so we all saw the big top.

We didn't speak Italian on the street. No, no. Oh, we would be called — you know what they would call Italians. They didn't call me that too often, because I had a good swing! But you just couldn't [speak Italian on the street]. And my dad, he wouldn't permit it anyway because he said, "This is your country and you learn English." But Mother always spoke Italian and we understood it but we would always answer in English. The younger sister didn't even know a word and wondered what the heck our parents were talking sometimes. You more or less had to speak English, because in our [neighbourhood] you had your coloured, you had your Japanese, you had your Chinese, you had your Russians — you *had* to speak English to understand each other.

Hobo Jungles and Hopping Freights

Edited by Daphne Marlatt and Carole Itter

David deCamillis was born in Vancouver in 1913 of Italian immigrant parents. His father immigrated to Boston in 1902 and his mother to Vancouver in 1910.

DAVID DECAMILLIS: Some of the men riding the freights in the Thirties were *sure diversified* — lawyers, doctors, engineers, anything at all. Coming into Vancouver, they'd try and jump off before they got in the yards, and run like heck. That's when a lot of them got killed. They used to call it the "bull horrors." If you go down the ladder and it's moving too fast, the train, and you've got a foot on the ground, it's pretty hard to get back up and you get dragged underneath. I've seen more than one like that, and a lot of them had heavy packs. Well, they'd be frightened to get arrested or chased by a dog or get clubbed by the police or yard workers. And that's why everybody would try to jump off before it got into the yards. The only way, I found out, was to wait till it slowed right down, then jump! When there was a lot, the police were there, "You go right down in there," and they'd show us. It wasn't too far from the tracks, and there's where you stayed. "Don't go into the town or city at all."

Most of these jungles were located where there was some sort of supply of water for these people. Like in Calgary, it was near the Bow River, you could have a bath and everything. Some of these jungles were well organized. You'd have to take turns to go out panhandling for vegetables, meat, or anything you could bring back. And you'd have a big clean garbage can. Well, there'd be two or three guys do the cooking. Great big mulligan, fill that whole thing right up, feed the whole works. There were soapbox orators, people standing up and giving speeches, how rotten the country is and how rotten the government is. Oh, a lot of good speakers. Most of the time you'd sleep on woodpiles, coal piles, any place you could sleep, that's all.

Some of the train crews were good, and some weren't. For instance, when we were going through those tunnels, going up so slow, they sent the word back, "Get off and walk," because you could suffocate from the smoke from the engine. That was an experience. Coming back, it was cold, so the engineer, he only filled his locomotive half full of water, then he'd stack us like cordwood on there so we'd get more heat. We'd be piled on the engine, well those who couldn't get into inside the boxcars, and you'd be burning on your back and your sweater would be frozen to your nose, it was that bad.

Shinichi Hara was born in Wakayama, Japan, in 1900. At the age of ten he went to work in an Osaka shipyard. He worked at a series of jobs in Japan until December 1924, when he came to Canada.

SHINICHI HARA: I went to Japan in 1929, and in 1930 I married there. *Then* start the hard times, yeah, the hard times.

I came back in March 1930 by myself. If you could see what I saw! People hungry and dying down on the beach. Three stakes and a sack, that was home for them. You just went down to the foot of Dunlevy Avenue where Hastings Mill used to be, and there were lots of them, both ways. Hungry people. And then the trouble in the city started. People had iron bars, they broke windows at Woodward's and everyone went in and helped themself. You see, they had no jobs and no food, and the police couldn't do anything with so many — a whole city! And the garbage cans: on Hastings Street, Granville Street, people ate from them. I saw a mother with a baby pull out some chicken bones, set them on the garbage lid and right away three, four kids were standing around eating chicken bones. I left Vancouver that spring.

I jumped on a train in the shipyard with half a dozen young fellows. We'd gone to a butcher shop because we were hungry, "Have you got any leftovers you can give us?" They gave us old bread and meat we put in a sack. Any butcher shop you asked would give you liver free. There were more than half a dozen of us, about twenty-five, twenty-six years old, on the freight train. We hid under the lumber and we wanted to go to the other end of Canada. But when we got to Vernon, it started to rain and we were all soaked, so we had to get out. Two of us went down the Okanagan and we had nothing to eat for two or three days — pretty hungry. We ate anything, we ate grass. We got a job with a fruit company picking apples, but we only picked sixty acres. Three hundred acres we didn't touch, they were lying on the ground. There was no market for them. In Vancouver apples were three dollars a box, three dollars! And here they were lying on the ground and people were hungry.

John Crossetti was born in Vancouver Island in 1903 of Italian immigrant parents. His father worked as a coal miner. After he was in a serious mining accident, the family moved to Vancouver and started the Europe Grocery store on Main Street.

JOHN CROSSETTI: Reverend Roddan's church [First United] at the corner of Hastings and Gore helped the poor people all the time. He used to give speeches, like on a Sunday after the church service. They had a big auditorium there and then his office used to be in the back. He helped the poor a lot, helped them with food and all that. He was a very good man, good speaker too, and every Sunday he used to have his program on the radio. He stuck up for the poor all the time, like when they had the jungle, he used to come over to see the boys there.

The Rev. Andrew Roddan of First United Church with a makeshift cookhouse, offering food to unemployed men in the "jungle" at the city dump on the False Creek flats (between Campbell and Heatley avenues), Vancouver, 1931. Photograph by W. T. Moore, courtesy Vancouver City Archives

They weren't being ignored, people were helping them all along. But gee, it was an awful-looking place down there. Oh, it was terrible in those days. But they conducted themselves pretty good. People seemed to get along, you know. I used to see people on relief come into my parents' store and sometimes my father would say, "Well, you haven't got enough, so wait till your next relief ticket comes in."

Mrs. Jean McDuff, who worked for years as a cook for First United Church, also remembers that time.

JEAN MCDUFF: They were coming every day off the trains. And then they got to know about First United and they came up and Mr. Roddan made this stew. They never sat down, they just came in and we gave them out plates. Some of them were so cold, you know, they could hardly hold their plate. Mr. Roddan would always say to them, "When did you hear from your mother last?" They didn't write, I guess they were ashamed to. And it would be, "Oh, years." And he'd say, "All right, before you get anything, I'm going to give you pen and paper and just write a wee note telling her you've been in to the church." [Reverend Roddan] was a real family man.

We fed all that was there and sometimes we sent out for bread and stuff. The bread line was every day, we made a stew every day in the morning. They'd come in about eleven or twelve to get it. Mr. Roddan used to go down to the stores too, and get bread and hustle up stuff. We made a joke about it. I said, "Oh, never mind, we'll get something, we'll make 'ends' meet." And I meant these oxtails, you know.

Mr. Roddan was on the radio twice, morning and evening. He thought the Thirties were terrible. He and Roy Stobie, when they went to the jungles [on the False Creek mud flats], they carried the big kettle of stew down, took it in the back of the car, and fed them down there.

Bootleggers and Gamblers in Hogan's Alley

Edited by Daphne Marlatt and Carole Itter

A rather wry recognition that the law serves the interests of those with enough money and power to make the law is common currency among the powerless. Strathcona had the reputation in earlier decades of being Vancouver's square mile of "sin." Yet two of its major illegal activities, bootlegging and prostitution, stemmed directly from a combination of poverty, self-reliance and minimally available social welfare.

Austin Phillips came to Vancouver from Athabasca Landing, Alberta, in 1935.

AUSTIN PHILLIPS: Corner of Main and Union was the Bingarra Hotel which has been torn down since the new viaduct opened. Then you went down the alley, down Park Lane, to this place called Scat Inn which was, oh, I'd say they cooked a few chickens and steaks and played a lot of music and people danced. They cut a few walls out of an old house, sold drinks, a regular bootlegger at that time. Whisky was twenty-five cents a drink, beer was twenty-five cents a drink — that's bootlegging prices. Then the real part of Hogan's Alley started right at Park Lane and it ran right straight up between Prior and Union, ended around Jackson Avenue — that's when you were out of Hogan's Alley, the rest was just called an alley.

Oh, the things that used to happen there! I came out here in '35 and that's about the first place I run into. I didn't know anybody in town and I just got off a freight train somewhere out here by the ocean and started to walking. Just walked right down as though I'd been in town before and ended up in Hogan's Alley. Going through the alleyway, you'd see some people laying on wagon wheels — they had a bunch of old broken wagons out on this old-time lot, with the grass maybe growing up around it about a foot high, two feet high. And people, some of them bums, would just sleep in the wagons, sleep in the grass.

There was one thing about it, none of them were big boys around there. They'd get all the play mostly from everybody coming in and out getting their drinks, and they'd have a room where you'd have a dancing space. Then there was Buddy's over on Prior. The chief of police remembers him from now. He was the only man that was known to take a set of square dice and throw from two to twelve on 'em and never miss. When he died, the chief of police made this statement in the paper. He says, "He's the only man I ever saw say dirt to me because I bet him two bucks he couldn't do it." He had an ex-fighter, most everybody knew him, Joe Wilson, and he used to play piano for him.

Another one down there, the big boss of the place, was Lungo. This was the big Italian, he was 310 pounds, six foot four inches. His house was in the middle of the alley, and they called him "The King." He made homebrew wine, you know. He'd make this wine and he would sell it for forty cents a quart, and the fella across the road from him, this West Indian guy, used to buy from him and sell it for ten cents a glass. So you can imagine the profit he was making.

There was nothing but parties in Hogan's Alley — nighttime, anytime, and Sundays all day. You could go by at six or seven o'clock in the morning and you could hear jukeboxes going, you hear somebody hammering the piano, playing the guitar, or hear some fighting, or *see* some fighting, screams, and everybody carrying on. Some people singing, like a bunch of coyotes holler — they didn't care what they sounded like just as long as they was singing. Oh, I used to go from one place to the other playing guitar. They never paid you a salary. They had what you call a kitty, a little tin box with a horn like a phonograph on it. People wanted to tip you, they'd want to throw a buck, ten cents, whatever it was — well, they'd throw it in the kitty. That was *your* money, that's what you made. Then if you didn't want to drink whisky, well, you'd ring for the houseman, the boss, and he'd bring you Coca Cola for rum and tea for whisky. Then you'd get that two bits for yourself, see.

So I can say, myself, I was making my money going from place to place, you know. There used to be a bunch of chop suey houses on Pender Street — always has been — and I would go from restaurant to restaurant and play from booth to booth. I've seen myself make as high as twenty-five dollars a night in those days. And then go back down and go into the bootlegging places again. I was playing the songs that come out then: "East of the Sun, West of the Moon" and "Don't Get Around Much Anymore," and oh, just mostly all those songs. "Stardust" was pretty well famous in those days, and "Am I Blue," that was one of the favourites. And "Beale Street Blues," "St. Louis Blues" and "Beautiful Lady in Blue," "Paper Moon." Those songs all got famous around '36, '37, then they died out. There's been thousands of them. I can't remember them now until somebody requests them, and then I try to remember all of 'em. I would take my guitar, throw it across my shoulder and go from one place to the other. I play all string instruments — piano, guitar, banjo, steel guitar, ukulele, mandolin, violin. Somebody want a party played for, I'd go all over town. I'm a pretty good singer in my time, and I always dressed pretty well, always ready for an occasion, and I've made a lot of parties.

Back in '38, that was after [Mayor G. G.] McGeer was out and Taylor was in, anything went. [Prominent people] would come in a place, and if they didn't want anybody to know, they would buy it out, say one or two hundred dollars a night — just whoever they wanted to stay there and drink with [them]. And Mayor Taylor used to come down and drink if he went to Buddy's or Dode's, or Mother Alexander's for chicken and steak.

There weren't too many guns around Hogan's Alley, it was more blackjacking and mugging and stuff like that. There was more killings in the West End, even at that time, than there were in the Alley. I can't recall of anybody except this one guy getting killed. Another guy was shot in there, and some of them was stabbed in there, but they all lived. But this guy, this Lungo's son, never knew his name — he's the only one that was really killed. Coloured guy killed him with a wrench over a dogfight. What happened was, this guy they called Ernie, he was setting back near the Scat Inn in the summertime, you know, and he was strumming away on my guitar. And the dog starts a fight down the alley right in front of Lungo's place. His son was hitting the other dog that was fighting *his* dog, and he hit him with a stick. All of a sudden, Ernie goes down and he says, "Don't ever hit a dog around me," he says, "dog saved my life overseas," he says, "you hit the dog again, I'll hit *you*." So the guy kicked the dog and, well, he hit him with a wrench — very light tap it looked to me like, but it was enough to kill him.

Well, there was always somebody in fights, or threatening. But then again, you take all the other guys bumming, no matter what nationality they was, they was on the bum for dimes and nickels — and some of those fellas was bumming could stand on a corner and they'd bum more than the average guy working a day. They could eat cheap, too, but nobody would refuse. These people that had the money with them, they'd give them ten or fifteen cents, a quarter. Some were generous, some made a winning and they'd hand a guy two bucks, tell him to "Go git your clothes cleaned," or something like that. But they was always good that way. Unless a man was something really out, like he was considered an informer or something, a stool pigeon. Then he wasn't liked, he wasn't welcome around that part. Even the police didn't like him. They'd use him 'til he was no more value to them, then, if the crowds want to get him, let them get him, he's served their purpose. But that's the way it run, off and on, like the fish in the sea: the big ones eat the little ones, if they could have them. You never know when that little guy might come into the luck and make something, might be able to get it back.

There was a guy came out of the logging camp — I think he was a donkey puncher, 'cause he was making good money. But he came down in this Hogan's Alley with a girl I knew, a regular clip-artist. She picked him up, or he picked her up, in the beer parlour there, and on a foggy night he comes down with eight hundred dollars in his pocket. Well, she give him the knockout drops in the drink, and he walked outside and she rolled him, and when he finally did come to, he was on a pile of rubbish out in the alley. He went down and he made a complaint to the police, and they says, "Have you ever heard of Hogan's Alley?" He says, "No, I really haven't." He said, "You've heard of the East End, haven't you?" He says, "Oh yes, I've heard of the East End." He said, "You mean to tell me you didn't have any more sense than to come down here?" He said, "I'm a policeman, I wouldn't pack that kind of money with me in this part of town, and I've got a gun." He said, "If you're stupid enough to go down that end of town with that kind of money on you, I would say you deserved it, and we're not wasting our time looking for nobody we couldn't find anyhow."

There was gambling going on practically every place. Sometimes there'd be guys over from the American side, and I seen as much as two or three hundred dollars on the table. And some of the little places had penny ante games you could buy into for twenty-five cents, and they'd play as hard for that as they would for the big stakes. Practically every house around there, they'd just start up a game, but there was only a few of the houses that had big games. Old Buddy, he was quite a man on the dice game, and he used to get all the big shots from across town, big-time gamblers, and he gambled them. They were shooting two hundred up to a thousand bucks a shot, rolling dice. But he was one of the rich men there, he was top bootlegger, and that's all he did was bootleg and gamble.

There was junk that passed around there too. But maybe out of a thousand you'd see one dope-fiend in those days, that's how few they were. Not because some of them couldn't afford it. Because it was so cheap in those days they could go down and get a prick of morphine for about a dollar and a half. But very seldom you'd see dope-fiends.

But every place you went to, practically every place in Hogan's Alley bootlegged. If you could afford a high-class place, you went to the Scat Inn, you went to Buddy's Beer Garden. He served beer and he'd serve hard stuff — rum, gin, whisky. Then there was the two Macaroni Joes: one guy was a little one, and the other a big one. The little guy, he sold everything from wine to whisky, anything at all, right up until he died he was still a bootlegger. But this other big Macaroni Joe — I'd been buying wine off of him for probably a couple of years, and he had good wine he was making out of apples, it was sweet, and I like sweet wine, and it was a little bubbly, you know. So I was setting in his place one Sunday morning, right on the corner of Prior and Park Lane, and I said to him, "Joe, how do you make this wine?" So he says, "I got some mash on now, I go show you. I making with feet." Well, I seen pictures of girls running around with their feet to make wine over in the old country — that's girls, they wash their feet. But this guy, he pulled off these blue woolly socks and his feet were sweating, and in between his toes you could see this black he called toe-jam. He rolled his britches up, and he's got apples in a tank about four feet high, and it's bubbling up, and he just stepped right in there. He never washed his feet and he weighed about 250 pounds. Oh God.

We used to know a few of the police in town. They used to come down — they liked to get in on that gambling. One night two of them was off the beat and they'd come in and they'd put their money in the bank together, and they were dealing. Blackjack. They had a whole stack of money and everybody was betting the table, as many people could bet. All of a sudden, in comes the chief of police. What he was doing there I do not know but he drove up; I guess he must have seen the car parked on Union and wondered where they were at. So when he walked in the door, he said, "What are you guys doing here?" They just *dropped everything* and went out, left their money on the table, they just went away! Well, everybody had a ball with the money, everybody was grabbing away. They used to be pretty good, pretty good. They didn't pay attention to prostitutes or pimps, they didn't bother them too much. What they were really hot on was dope-fiends, and there wasn't many of them. If they caught them, bingo! And anybody that was selling it, well, that was it, because they're worse against that than they are on murder. They didn't bother about gambling.

This town, it just run itself, practically. Some of them were paying off. That's before Gerry McGeer took over [1935]. When he got to be mayor, he closed everything in town up, everything. He tightened on and he chased all the prostitutes out of town; all the bootleggers, he was clamping down on them, he just cleaned up the place. The only good thing that he done, that I said to myself, was when he put Joe Celona in jail. That's a guy you couldn't even be decent with — the guys he was paying off to, the cops he was paying off to. And he was just a young man but let go long enough he'd of become another Al Capone. But he ended up with a twenty-year rap on him. He got that time just before I come out here in '35, that's when he first got sentenced. He did half his time and they finally gave him parole and he was out *one week* and the church people, all the people, signed a petition to put him back in. He did his time.

There was quite a few black people around. That old Mrs. Pryor, that big woman, she used to weigh about 350 pounds, I liked to see *her* come in. She'd come down about once every three months. She used to bring a sack, one of them leather bags, and she'd have it full of silver dollars and fifty-cent pieces. And she would set me on her knee and say, "Play my song! You come on and you play 'Maggie'." I didn't know "Maggie," I'd just sing what I knew of it and everytime I'd sing "Maggie" for her, she'd give me a silver dollar. And curse me out, curse me out all the time! "Oh, play me that song 'Maggie' again!" Probably have to play it for her about fifteen times a night, but if you got through, you got a dollar for every time you'd sing it.

Most everyone from Hogan's Alley is dead. I'm about the only one that was ever around there that's still living. And that is the lowdown rundown on the way things went at that time.

The Internment of the Japanese
Edited by Daphne Marlatt and Carole Itter

George Nitta is a third-generation Canadian citizen, even though he was born in Japan in 1903. His father and grandfather before him were fishermen on the coast of British Columbia.

GEORGE NITTA: My mother was visiting in Japan and she went over for a little longer than what she expected, so I was born in Japan in 1903. That meant I was supposed to be Japanese, so when I got to be eighteen or nineteen I was naturalized in order to get my rights as a Canadian. My grandfather had come over here about one hundred years ago, and then he called over his son, my father. My grandpa was a naturalized Canadian and so was my father, so my children are fourth-generation Canadian.

Those were the "dog days" then. Discrimination was floating in the air. For example, they wouldn't allow anyone of Oriental descent into the White Lunch Restaurant. And it was the same thing in the public swimming pool. In the movie theatres, upstairs was for coloured people, including us. I was kind of fed up after I found out that I didn't have equal rights, and I thought I'd better go to some other country. But after the war, everybody realized discrimination is real bad for all of us, and now it doesn't matter what colour your skin is, a Canadian is a Canadian. But it wasn't like that before the war.

So, I was helping my father and I didn't even get the chance to go to school. Because those days we worked all year round, we sweated, and no eight- or ten-hour day, either. We worked twelve and fifteen hours a day and maybe we managed to save three or four hundred dollars a year. The only reason we survived was because everything was cheap then. Once the fishing season was over, then it was another job, eh? And you couldn't choose, you know. You went to work at sawmills, logging, railway, anything you could get. Well, so I had to help my father support the family, and the only time off he gave me, when I could go to school, was after January first to maybe the beginning of May, when we'd go back to fishing. So I'd study only a few months a year, and I'd have to keep starting and starting — night school, eh? Even for white Canadians it wasn't easy then, so I had quite a few white schoolmates at night school. One of them was called Blackie and later he was on staff at the RCMP office in Vancouver.

I was surprised when the war started, and we Japanese-Canadians had to be registered and go once a month to the RCMP office to state what we were doing, you know. Because the first time I went up to the RCMP office I met Blackie there. That was almost twenty years after we quit night school. And I was a friend, so he treated me real good. He always gave me a special permit if I had to go to a different town to look for a job.

[In 1941] we had a fish-processing plant on Mayne Island, working seasonally. We'd been doing it year by year for almost fifty years and we depended on it for a small income during the winter months. I also owned three or four boats, and everything was seized. The Coast Guard forced everyone to bring their boats up the Fraser River to Annieville — oh, there were a thousand boats. They didn't give us credit as Canadians. They just took us for "enemy aliens" for the duration of the war. How do you like that? Even if you were a Canadian citizen or Canadian-born, as long as you had black hair on your head and a Japanese face you were an enemy alien.

I had my own property and my own business, and it took three generations to build up what I lost. That's why I sued the government, and I won the case. Although I won the case, the lawyers took the biggest part. I got maybe twenty-five per cent of the money the government paid us. I felt like suing the lawyer, you know, but we gave up. In the United States, the American government returned everything owned by Japanese-Americans, they just held and protected all the property and then they returned it.

Anyway, Blackie was with the Security Commission and he told me, "Whether you are my friend or not, you've got to evacuate. So you'd better check around and find out where you could survive the duration of the war without any big income." He gave me permission to take a trip, so I went to Kamloops to see my uncle who was farming there. He said, "Well, I've got enough money to keep us from starvation for five or six years anyway, so you'd better come to Kamloops and stay with me." My wife and children stayed with him. while I worked at anything I could get within fifty miles on either side of Kamloops — you needed a permit to go more than fifty miles — farming, logging, sawmill, anything I could get. We went as a self-supporting family and we stayed in the Kamloops district for about seven years, because they didn't allow us to come back to the coast until a couple of years after the war was over.

Wartime is an entirely different picture, you know. For the duration of the war, there was big propaganda floating in the air *every* day by radio, newspaper. Lots of simple-minded people believed it, and lots of places in the countryside we couldn't even buy a packet of cigarettes. Soon as they knew we were Japanese it was, "No, you get out. No, we have nothing to give you." It was real tough going.

But many groups of people understood our situation. And especially the chief of police in Kamloops. I knew him when he was chief of police at Prince Rupert. Those days very few Japanese spoke enough English to understand it, so Inspector Barber was always picking me up to act as interpreter for people.

When I first got back there were very few Japanese in Vancouver, but gradually, slowly they came back, a few hundred every year. I had taken a little money with me when I went to Kamloops, but I spent it all, and when I came back to Vancouver, I was very close to coming back barefoot and bare hand. So I had no choice, all I knew was the fishing game, working on water. So I took an opportunity and went to Skeena River fishing, and the company rented me a boat. They welcomed us back because they knew we were good fishermen.

Before the war there were eight thousand Japanese in Vancouver. Alexander and Powell and Cordova streets, from about the hundred to the seven hundred block, was Japanese. White Canadians used to call it Little Tokyo. It was said to be the cleanest spot in the whole of the city. They got up early, those old-time Japanese, they'd get up about seven o'clock, and the first thing they'd do is sweep and even wash the street. Talk about clean! After the war, Powell Street was nothing but a ghost town.

War is a bad game, you know. Everybody gets so excited, they can't even think any other way. Near the beginning of the war, this young soldier held up a confectionery store on Commercial Street that was owned by a Japanese young fellow, Canadian-born too, and he shot [the owner] to death. It made me real mad, you know, because everybody talked like he was a hero, said, "Never mind that he killed a Jap, send this soldier to the front." And we believed we were protected by the law, by the justice of the nation. You couldn't even think about this in the common, ordinary way. There is a monument in Stanley Park to the Japanese who sacrificed their lives in the First World War.

And people were screaming their heads off, "Move that monument!" I was so sad. Those men only had one life, and they had willingly sacrificed it for Canada's sake.

Discrimination is real bad. We've got to avoid such nonsense in the future. Those things my grandpa, my father and I myself built up before the war are all gone. I've had to work.hard enough for three generations in my time. Fortunately, I've built up inch by inch, and I'm going to continue another few years. Because if you have no hope in the next day, that's bad, you know. So I don't think I'm going to quit completely. If I'm lucky enough to live to be eighty years old, I'll still do something every day.

PART III: HOPES HIGH
DOLLARS FEW —
WORKING PEOPLE

A high rigger, the man who tops the spar tree, circa 1926. Courtesy Provincial Archives of British Columbia (Roozeboom Collection) / 67903

MEN OF THE FOREST

*L*ogging was one of British Columbia's first industries, and still is of prime importance. In the late 1840s there were only three small sawmills, but national and international demands for the province's excellent forest products grew quickly. By 1910 there were about 350 logging camps in the province.

Loggers cheerfully took on the hard physical labour and constant exposure to bad weather: that was all a part of the job, as was the dangerous nature of the work. But dismal living conditions in the camps and unsafe working conditions in the woods made them determined to unionize.

Those Days in the Woods

Edited by David Day

*R*obert Swanson is probably British Columbia's most popular rhymster poet. His volumes of verse on the West Coast logging camps have for many years been a source of entertainment in the Pacific Northwest. His books include *Bunkhouse Ballads* and *Rhymes of a Western Logger*.

ROBERT SWANSON: Well now, in those days in the woods . . . you asked me what kind of a day you'd have. Nobody said have a good day. This is a new saying. But we had a good day anyhow. You see, you'd be sleeping in a bunkhouse with probably, in my time around the woods, there'd be four, six or eight of us in a bunkhouse with a big stove, a lumberman's stove, made like a big oil drum in the middle with a pile of wood alongside of it. And if it got a little cold towards two in the morning, one of us'd get up and throw a couple more logs on. And somebody'd say, "Go to sleep, you noisy so and so!" But pretty soon you'd hear everybody snoring. If a guy snored too much you threw a boot at him. That was the normal thing to do, to throw a boot at him. That usually stopped him. However, you were awakened from your slumbers by a locomotive whistle blowing the longest, mournfullest sound you ever heard in your life at about, I'd say, maybe six o'clock in the morning. Now, the story in the woods was, the bull of the woods came around the bunkhouse and said, "It's daylight in the swamp." Well, anyway, the watchman, or the man that was steaming up the locomotive, would look at his watch and at six o'clock he'd pull on that locomotive whistle in just a long, mournful, discordant wail, you know. And then pretty soon you'd hear action. The light lamp would be going and everybody'd be getting up and you'd go to wash, and if there was no hot water you washed in cold water. You lined up for that cookhouse and boy you got in that cookhouse just as fast as you could. And you sat down at the table and you had a half-dozen eggs and hot cakes. Some of them had beef steaks. Some of them had fruit, corn flakes, everything you can think of was on that table. But they were out of there in less than six minutes. And they stuffed some in their pockets as they went, and they went past the lunch room and they got a lunch that was made the night before.

Now, that was later in the woods, the lunches, but prior to that, when I first started in the woods, they didn't carry a lunch, they had what they called a "mulligan car" went out at noon from the cook-house with a couple of flunkies, and it went out with the locomotive right out to the woods, and the crew would come and sit in this car or on stumps all around the car and eat hot bowls of soup and hot meat. And then they'd get back to work. They'd take an hour for lunch in those days.

However, to be specific — in the morning, they'd say, "All right, come on. It's getting time." And everybody would head for a certain place to get on the crummy, and the engine crew would be down at the engine and she'd be all ready to go, maybe three or four engines steamed up, locomotives. In my own case, I'd take the locomotive, and you'd have the crummy already hooked on, usually, and you'd back the crummy up to the place where the men got on and they'd all pile on, and then somebody'd give you the high ball, "Come on, let's go!" And wow wow on the whistle and wang on the bell she'd ring, and off chu-chu-chu-chu-chu away she'd go, usually up to a back switch, and then from the back switch you'd have your headlight boring a hole in the darkness in the winter and you'd be riding on her kind of warmed up for the day. This was a little hot or a little cold or something and you'd be looking over at the fireman, and then he'd nod back to you; everything was all right and you'd be looking ahead. The odd deer crossed the track, you know, and you'd go way up the woods. You'd stop at a certain place and five or six men'd pile off here and they'd walk off to one place, and five or six to another, and finally you get to where you were going to, side one or side two, and everybody'd get off. And then when they were all off, the locie would back away, shove the crummy in a siding somewhere and start "bull-cooking around" as we called it. Bull-cooking is just doing general chores. So you'd bull-cook around for an hour or so and switch cars in here and there and pretty soon you'd hear the machine whistle for the locie. They had loads. So then you'd head up there with the empty locomotive, hook onto the loads, pump up the air, he'd let off the brakes, roll. . . .

But this was your day. And when it came to around quitting time, everybody was ready. The main-line engine was taking a big turn into the beach, maybe working overtime to do it, but the smaller engines, the bull-cooking type engines, would take the crummies and would be up there to pick the crew up on time and get them back to the cookhouse.

So when you got in the cookhouse, you'd be in about fifteen or twenty minutes before supper and you'd pile off. You always got off a hell of a lot quicker than you got on. And you headed for the bunkhouse. Dropped your lunch bucket in as you went by the cookhouse, got down to the bunkhouse, got your cork boots off, got another pair of shoes on, got washed, and by this time you'd wander up to the cookhouse because the bell would go. Just about the time that bell went you'd head in. And it was a mad scramble to get in because you were only going to be in there not more than seven minutes and you were out again all fed. It seemed to be, for some reason or other, if you didn't go fast, well, all the good stuff was gone first. Actually, one fellow at Hillcrest many, many years ago, over thirty years ago, he was coming back from the cookhouse and I was a little late — because I was always a mechanical man, I always was doing something and we'd get up a little later sort of. I never believed in being a fast eater, but loggers, you know, you had to eat with them. I said to this fellow, "Well, what's the matter?" "Oh," he said, "My foot slipped on the way in. I knew I'd never make it so I'm giving up." Well, I thought nothing of it at the time, but it got to be quite a joke. If your foot ever slipped going into the cookhouse and you lost about that one step, you might as well not go in at all. However, this actually happened. This fellow said, "No, my foot slipped and I'm just giving up on it. It's no bloody use," he said.

Well, it was sort of true; if you were late in getting in there, you didn't get the choice of anything. The best steaks were gone and the pieces of fat were left. The best potatoes were gone or the plate was empty, and the flunkie didn't want to bring any more. In the morning the hot cakes were cold and this sort of thing. So, it was a case of necessity you see, which prompted the lines and the "Loggers' Ten Commandments," which I wrote one time.

That's how it was. But it's quite a thing, the life in the woods. Sundays, some of them played horseshoes, some of them rested up, some of them washed their underwear, some of them washed their socks. Of course, me, I always monkey-wrench a locomotive or a logging donkey or something. I always worked every Sunday, you see. You were always wet-nursing a piece of equipment somewhere. If you didn't do it, it wouldn't work, and you were sent down the

*Yarding and loading logs at a railway logging operation, Menzies Bay,
B. C., circa 1926. Courtesy Provincial Archives of British Columbia
(Roozeboom Collection) / 67778*

road. You had to keep that thing running. You knew how to do it. And you got overtime for it. It was straight time, mind you, but we worked Saturdays, just like any other day. Then Sundays, the machine shop always ran and the locomotive men all worked. They washed out the boilers. The donkey punchers went out and they all worked. The greasy gang, the black gang, would come in around five o'clock, a few minutes early on a Sunday, and get well washed up. They'd be smelling of soap, you know, and they'd head into the cookhouse. Somebody'd say, "What the heck you been doing today?" "Oh, I had an awful time today," you know. However, that's what we did and we liked it. It was a good life.

My idea writing poetry is, you've just got to love it. You've just got to love the sound of the ravens, the sigh of the breeze in the trees, the height of the mountains, the clarity of the air, the roar of the waves. It's all just beautiful! And you've got to want to be part of it. If you don't do that, you're not writing poetry. You can't write protest poetry. A man that says, "I hate the sound of a bird! I just can't stand the sound of a robin." Well, the guy isn't human. He's got to think of a robin as a little person and has as much right to live as he has. And a good logger, a real good big-shot logger is like that. P. B. Anderson, who was one of the old-timers, he took some of us around once, and I says, "Why aren't you logging that corner?" He says, "I will show you. Come over here." It was a hummingbird's nest and he didn't want to disturb it. So he moved the rigging over here. He says, "There's lots of time. The little birds'll be hatched by the time we get back to here again." These are the kind of people that are human beings, you see. And there's more to it than just making money. It's a way of life. It's something that you're doing, that you feel you have a right to be doing. And if you don't have that feeling, I don't think there's much point in working.

Roughhouse Pete and Other Characters

Edited by David Day

AL PARKIN: Camp cooks were lord of all they surveyed. They were pretty much supreme and they should have been because they were good men. A good camp cook was a highly skilled man — almost an artist. But

Riggers, either going up or coming down, circa 1926. Courtesy Provincial Archives of British Columbia (Roozeboom Collection) / 67828

there were many odd characters. Caraway Seed Bill began to use caraway seeds first in cookies, buns and things like that. He'd get his bread-maker to put them in. Then he began to introduce it into all sorts of foods including, they tell me, the porridge in the morning and into the batter that made up the hot cakes, and he sprinkled it on the bacon and eggs, which I think was a little bit too extreme.

But anyway, after this had gone on for some time, the crews began to grumble whenever he appeared in camp. And so the camp superintendents began to censor his mail; whenever he'd send an order down and he had caraway seeds, they'd cross it out. So he began to circumvent this by bringing it up to camp every time he went down [to Vancouver]. When he came up to a new camp or went down for a while and came back, he'd bring up pounds of it in his packsack, and he finally got so bloody unpopular that no camp would hire him. He literally seeded himself out of the industry, if you like. But the amusing thing, of course, is this odd fixation that this man had developed, and no one seems to know why . . . odd stories like that.

The logging camps were filled with these kinds of characters. There was another man named Bullshit Bill. It was said, and I think with justification, that had he become a lawyer or something he'd have made a name for himself, because he was a beautiful speaker, and he could hold people, you know. He was another instance of characters. The woods were filled with people like that.

Really, they were outstanding, unusual people, so many of them with good educations.

There was another man, Johnny-on-the-Spot. He was a man who in any other walk of life would have been perhaps a university professor: a very scholarly type, a man who would drink like a crazy fool when he was in town, and the moment he went out to camp he was just finished with it and would always take books with him and study; the soberest, most serious-minded, most upstanding-looking person you ever saw. He came to town and he just became *mesachie* [a Chinook word meaning bad or evil] — a real 'rangutan. But there were so many people like him.

Roughhouse Pete — he was a terrible character. Some amusing stories are told of him. In one case he had a feud with a camp cook. Now, these were the days when there was no union, and there was only one way of expressing disapproval to the boss or anybody else, and that was by individual action. So he walked into the cookhouse one night, sat down and looked at the usual stew, I guess it was, that he took exception to, and had been taking exception to, and decided that he had enough of it. So he just simply got up and started down from one end of the table to the other, kicking all the food off as he went along. A lot of it landed in the laps of the poor devils — fellow workmen and so on — you know, hot potatoes and gravy and so on. He didn't care; he was a complete fool.

In another instance he was in the camp where the camp superintendent had to go down to the city. Now, this was at Rock Bay, I think. He had to go down to the city for some business and he temporarily left the accountant in charge for two or three days. He'd left some instructions which the accountant promptly mixed up [and] got confused about, so he issued an order one morning stating that all workmen, all the men on the job, would have to bring their tools in every night. Apparently, some of the fallers had been leaving their axes and saws out on the job and they'd been losing them behind a stump — forgotten where they'd left them, you see. So he issued this. He put this letter out and hung it on a bulletin board, and there was a bit of an uproar about it. On the second day Roughhouse Pete decided to do something about it.

Now, he was what they call a sidepush. In other words he was in charge of two machines and a crew, which meant that he had a great big machine under him, a big trackside machine which yarded the logs in from the cold deck machine into a cold deck pile at the [railroad] track and then loaded them from there onto the flatcars. So he decided to quit, apparently, and carrying out the accountant's instructions to the letter to bring his tools in. What were his tools? Well, his tools were this bloody trackside machine — an enormous machine, you know, with a great big steam boiler on it and all sorts of drums and levers, a very intricate piece of machinery. It was all rigged up with guylines on a spar tree and a bull block and a skyline

Topping a spar tree. Courtesy Provincial Archives of British Columbia / 68007

going out to the cold deck pile — oh, a very intricate sort of a system that took several days to set up. He had the whole damn thing dismantled. I mean, that was his tool!

So he was going to bring them in. He had them take down the rigging and load the main-line and the bull block onto a flatcar, and he had this trackside machine pull itself up onto a flatcar and call the locie, and they rolled the whole thing into camp and spotted it right in front of the commissary, right in front of the office. It's said that the accountant came out just white with fear, realizing what happened. He asked what he done. "You wanted my tools, there they are. Now give me my time!" says Roughhouse Pete. Of course, nobody dared to touch him because he was such a battler and such an insane person. He was blacklisted, finally, for stunts like that.

In and Out of Camp

Edited by Derek Reimer

George Lutz and Jack Vetleson, though not old, are members of a dying breed, the old-time coastal logger. Their stories have become part of the folklore of British Columbia logging.

JACK VETLESON: Well, some guys stayed [in camp] three months. Some guys stayed six months. Some guys stayed a year, like George says . . . but there were guys like Eight-Day Wilson. He never worked more than eight days in his life. He's an old-timer. He's long gone, years ago, you know. He was proud of the fact that he'd never worked in a camp more than eight days. And he was a good man. He could always get a job. He did his work and he did it well while he was there, but he never worked more than eight days. There was Eight-Day Wilson, there was Panicky Bill, there was Panicky Pete, there was Hungry Bill and, oh, you could go on and on with these names. . . . I remember this Hungry John we used to have here. When the penicillin first come out, he read in the paper where they got this penicillin from mould from the bread. He used to take bread down to his bunkhouse and get it mouldy and eat it. He figured that was good for his health.

GEORGE LUTZ: There wasn't the turnover in men as there is today, at that time. A man would come and he would work for six months or a year. Some would stay on longer. Like, this camp here . . . I travelled the coast before I came here . . . I worked at "gyppo" outfits, and I just moved

A Duplex four-wheel-drive truck loaded with 4000 feet of logs, Gerrard Lumber Company, Trout Lake, B. C., circa 1919. These trucks ran on a fore-and-aft roadway in the bush. Courtesy Edna Daney

from camp to camp and just went all over. I was looking for the right place, I guess. I don't know, but this was the trend. But when I came here, it surprised me that there were so many people that had been here for a long time, and the turnover at that time wasn't that great.

I quit myself, in '45. I got into a row with the boss and I said, "All right, that's it. I quit!" And he says, "No way, man. You're fired!" I says, "Oh, no, I beat you to it! I *quit!* And I *did.* I left and took everything with me and I went to town and I stayed in town, I guess, two months. You know, I had quite a stake and everything like that, and staying in a hotel. Finally, I was getting low on funds and I got a job with the bridge crew at Port Hardy. I was just hired out for there, when our "man-catcher" — he's the fellow in Vancouver, in the office there — they would phone down and say, "Now look, you find that fellow and get ahold of him, and send him up here!" So that fellow — he'd go out and find you, you see. Well, this fellow, our man-catcher, Arnold Smith . . .

JACK VETLESON: We call him Two Dollar Smith. You'd ask for a "drag" before ya left town . . . that was the common thing. You'd hire out and you'd be broke. You wouldn't hire out until you didn't have any money left, so then you'd say, "Well, I'd like some money so I can get a bottle to take back to camp with me." Well, most outfits would give you fifty bucks, some would give you a hundred, you know. Arnold Smith would offer you two dollars. . . . They call him a personnel man today. They're more refined. Some of them are even personnel managers, you know. And they've got an office and everything, and a telephone, and they don't do anything, but them days the guy had to get out on the streets and go around the beer parlours and look these guys up. Most of the big outfits had one.

GEORGE LUTZ: If they wanted to get hold of a certain fellow they'd send him out, and he knew where to go. He'd go into a certain beer parlour. We all hung out at the Belmont, and he'd just go in there, and, of course, being the man-catcher, he was known by everyone and he'd just say, "Have you seen Lutz around anywhere?" And the guy says, "Yeah, by gosh, he was in here just a few days ago." "Well, have you any idea where he's staying?" "No." Well, as a rule, we always stayed in the same hotel. We either stayed at the York or the Belmont.

JACK VETLESON: You only had to go to six or seven hotels in Vancouver at that time. You'd find eighty per cent of the loggers in these six or seven hotels. Maybe ten hotels. And if they weren't there, there would be somebody there that knew where they were. A guy stayed at the same hotel for years and years. Some of them left their clothes there. When they went back to the woods their clothes would be put away for them, and when they came back their shirts would be ironed and their suits would be pressed. When you went broke, you never worried about a hotel bill. You worried about changing the desk clerk, because there might be a new guy on there, and you come in three o'clock in the morning and need twenty bucks and you wouldn't know the desk clerk, and that was your biggest worry. If you stayed in the same hotel you'd just walk down there and say, "I need some money," you know, and out it would come. They gave it to you and you always went back to that hotel, because if you *didn't* go back to that hotel, nobody knew where to find you when you got to town — you were a stranger. And loggers, them times, went to a beer parlour and they always sat together. At two o'clock in the afternoon their table would have twenty or thirty . . . and you knew everybody at the table.

GEORGE LUTZ: That's what loggers do. They go to Vancouver — they do all their logging in the beer parlour, then they come back here and they do all the girls back here. But you go back thirty years ago, or even a little longer, if you want, and I know myself — this one incident — I was going around with a girl in Vancouver — quite a respectable girl, and everything. So her parents wanted to meet me, you see, and she'd told them that she'd met a logger. Well, that was no problem. Certainly! So I went up there. They invited me for dinner. Well, I was always a well-dresser, and most loggers always were. Most people I knew were always well-dressed. And when I got up to their place and knocked at the door, I tell you, her mother just turned white! I think she expected me with cork boots. After a while we got talking, and they asked me about camp and they were surprised just how well we *were* living. They didn't know. Most people in Vancouver just thought we were . . . I don't know what they thought we were, but . . .

JACK VETLESON: Loggers used to make good money, you know.

GEORGE LUTZ: . . . and really raised hell in town, and this is where they got the bad name. But it was just that you didn't have time. Loggers were out for six, seven, eight months at a time, then they'd go to town and they've only got two weeks. Well, I know they'd blow thousands of dollars in that two weeks, and at that time that was a lot of money. And everyone came back broke.

JACK VETLESON: The old *Maquinna* that used to travel the West Coast would call in on the radio somewhere between Victoria and the coast and they used to say, "We've got a hundred and fifty loggers and fifty passengers." That's the way they defined everybody.

GEORGE LUTZ: [It would stop at all the camps on the way up.] Oh, yes, that is what took so long. We were put off on a little float out in the water, just a little twelve-by-twelve float. If the wind was blowing, you hung on for dear life! Then you'd see one of these great big boats come in and try to tie up to that little thing. They wouldn't even tie up — they'd drift right into it, you know, and then they'd open up the side doors — at the side of the hatch — then they'd grab you and bail you aboard that way. There was no such a thing as putting a ladder down.

JACK VETLESON: They've been known to let loggers off on boomsticks in the middle of the night, and their suitcases and everything. That wasn't too uncommon. The little "gyppo" camps didn't have a float and we made it. I never hear of anybody drowning.

GEORGE LUTZ: A lot of people fell in, though!

JACK VETLESON: I've been in camps where they didn't even have boomsticks, and the big boat wouldn't even stop. They'd open up the doors in the side of the boat, and the other boat would pull alongside and they'd both be moving, and you'd bail into the big boat. Right out in the water . . . and the big boat only slowed down for them.

DOWN IN THE COAL MINES

*C*oal mining began in 1849 at Fort Rupert on the northern end of Vancouver Island. The coal there turned out to be of poor quality, but as coal at that time was fetching forty dollars a ton in San Francisco, the search went on. Shortly afterwards, good coalfields were discovered at Nanaimo. Soon, coalfields were in production from Namaimo to Comox to fuel steamships, locomotives and factories. By the 1890s, Robert Dunsmuir's mines were shipping out 400,000 tons (363 000 t) of coal a year.

In common with other workers in resource industries, coal miners did hard and dangerous work for low wages, and did so under unsavoury and unsafe conditions. Their attempts to organize unions were met by harsh and violent measures.

"The Big Strike" of 1912

Edited by Patricia Wejr and Howie Smith

*I*n the early 1900s Vancouver Island coal mines were known for both their high quality coal and their extremely dangerous working conditions. Without strong union support, the fight for safety was a very difficult one for coal miners. In 1912 the longest strike in B. C. history started in the coal mines of Extension and soon spread to all the coal mines in the area. This strike for better working conditions continued for two years and resulted in the destruction of the union. Its impact is still felt by the people who remember it today.

In the dying days of the strike, when many striking miners were facing court trials, the B. C. Miners' Liberation League was formed in Vancouver. Its object was to obtain the release of those miners already sentenced and to prevent further sentences. To aid their cause, the league issued a pamphlet by J. Kavanaugh in 1914, describing the strike situation in detail. Excerpts from this pamphlet, *The Vancouver Island Strike,* are used here to narrate the story of "The Big Strike."

In the twenty-eight years prior to 1912, 373 men were killed in the mines on Vancouver Island in consequence of explosions of coal gas. Wellington accounted for 83, Nanaimo for 180, Extension 50 and Cumberland 69. The last explosion took place at Extension as late as 1909.

BEN HORBRY: Conditions were always more or less bad. You went into your place with your lamp held halfway between the roof and the floor. (It was all open-flame lamps, just little teapot fish-oil lamps.) If you put the lamp down, it went out in black damp, that's a heavier-than-air gas. If you put it up, you lit the explosive gas on fire.

My uncle got burnt. He started a fire and singed off his moustache and eyebrows and stuff. When my father came down, my uncle told him: "The tools are there (at that time they owned their own tools); you can go down and get 'em or you can leave them. I'm not going back." So my father went down and got the tools, and they transferred to another mine. Then they kept after their brother-in-law, who was working in Number Six, to quit and get out of there. He did, and it was about a week after he got out that everybody in the mine was killed.

HENRY GIBSON: When that explosion took place in Number Six, it was a month before they got anyone out, there wasn't a soul. They had to flood the mine to get the bodies. Every man was killed in it.

It is not due to the negligence of these miners that these gas explosions have taken place, nor would it appear on the surface to be the fault of the government, which has instituted laws designed to prevent such accidents. The Coal Mines Regulation Act of 1911 makes provision [for mine inspections and gas reporting]. It would appear that the miners were amply protected, but it was found that if a gas committee discovered gas in dangerous quantities and made a true report of the same, much difficulty arose in finding a "place" in which they could work, and ultimately they would have to leave the camp.

On June 15, 1912, Isaac Portrey and Oscar Mottishaw, the gas committee appointed by the men, reported having found gas in several places in the No. 2 mine at Extension. This report was forwarded to the Inspector of Mines, who verified the same in July 1912.

JIM GALLOWAY: The miners were allowed to elect the gas committee, two men to go around one day every month and inspect the places for gas or anything for safety. Then they come out and write a report. Well, that's what happened with Mottishaw and his partner. They found gas in some place and reported it. The company didn't like it and I guess they fired them. And one [Mottishaw] come up to Cumberland and got a job there and the contractor laid him off.

The miners then decided to declare a general holiday at all the mines in Cumberland on Monday, September 16, 1912, in order that this question might be discussed. At the meeting, a committee was chosen, consisting of union and nonunion miners, to again visit the managers. This committee met the same fate as previous ones. [Managers refused to meet with them.]

On the miners returning to work on the morning of the 17th, they discovered notices at the mine entrances notifying them to take out their tools, the only condition under which they would be permitted to work being: that each man desiring to work could do so, provided that he signed an individual contract agreeing to work under the old conditions, for a period of two years. Thus commenced the strike on Vancouver Island — by a lockout at the hands of the mine owners.

BEN HORBRY: Everybody that was on strike was forced out of their houses. My grandfather and grandmother were forced out because they lived in the camp which was company owned.

BOB McCALLISTER: We all got a house each down at the camp. And you were notified to get out. "You're not working for the company anymore." You got four dollars a week from the United Mine Workers Union. I got four, Dad got four, two for Mother and a dollar for each child. Well, you can't pay rent and light and water on that, so we moved down to what they called Striker's Beach and lived in tents the first winter. We got enough lumber to put a floor and a three-foot wall in. The kitchen stove was sitting out on an old road next to the main highway, and we built a lean-to over it.

> The next spring things didn't look good, so we got a little more lumber and built a place for us to live and we stayed there. Others stayed there, too.

In the meantime, the miners working at the Extension mines, Ladysmith, operated by the same company as at Cumberland, The Canadian Collieries ("Dunsmuir") Ltd., had taken one day's holiday to discuss the situation as it applied to them and on their return to work, were met by the same notice which had been posted at Cumberland. By the beginning of October all miners employed by the Canadian Collieries Ltd. had been locked out.

JIM GALLOWAY: The mines were open all the time; it was all scabs. They went over to England and brought in some men. We got some to quit, and some went to work. You couldn't blame them in a way, I guess. They were told they were coming out here to work; they came out, and I guess they had nothing. You know, you could meet them coming off the trains and offer them strike pay, but that wasn't very much encouragement to them, coming out from the old country to make a fortune.

BEN HORBRY: They were told: "Don't go to Cumberland, there's a big strike on." But a man's tied up, he's got his family. Of course, that's an excuse; some of them didn't come. Some of them have said to me that they felt they had to come because they were obligated, their fare had been paid and all that.

BOB McCALLISTER: We couldn't stop them.

HENRY GIBSON: They had thugs from the States with pistols stuck on their sides!

BOB McCALLISTER: The company had their own police — they hired them. And then there was the provincial police, see.

A United Mine Workers' parade in Ladysmith, B. C., during "The Big Strike," 1913. Courtesy Provincial Archives of British Columbia / 80650

Although Cumberland was, if possible, more peaceful than ever, approximately 100-foot and 20-mounted special policemen were sent into town.

It had been decided at an executive session of the miners to declare a general strike of all miners on Vancouver Island, in an endeavour to influence the government to intervene and bring about an investigation into the circumstances responsible for the lockout. May 1st being the day celebrated by the miners as Labour Day, it was finally decided to issue the strike call on the evening of April 30, 1913. In Nanaimo, a mass meeting was held on the night of May 1st. The feeling in favour of the strike was overwhelming and the strike of all miners on Vancouver Island had commenced.

Various attempts were made to provoke the strikers into committing a breach of the peace, in order that the special police might have an opportunity of earning their pay.

BEN HORBRY: One of these special policemen would come along; you might be walking on the sidewalk, and he'd bump you off, stagger into you. You'd retaliate and you were pinched for assaulting a police officer. You know, the younger generation doesn't see any of that. They can't understand how you were aggravated into retaliating. It was just how it happens in hockey — one man gets away with it, then the man that retaliates gets chucked off the ice. Well here, they put them in jail. That went on all during the strike. It was just a way of life.

On July 16, 1913, the Cumberland strikers received word that a man named Cave, a big husky fellow who was acting as a scab herder for the company, had declared his intention of coming into Cumberland and cleaning out the strikers. On the

Striking miners being marched to jail in Ladysmith, B. C., in 1913.
Courtesy Provincial Archives of British Columbia / 78704

evening of Saturday, July 19, Cave, accompanied by about 15 others, came down the street leading from the company's property.

JIM GALLOWAY: They had what they called a bit of a riot. That was when the scabs come marching down the street to the post office. They came in Indian file, walked right down, and all shouting. We was across the street, and of course the fight started then.

BEN HORBRY: There was men and horses and everything going in all directions. They had clubs three feet long — pick handles and one thing and another.

JIM GALLOWAY: I was right there. And Joe Naylor wasn't there. Joe wasn't there but he got arrested anyhow.

Some two weeks later several of the strikers were arrested, among them being Joe Naylor, President of the Union, and charged with being members of an unlawful assembly. Neither Cave or any of his companions who were the instigators of the trouble, have been arrested. Those arrested were refused bail.

In the meantime, the strikebreakers at Extension were becoming particularly offensive to the strikers residing at the mining camp. The miners received the impression that some attempt was to be made to drive them out of the camp. They therefore approached the "Bullpen" where many of the strikebreakers were lodged. It was necessary to proceed carefully as many of the strikebreakers were possessed of firearms. As they drew near the mine, the strikers were met by a fusilade of bullets. This drove them to shelter.

ELLEN BOWATER GREENWELL: They shot right in the mine. They must have had their guns already loaded. Oh yes, one guy here by the name of Baxter got shot right in the arm. I was lucky I never got shot. I was as lucky as . . . I was running right back up the hill, but I didn't get shot.

The militia was sent from Vancouver and what a time they had in Vancouver! The people was down at the boats calling them everything they could call them, for coming over here to the strike. And then when they got here, they headed for Extension. And people in Nanaimo said, "Oh, by god, you'll sure hit dynamite if you go up that road to Extension! There's all dynamite laid for you, you'll get shot up!" You know, four or five fainted on that road going up to Extension. Sure they did! They scared the devil out of them here in Nanaimo!

I can tell you lots of things on that damn strike, you know. My sister lived down at South Wellington then, and of course they lived in company houses. Well, here when South Wellington come out on strike, first thing, they shipped them out of their company houses. Well, here's what happened.

When you get into Extension, there's a big "special" [policeman] here, there's a big "special" there, and they've got a great big police dog. So here my sister and me goes down there to load her furniture up 'cuz the men's in jail. Well, you know, they had them fancy hanging lamps with the dinglers on and gold-framed pictures. Well, here I've got a kid's picture under this arm and part of the hanging lamp under this arm, and she's got her husband's picture and the other part of the hanging lamp under the other arm, and we've got to walk four miles with these things!

Well, when we're getting up to Extension, this big dog comes grrrrrr after us, and those two guys standing there. I guess they thought we had been stealing stuff from the riot. My sister said, "Get the devil out of here!" (We didn't care in those days, I'm telling you!) So here the cop looks and he says, "Don't worry, it'll just take you by the hem of your skirt with its teeth and bring you up to me." My sister said, "Well, you know, that's funny, but it'll be a damn dog bringing us to a dog!" Oh, we used to cheek them! We didn't care. Oh God, we used to be fighters. That 1912 strike is a great lesson to me. If I would have knew then what I know now, boy, I sure would have been up on the road, a fighting devil for labour!

On Monday, August 18th, notice was issued that a meeting would be held in the Athletic Club, Nanaimo, for the purpose of considering a proposed agreement between the Vancouver and Nanaimo Coal Co. and the Union. The meeting convened at 7:30 P.M., some 1,200 men being present. Shortly afterwards, the hall was surrounded by troops, under the command of Colonel Hall.

Colonel Hall recorded some splendid tricks in Nanaimo and district. He seemed to be invariably under the inspiration of some brilliant stroke of generalship. Anyhow, something had him going. This was most marked at a public meeting held by the miners to consider the Jingle Pot Mine proposal, when he appeared to think a good time had arrived for the display of some nice stage effects. When the meeting was in progress, he rushed his troops to the scene under cover of the night and surrounded the hall and placed his machine guns at the back door.

Some of his trustees peeped through the cracks and alleged that they saw the miners with guns and knives and every conceivable weapon. He thereupon sent an officer into the hall, who told the chairman that he had two minutes in which to clear the place. There were probably 14 or 15 hundred men in the hall and you can imagine what effect an order like that would have. I can conceive of many cases wherein a similar blunder might have led to a terrible tragedy in the struggle for exits.

— ANONYMOUS ACCOUNT

The Colonel then said they could have one hour in which to finish their business. Later, he desired to address the meeting and on this being granted, said they could go ahead and finish their business, but that he was tired and was going to bed. Strong suspicion is entertained that the gallant gentleman had been gazing on the wine that was red.

When the meeting had closed, the miners having voted to accept an agreement with the Van. & Nan. Coal Co., they were marched out in groups of 10, single file, in charge of special police, a guard of soldiers with bayonets fixed on either side, and marched to the courthouse. There each man was searched, his name taken, and if he was desired, placed in detention. The remainder were then marched out on to the ground at the front of the courthouse and kept there under guard. Forty-three were detained, the remainder being kept under guard until 2 A.M. before being allowed to disperse.

The Colonel came along the next morning and tore up the floor of the building. Perhaps he was looking for the provincial prosperity of which we have heard so much, but certain it is, that he did not find any ammunition, such as was alleged to have been deposited there.

— ANONYMOUS ACCOUNT

At Ladysmith the miners were not holding a huge meeting, therefore, no spectacular arrest could be made. However, commencing about 1:30 A.M. August 19th, 1913, the special police and militia went around to the houses of some of the strikers, woke them up and told them they were wanted at the police office. Here they were arrested. Among them was Sam Guthrie, President of the Union, and one of the greatest factors in the keeping of peace in Ladysmith.

ELLEN GREENWELL: They took my father and my brother in, you know. They come at two o'clock in the morning. The first thing my father said was: "I'm not going out in them ranks at all, not until you give me a warrant." They said: "We don't need a warrant now; you're under martial law!"

In all, 179 miners were arrested and thrown into prison where they were held, bail being refused. At the preliminary hearing in Nanaimo, the visitors to the court were treated to the edifying spectacle of Magistrate Simpson retiring to the judges room in company with Prosecuting Attorney Shoebotham, any time he happened to be in doubt as to what course to pursue.

The trial was to take place during October. Contrary to expectations, however, Judge Howay of New Westminster was brought over to try the cases. Thirty-nine men were tried. The sentences ranged from two years to nine months, the sentences below two years carrying additional penalties.

> *Mr. Shoebotham made the statement that the sentences imposed upon the miners would break the spirit of the others. Now what kind of a joint is the Attorney-General running? Is he running a strike-breaking business or is he administering the law as we are all supposed to expect he has been doing? If Mr. Shoebotham's statement represents the attitude of the Attorney-General, what particular brand of justice can we expect to be meted out in B.C.? As a matter of fact, it is perfectly clear that there are two brands of justice in this province.*
>
> — ANONYMOUS ACCOUNT

Previous to delivering the sentences, Judge Howay vilified the prisoners because they did not cringe before him. On his return to New Westminster, he issued a statement to the press justifying himself, which was calculated to influence the jury, before whom the remainder of the prisoners would be tried, the venue having been changed to that place.

ELLEN GREENWELL: They had my brother up for arson and they had his pal up for attempted murder! The biggest lies that God ever put breath in. And you know, they never let my brother out of jail for six months. They let him out the day before Christmas on ten thousand dollars bail! All them years ago, ten thousand dollars bail. And then he had to go back. And the other one, who was up for attempted murder, they never did let him out until he got out when the real trials come up.

And them was some trials, you can believe me. For three months we went every week to that Westminster. And I'm going to tell you, that was a hell of a hole for men from Vancouver Island to go to! I was up in that witness box on every case from Extension. And the old judge, oh, he was an old bugger, I can see him now, big red face ... he said, "You know that there Miss Bowater [Ellen Greenwell's maiden name], she's about the brazenist, brassiest thing I ever seen in my life!" Anyhow, when my brother come up, they had him four hours in the witness box, a kid sixteen! Four hours! On arson. But the jury disagreed, and he went back, but he got off the next time just like that. At last they got so sick and fed up with him they threw the whole thing out. They got sick of those scabs telling lies!

JIM GALLOWAY: The strike ended, I guess, about a month before the war started (late August of 1914). You see, the war was coming on, and I guess the mine workers were having lots of trouble down in the States, too. So I guess the money was going short, and they cut us off the strike pay.

BEN HORBRY: It wasn't a total loss. It was as far as wages and that were concerned, but in another way, you've got to strike to keep things on a balance.

> *Included in the terms of settlement of the strike was the statement: "The companies will employ all men in their employ at the beginning of the trouble, without discrimination and as rapidly as physical conditions of the mines will permit."*
>
> — *B. C. Federationist*, 28 August 1914

ELLEN GREENWELL: My husband and his brother had to go up to Coalhurst, Alberta, to get a job. They wouldn't hire them back. No. When my brother went over, they said, "You've been walking around for two years, get out and walk around for two more!" Lots of them never did get hired. They even went down to Australia.

[The last of the jailed miners was released on 25 September 1914. The only one never to gain freedom was Joseph Mairs (Jr.).]

ELLEN GREENWELL: This young Mairs was in jail and he took sick. And I guess they didn't bother about him at all. He died right in jail. My brother and me and my father came over on the boat with his mother and the body when he come over. And Ladysmith erected a big headstone down there for him when he was buried.

The inscription on the headstone read:
> *A martyr to the noble cause — the emancipation of his fellow man.*
> — *Erected by his brothers of District 28, United Mine Workers of America.*

Sixteen Tons a Day

Edited by Patricia Wejr and Howie Smith

After the breakup of the union in 1914, coal miners were without a labour organization until the 1930s. The contract system of paying for the amount of coal mined, rather than straight wages, caused many miners to push themselves past the point of safety.

BEN HORBRY: If you were·caging down in the mines, you'd maybe push three or four hundred two-ton cars a day onto the cage and bell 'em up, send them to the surface. They had two-ton cars on rails down there to

Coal miners at the Alexandra Mine in South Wellington, B. C. Courtesy Provincial Archives of British Columbia / 50764

bring the coal out. How do you push a two-ton car? You get your back to it, your heels dug in, and push! If you were picking coal, it was just pick and shovel and blast, no machines, and you got eighty-six cents a ton for coal mined off the solid. I've turned out sixteen to eighteen tons a day. When you first started at it, of course, there was two or three weeks that your bones really ached by the time you got finished. A sixteen-ton was a good average if you had the coal to do it with.

At that time, it was all pillar-and-stall mining. Every hundred feet there'd be a pillar holding the roof up, and the piece of coal around the pillar would be left. After you got to the end of your boundary, they'd come back and take the pillars out, one at a time. And then the roof would start to talk. First of all, there would be a few rumbles, and this might go on for three or four days. During that time, you cleared all your equipment out. The section would collapse, and then you'd go back in. I've been knocked down by the push of air when it collapsed, because I waited too long getting out. When the roof was coming down, there was also a pressure on the face coal, and the coal came easy. You could take it with a pick and pull it down in big chunks. Well, if you got greedy, if you were loading coal fast and the empty cars were coming in to you, you stayed until the last minute. And then ran!

You were forced into it, in a way — the contract system does all that stuff. In the Thirties we threw out the contract system, but it was a big fight, because as long as the coal miner was on contract, the company didn't need anybody to push the drivers and all the haulage crew who were supplying the empty cars. The miner pushed them — he wanted more money, he hollered for more cars. It was stupid, in a way, because a lot of the men would load coal and load coal and load coal. Then, when they drew their pay, they'd find out they weren't paid for half of it. The contract was written out in such a way that it seemed like the more coal you loaded, the less you got paid.

In those days, about the end of September, grain shipments were leaving Vancouver. They didn't ship grain in a ship that burnt oil, so it was all coal-burning ships. Then the work was really steady. They wanted you to work seven days a week. I didn't and I got into a lot of trouble over it. I like to go hunting at that time of the year, and the boss would come around and say: "Well, I'll give you a choice. I know you don't want to work the whole weekend, but you can work Saturday afternoon or Sunday morning." It turned out I didn't work either! The superintendent come in on Monday and said, "You didn't show up either day. You know, this company has been keeping you employed and paying you good wages for a long time." Well, the only answer I had for that was, "Yeah, and I've been making profits for the company for a long time, too!"

FISHING THE SEAS

Salmon fishing became a major industry in 1882, with the establishment of British Columbia's first cannery at Rivers Inlet. By the turn of the century, scores of other canneries — each with its own fishing fleet — were set up on the Skeena and Fraser rivers, as well as on Rivers Inlet. In 1901 a record-breaking 1.2 million cases of salmon were shipped to market, and each case held ninety-six half-pound (225-g) cans.

In the early days canneries owned the fish boats and paid fishermen a monthly wage. Later, canneries paid fishermen by the fish. Fishermen first organized, then formed unions, to force canneries to negotiate rather than simply set the price of fish.

Gill Netters on the Skeena

Edited by Allen Specht

The fishing industry on the Skeena had undergone continuous change, but in this period, fishing boats were owned by the canneries, and the fishermen were like employees of the companies. At first Indians did most of the fishing and canning, but later Japanese, Chinese and whites formed a large part of the work force.

Mrs. North is the daughter of Peter Herman, one of the most prominent citizens of Port Essington.

MRS. NORTH: Every Sunday evening the guns went off, and the boats started for the canneries. You see, there was a curfew on fishing over the weekend. And the tug would start out from the cannery with her tow of boats. Now, the tow consisted of a long line from the tugboat, which would be two to three hundred feet long, or more. And all their fishing boats would tie up to this rope and be towed out to get out in as short time as possible to the fishing area. But nobody moved until this gun sounded.

They were only allowed to use sail. Of course, when they were taken out, their sails would be down. [Later] I'd see them in the

Fisherman hauling in a gill net. Photograph by Clifford R. Kopas, courtesy Lester R. Peterson

mouth of the river with the sails all set. As I remember, most of them were a kind of orange-brown-khaki.

WALTER WICKS: There were two men in a boat, and the first partner that they picked for me was a Japanese who had always been what we called "high boat" — that is, brought in more fish than others. They always put me where the most money was, so it seemed, but he was a wonderful man, that Japanese. I fished with him for two years.

In the central mouth of the Skeena River — the passage between two islands, Kennedy and De Horsey — this passage was called "the gap." There was a neck of land that stuck out just below the passage, stuck out well into the river on this low stage of the tide. When the salmon came in with the incoming tide from the ocean, they would come in behind this point. The tide striking that point would swirl around in a semicircle, and the momentum of the tidal current made a complete vortex, and in this vortex the fish would become bewildered and they would circle around there. Well, it was a great place for the fishermen to get in. Thirty and forty fishermen would get into this hole — we called it "the glory hole." They would throw their nets in every and all directions, crisscrossing one another, cursing one another, fighting one another, to get this salmon as much as they could; but as the tide came up and found its higher level, then the tide would slow up in its movement, and the fish would continue on around the point and upriver to the spawning ground. But there were some terrible fights in that glory hole. Indians trying to keep the Japs out, they would jump on their boats, cut their anchor lines, throw their anchors overboard, rip their sails to get them out of there. They never bothered the white much. They hated the Jap because they felt he was a despoiler, for the reason that they would fish night and day legally or illegally, and the Indian felt that the Jap was taking more than his share. That was the reason. There was always an enmity between the Indian and the Japanese fisherman.

There are small incidents that happened here and there, but I don't offhand at the moment know what would be of particular interest, except to say that it was really a rough life. We didn't think so then, but I look back and I wonder how a boy of thirteen followed that kind of a life even for two and a half months in the better weather, ever survived it. And I have seen drownings in bad weather.

We had at that time steam tugs that would tow us out in the mouth of the river in the first part of a fishing season, and having no power but oars and sails, the steamboats tugged us out into deeper water where we would be cast loose, and cast out nets and drift for the night and the tugs would come out in the morning and pick us up again. Or we would make some cannery fish camp that had been placed at strategic places along the coastline that would take our fish if we didn't want to go back in the cannery that day. Sometimes it was long distances. I remember one time we went out and one boat was missing. I couldn't find it, and they kept towing us around for hours and hours, and finally they gave up the search; and on the way in they spotted the boat laying sideways with the sail flat on the oar. If a fishing boat capsizes, its sail is up; it never turns bottom up. They pulled on a heavy line when they got to the boat, a weighted line, pulled it up, and on the end of it was one of the drowned fisherman with the rope tied around his wrist. The other man was never found. They were what we called *cheechakos*, [Chinook for] greenhorns, beginners who didn't understand the game. Well, we grouped around the body that was wrapped up in a piece of sail on the wharf later on and we heard a lot of remarks that were not very favourable to the cannery management. One person I remember saying, he said, "If those darned cannery managers wasn't so greedy, these boys wouldn't have got drowned!" They wouldn't have allowed those *cheechakos*, or greenhorns, to have gone out there with a boat and net, and they couldn't even pull the boat or handle the net or the oars and yet they were sent out there to get as fishermen. There were a lot of remarks made there that I don't care to repeat, but like one cannery man said, it was not necessary to send these men out there to their deaths. They could have gotten work there in the cannery that they could have handled, and now two mothers in England would be opening up their letters to read this.

Chief Jeffrey Johnson of the Gitksan village near Hazelton talks about the earliest period of fishing activity on the lower Skeena, most of which was carried on by the Indians from the coast, upriver and from the Queen Charlotte Islands.

CHIEF JEFFREY JOHNSON: They travel by canoe from upriver. Four or five familes to one canoe, and came down here early in spring. . . . And the women work in the cannery and so on like that.

These women at the cannery early in the spring, they're knittin' the sockeye net. . . . There's a carton of twine. I think women get two and a half to make a net.

And during the summer, when the canning was on, the women got three cents a tray, filling the cans; one hundred and fifty trays to a [rack.] That's a lot of money for them, because it's an awful lot of fish in those times.

Mother used to make a [rack] a day, and they were surprised how much money — seven dollars and fifty cents a day for that [rack.]

And fishermen they went out. They don't sell fish by each fish the same as we do today. They only get paid by the month — thirty dollars for a captain and twenty-five dollars for a boat puller. And it's only two months in a year they fish. They fish day and night for that thirty dollars a month.

And they use the flat-bottom skiff with no shelter, just open skiff with two pieces across to sit on. You know how much wind and how much rain are here! And these people would sit out there, and the

Gill netting with sailboats on the Skeena River, 1920. Courtesy Provincial Archives of British Columbia / 31219

rain and the wind blowing. They didn't have enough money to buy slickers. . . . In those days a lot of people died.

They don't care how many die.

And there's nobody else besides our native people doing the fishing in those days. No other race of people before Japs and whites.

Now, gradually, the companies came in. They must have heard that there was an awful lot of fish in those days. Father says there's about three or four feet dead fish on the beach. The cannery, they don't can pink salmon. They just throw them away. They just pickin' sockeye and they getting the sockeye by the thousands, each tide. At the peak of the run each fisherman brought in a thousand, from eight hundred to one thousand each tide, those days. So they don't care for pink salmon.

WALTER WICKS: Sockeye, of course, was the highest grade salmon. They were the fish that they could get a better price [for]. Then the dog salmon, or [what's] called chums today, we had to throw them overboard. [For] the humpback we were allowed approximately two cents, two to five, then when the humpback salmon came in heavy schools — would last only ten or fifteen days — the canneries would become overloaded. Being unable to can the salmon quick enough, they would sometimes become spoiled so that they could not be packed and then they would have to be thrown overboard. The result was that the heavy run of the humpback salmon, which were known as pinks, they would limit us to a hundred fish per boat per day, at one cent apiece. Now, there were times when they were running heavy, yet we would have to unentangle five thousand humps and then bring in only a hundred at one cent and divide one dollar between two men.

Now, let us take a few figures. We had thirteen canneries — it happened all along the river. Each cannery would have forty-five to sixty boats; practically every boat was doing the same thing, the canneries were flooded, and so we were all given the same choice — bring in a hundred, that's it, that's all we can handle. Throw the rest overboard. The dog salmon, they were not canned at all. There was what we called the springs, the cohoes, the sockeye and a limited amount of humpbacks, and that's all that was canned. Everything else was thrown back overboard. Now, all salmon are supposed to be red or deep pink, but there also is a white spring salmon. Sometimes they are crossed in spawning, and you get a pink, but the white was never canned, it was dumped overboard, and I have seen spring salmon forty and fifty pounds in weight, each fish, and dumped overboard just like garbage.

The fishing industry, vital to the economy of Port Essington and the major employer in the lower Skeena, underwent rapid changes that ended the prominence of Port Essington and spelled the end of the numerous small canneries. As the supply of fish diminished, the fishing boundaries were shifted downriver, and this left the upriver canneries far away from the supply. The introduction of engine-powered boats made it possible for boats to fish over a wider area and to bring their catch much greater distances. Canneries became further mechanized, thus being able to handle larger volumes of fish, causing the canning process to become centralized in a few large canneries. Significantly, the canneries that did survive were those on the railway line. Over time the bulk of the fishing industry shifted to the new port city of Prince Rupert.

Trolling off the West Coast
Edited by Bob Bossin

IAN McLEOD: Fish always go in a clockwise direction in the northern hemisphere. You know that when you're fishing. That's how the fish traps worked in the real early days. A net would go out on maybe a thirty-degree angle from the shore at a narrow place, and the fish would funnel into it. Once they went through a certain section of the net, they couldn't turn around, and they didn't have the brains to go back the way they came in. If they went the other way, they could get out, but they are not smart enough. They always go clockwise, like a bunch of sheep.

All these boats you see here are trolling boats. When we first came to Tofino, there was only one or two white men fishing, that is trolling. I was about the third one. The rest of the fishermen were Japanese. They came here in the early years, half a dozen at first. One old fellow called Suzaki brought the technique from Japan with him. And that mushroomed from Tofino all along the west coast. Even the Americans ended up with our method of hook-and-line trolling. But this is where it started years ago, and it was Japanese right until the late Thirties.

I first went out trolling with Japanese fellows on weekends for fun. I liked the thrill of catching salmon and the sport that was attached to that method of fishing. We could get a boat for about eight hundred dollars and away we'd go fishing with a two-cylinder gasoline make-and-break system, chug-chug, chug-chug, no high speeds in those days.

Of course, we didn't have weather reports. You used the signs around the sun in the morning and the atmospheric pressure — you could feel it on yourself. You watched how fast the clouds were moving. How it looked the day before had a lot of bearing on it. But we had better weather in the summer in those days.

The Japanese were the greatest people on earth when it came to fishermen. They co-operated so well. There were no radio telephones, but there were methods of communicating. If a man was in trouble, he raised one pole. That meant he was in distress. Then the first law of the sea came into play, that you should help your fellow man. You'd tow him in. Everybody would do that, certainly. Another thing: you didn't try to prove a point or be tough, or stay out too late. If the weather looked bad, everybody would stay out until a certain point and then they'd all go in together. They wouldn't leave one guy by himself. That just wasn't done.

One fellow I know — I won't mention his name — tried to pull a fast one. He used to put his pole up late in the day, and somebody would tow him in. He would do that to save gas, but he did it too often, and we got wise to him. One time he really broke down, and the wind was coming up fiercely around Lennard Island, and everybody passed him by. Luckily, there was an old Indian coming in late in the evening, one of the last boats, and he took pity on him and towed him in. He was just about on the rocks. He cried fox, you see.

We exercised extreme caution. We had small boats, smaller than they are today, but they were good boats, sound and well built. And you had a class of fishermen that were brought up to the sea for generations, and it was bred in them to have respect for the ocean and anything pertaining to it. Everybody obeyed the rules of the road and practised good seamanship. That's neglected a lot today. Two of our boys pretty near got run over in the fog by a big steamer who

Fisherman Tom Kimoto with a sixty-pound salmon off the west coast of Vancouver Island, 1938. Courtesy Tom Kimoto

wasn't blowing his horn. If he had been blowing his foghorn, the way he is supposed to according to the international rules of the road, the fishermen would have seen him in time and turned away. A lot of them don't blow their horns anymore.

JOE MCLEOD: Ian McLeod and I started trolling about the same time and they helped us no end. I went fishing with Johnny Madokoro for a week just to find out how to catch fish.

TRYGVE ARNET: Boy, they were good! They made all their own spoons. They'd get these big pieces of brass and cut them and polish them up and bend them the way they wanted them. Then they'd try them in the water, pulling them along to see that they worked right. I fished right amongst them. They were really good.

JOE MCLEOD: The Japanese were the main fishermen around here in those days. But they were never allowed up around Kyuquot or Winter Harbour or those places. I guess the Japanese were pretty good fisherman, and the white men just couldn't cut the mustard, so they ostracized them a little bit.

TOMMY KIMOTO: I became a fisherman because there was no other job. Then, when an old Japanese retired, I took the boat off him. In those days there was a quota on fishing licences for Japanese. That was in 1937, I think. We weren't allowed to go past Bajo Reef. The Americans were allowed to, but we weren't, even though we were Canadians. You needed to be a naturalized Canadian to fish, but we still couldn't go there, because the Norwegian fishermen and the Finn fishermen didn't want us. But there was virtually no trouble because we didn't go.

Around Tofino there was no rivalry because most of the young fellows here were taught by the old Japanese fishermen, the old-timers before us. But those square heads around Kyuquot, they were real bad. The politicians didn't help any. They were working against the Japanese. Only the old CCF party was good to us. They tried to stop discrimination and get us the right to vote. We never voted until 1950. It didn't make any difference if you were born here. That's democracy, eh?

JOHN MADOKORO: One year there were no fish at Tofino and no fish at Ucluelet. We were starving, more or less. So I figured let's go up to Kyuquot, there's lots of fish up there. So we took the packer with a full load of ice. I was the pilot. We fished up there half a day. Then, when we came to go into harbour, there were boats anchored all around the outside. The secretary of our co-op was aboard. We had to have a secretary to run the business, to plan everything. That was Mr. Yanamura, a UBC graduate. He couldn't find a job because he was Japanese, so he came up and worked for the co-op. So Mr. Yanamura went into the village and got the word. "The white people don't like it," he said, "they don't want us here; we'd better beat it back." So, okay, we can't do anything. We just came back to Nootka and fished at Hot Springs. From then on the government made it so our licence was good only up to Bajo Reef.

FIGHTING FOR LABOUR

The years 1910 to 1919 were characterized by widespread unrest and violence in Canada. Extremely rapid economic growth accompanied by massive immigration created a climate conducive to the expansion of labour organization, and as a consequence of this, unrest and conflict. Trade unions grew rapidly during this period despite the employers' opposition. Many strikes resulted and while most were lost, the labour movement persisted. It was a difficult time for labour because, for the most part, federal, provincial and local governments favoured employers rather than organized labour in conflict situations. Companies were allowed to hire special private police, and militia and armed forces were also employed.

During the 1930s, despite a worldwide depression, the labour movement in British Columbia actually made some gains. The greatest organizing drives occurred outside of the working labour movement. They took place among the countless number of unemployed workers who were struggling to organize against deplorable living conditions.

— Patricia Wejr and Howie Smith

Hunger Marches, Relief Camps and the On-to-Ottawa Trek

Edited by Patricia Wejr and Howie Smith

During the early 1930s, one form of unemployed protest was the hunger march. In hunger marches, people demonstrated to try to force the government into action that would solve some of the pressing problems of the Depression. A number of these marches took place in Vancouver and Victoria in 1931 and 1932. In the last hunger march in Vancouver, a riot ensued after thirty-five mounted police attempted to clear some two thousand marchers off the street in front of the City Hall. This resulted in Vancouver Chief Edgett announcing that no more parades would be allowed in the city. The hunger marches in Victoria were smaller and much quieter. One march took place to demand the introduction of unemployment insurance, and the Women's Labour League was among those who took part.

JENNY SHOULDICE: The wives in Ladysmith, particularly the Finnish women, were union conscious and conscious of what was happening — and so the first organization of women was formed, the Women's Labour League. My mother belonged, so I was totally involved with what they were doing. And that was discussing the things that were really important and relevant to helping the men. It also meant being involved in the news and what was happening in the day, so they were a very progressive group. A lot of these women, then, did participate in this big hunger march. It was to get unemployment insurance so a depression wouldn't hit like it did, without people having something to fall back on.

The hunger march took place in 1932. It was really quite exciting, because there was a lot of talk beforehand. It was being organized all through the province, because people cared. They really felt that something could be done by going to see Premier Pattullo and getting him to at least try and do something about unemployment insurance. My brother was going down from Ladysmith with a car, because being farmers, we had a car. People with cars went in a cavalcade — those who couldn't walk so well went in cars, and the rest walked. It took them days from Port Alberni or other places, but all along the way people had big dinners and a sendoff as they passed through. And there was a tremendous reception in Victoria — there were billets and food.

All the while there was a continual procession to the parliament buildings, walking there and demonstrating there while the delegation tried to see Duff Pattullo. It was supposed to be kind of an overnight thing, and the delegation and people thought they would reach Pattullo in maybe two days at the most. Well, that didn't happen, so there was a unanimous feeling that they would stay until Pattullo would see them. During this time, the government was doing nothing. The people were in constant touch, but there was no response. I was at the hall when the word came that Pattullo would see the delegation, and it was sort of a victory, because, before, he had absolutely refused. So on that morning, I drove the delegation (they were Arthur Evans, Peggy Harrison and, I think, his name was John Godreau) down to the parliament buildings. The delegation went inside, but I didn't. Pattullo had agreed to see a delegation of three; that was it. So I sat out there and waited for them. Oh, that I can remember.

It took two or three hours, but they were happy when they came out, because Pattullo had made the statement that unemployment insurance would go on the statute books then, in Victoria. That did happen, but it was some years later before it went through all the provinces. It was a Canadian thing, but each province had to pass the

Unemployed hunger marchers being prevented from stepping on the lawn of the provincial parliament buildings in Victoria, B. C., 1933. Courtesy Provincial Archives of British Columbia / 70521

bill. So in 1932, it was at least agreed that it would be presented to the floor of the house in B. C. That was as a result of the delegation. That was what they got.

Despite this small victory, unemployment insurance did not come into effect during the Depression in British Columbia or any other Canadian province. In 1935, the federal government under Prime Minister R. B. Bennett did introduce a bill that proposed that a form of unemployment insurance be established. The bill passed, but was never enacted. In the federal election held that year, Bennett's government was defeated, and the new prime minister, Mackenzie King, referred the unemployment insurance bill to the courts for a ruling. Eventually, it was ruled outside the jurisdiction of the federal government, and as the provinces did not move on the issue, there was no unemployment insurance until 1940. At this time, due to the War Measures Act, the federal jurisdiction was extended to cover areas normally under provincial jurisdiction, and the Unemployment Insurance Act passed in the late summer of 1940.

ART CLARCK: I walked to Victoria twice in what was called the hunger march. The walk to Victoria was seventy-five miles. First, we'd walk to Duncan, which is a little over thirty miles, and we'd stay there overnight. Then we'd walk to the top of the Malahat, where there was a relief camp. Nobody was in it, though, so we used to take it over and we'd stay there for a day. And then we'd move on to Victoria. We used to have about eighty-five or ninety on the walk, and all the way down we'd stop at farms and bum. People gave us chickens and eggs and veal — we really lived right off the hog on that walk. It was better than staying home!

But one time, I never laughed so much in my life. There were old-timers on the march and they had to have their tea. Well, Old Squint Haiken from Extension was the bull cook, and one night when we got into Duncan the old-timers told Squint they wanted a good cup of tea in the morning. So we put the pot on, we let 'er boil all night. So you can imagine what the tea was like the next morning! Well, the old-timers said it was the best tea they ever had and they said, "How did you make that tea, Squint?" He said, "You know, you wouldn't drink it if I told you." And they said, "Oh yes, that's the best tea." And he said, "Well, we took our socks off after marching from Nanaimo down to Duncan and put them in the pot."

Anyway, in Victoria, when we got there, we used to have a parade. There was a fellow who used to lead the parade. He was blind and he had a police dog with him, and we called him Blind Bill. Well, the parade got down to the parliament buildings, and they wouldn't allow us to put a foot on the lawn. They had police strung right around it with sticks, and wouldn't allow you anywhere near.

By the time the hunger marches were finished, some two hundred relief camps had been built in isolated areas throughout British Columbia. After the federal government took over the camps in 1935, it wasn't long before the men became discouraged with the reduced wages and military atmosphere of the camps and were ready to unionize.

RED WALSH: We had a union, the Relief Camp Workers' Union. It was a little difficult to organize at first, but in the latter part of the organization it was comparatively easy because of the conditions. You worked eight hours a day for twenty cents a day. And the food wasn't very good. The camps were controlled by the army, federal government. The provincial government took them over first and they went broke (or were supposed to have gone broke) and they turned them over to the federal government.

I worked in two camps, one in Spences Bridge and one in Hope. We were doing road work . . . the Hope–Princeton Highway was built by slave labour. I was fired in Hope because I was trying to organize the camp and they knew it. I come into town and got blacklist relief. No more camps.

During the relief camp strike of 1935, thousands of single unemployed men came from the relief camps to Vancouver to present their demands: work and wages at fifty cents an hour, an end to military control of the camps, the right to vote and recognition of camp committees. In order to call the men in to the city, union "runners" were sent out to camps. Pat Foley was one of these runners.

One of the young men who went to Victoria, B. C., with a large number of unemployed youth to appeal to the government for jobs instead of the proffered relief camps at twenty-five cents per man per day. His dignified appeal was symbolic of the attitude of these young people. Courtesy Kenneth McAllister

PAT FOLEY: We sent a runner out to each camp: one runner went up the Chilliwack area, another runner went up the coast, and of course they always gave me the hard end because I was the oldest in the group. God, I was way up in my fifties. So I had to go to the interior and down there, from camp to camp.

Of course, we had a lot of support from the old stump ranchers, the railroad guys, you know. They'd always tell us when the ten:ten freight was going out and the other freight was coming along. And if there was one that could open the sleeping car, well, we'd get into it and ride back into Vancouver and so on. This is how we worked things out, you see. We had no trouble in breaking up the camps because the unemployed was getting fed up and we knew that.

Then they sent me and another fellow up to a camp in Powell River. We had a meeting on Friday, and then the boss went over to Squamish for the weekend, so we were all laying low Saturday and Sunday. Monday morning, he come back with two policemen. There was a ticket in my bunk to leave, and one in the other guy's. So then, we had to call another meeting and we told them, "Now let everything be still, don't come down and make any howl about it. We'll go peacefully to the boat and go back. But I'll tell you what you fellows better do. When you get out on the job, tell the boss that unless he opens the commissary and gives ye your cigarettes and what's coming to you, you're not willing to go back to work. And then lay low. Lay down." Which they did.

When the boss come up, the first thing he seen, they were all laying down, smoking, talking. He says, "What's going on here, are you fellows going to work now?" "We're thinking about it," they said. He says, "You'd better all come back to camp." So they all come to camp. Now, he says, "How many among you here's willing to go out and go to work?" There was only three or four put up their hands. "All right, that's enough," he says, "We're going to close the camp down." So they all come back to Vancouver.

This is how the thing happened. It was an easy matter to pull the camps out after the young fellows was fed up after a couple of months. We knew that, so we pulled every bloody camp there was. And once they were in Vancouver, oh boy! oh boy! It was nothing then. They were raring to go!

RED WALSH: About two thousand answered the strike call. It started in April and we stayed until June. Our good fortune was that we had the people of Vancouver with us. During the strike we took over the old museum on Main and Hastings and held it for several days. There were about six hundred men in there. We placed a leaflet outside of the window, and when people were coming along, we would lower a rope down, and they would send up food to us, the people of Vancouver. They would put it in the basket and we would take it up. We left it the same as when we went in there.

On to Ottawa!

Relief Camp Strikers have decided to continue the strike on a National scale in order to bring before Premier Bennett and the people of Canada the hopeless outlook for OUR BOYS of the Forced Labor Relief Camp System.

A Mass Trek to Ottawa by Relief Camp Strikers leaves via C.P.R. freight, foot of Gore Avenue at 10 p.m. Monday, June 3rd.

You are asked to assemble at 10 p.m. at the foot of Gore Avenue to give OUR BOYS a farewell send-off in their determined fight for the right to live as human beings.

●

For . . . WORK AND WAGES
and AGAINST SLAVE LABOR

●

**ALL OUT: FOOT OF GORE AVENUE
10 P.M. MONDAY, JUNE 3rd**

●

Demand that McGeer, Pattullo and Bennett keep their hands off Relief Camp Boys on their trek to Ottawa.

Courtesy Special Collections Division, Library, University of British Columbia

Then about a thousand of us converged on Hudson's Bay. We moved in there, and of course people couldn't buy anything because there were too many of us in there. I got arrested that time and was thrown in jail. Got two weeks, I think, that time.

We put on a tag day without a permit during that period and we took over the streets. I'm not saying that the police couldn't clear us out of the streets, but they didn't try. We collected five thousand dollars, which would be now at least twenty-five thousand. It was wonderful!

We were trying to get some reaction from the city. Gerry McGeer, the mayor, we drove him up the wall! Of course, we knew the city had no connection with the relief camps whatsoever, but they had money, and we wanted relief. The question was, how long could we stay in town? There were men leaving individually on freights and going east, and we didn't want the organization to fall apart. So, we suggested a trek to Ottawa.

RED WALSH: Everybody was passing the buck. The city government, the provincial government, they had no control over the camps. . . . "We can't do anything, you'll have to see the federal government about that." Couldn't contact the federal government, so we organized a trek to Ottawa.

The "On-to-Ottawa" trekkers boarding railcars to leave Kamloops, B. C., in 1935. Courtesy Public Archives of Canada / C–29399

Early in June of 1935, under the leadership of Arthur Evans and members of the Relief Camp Workers' Union, about a thousand men boarded freights in Vancouver to take part in the On-to-Ottawa Trek. The goal was still to get decent wages and improve conditions in the relief camps.

RED WALSH: The first stop was Kamloops at a fishing plant. There was no preparation there, and we knew if these people didn't get food and some kind of shelter, we'd lose them. So from then on, we sent a delegation of about twenty ahead. The next stop was Golden. Five o'clock in the morning. I was never so cold in my life after I got off that freight after coming over the mountains. But at Golden the people must have been up all night. They had food ready for us when we went in.

People joined us along the way, particularly from Alberta. And the government noticed that the people were behind us and with us all along, so they decided to stop us in Regina. If it kept going on, they knew what would happen in Ottawa — there would be 150,000 unemployed there. They stopped all freights going east out from Regina. So to go, we'd have to walk, and of course we couldn't do that. [The government] sent two cabinet members to Regina, and they suggested a delegation go to Ottawa. At that time the Tory government was in power under the leadership of Prime Minister R. B. Bennett. We met him, but there was no results from the meeting.

Arthur Evans presented the demands that we had written out: for the camps to be turned into work camps with wages on an eight-hour day base, and the workers of the camp should be given the right to vote in elections. Bennett's reaction was hostile, very hostile. I thought that the whole delegation would be arrested. He told Arthur Evans he was a liar when he got up to present the demands, and Bennett accused him of being a thief.

We went back to Regina, and a few days later the riots started at a mass meeting in market square. It was a planned attack by the RCMP. There was a mass meeting called to explain to the people of Regina what happened in Ottawa, and that meeting was attacked by the RCMP. And they just beat up anybody that happened to get in the way. They came in by truck, surrounded the meeting and moved right in. There was a federal warrant out for the members of the delegation, and they arrested Evans right at that time. Well, then, the riot started. The rest of the trekkers started to fight back with the police, so they started to use guns. We know some got shot and some could have been killed, taken away and buried and we not know anything about it. It was a bloody fracas, I tell you!

The next morning we had a meeting with Premier Gardiner and we made arrangements with him for the two trains to take our organization back to Vancouver. See, that was in the summer of 1935. In the fall there was an election, and the Tory government was defeated and the Liberal government was elected. And then the camps were turned into work camps. I think the trek was the instrument that defeated the Tory government at that time.

The "Bloody Sunday" of 1938
Edited by Patricia Wejr and Howie Smith

*A*fter the closure of the relief camps in 1937, Vancouver was once again the scene of thousands of single unemployed men. Under predominantly communist leadership, the unemployed were organized into divisions to carry out various activities to gain funds, such as tag days and tin-canning. After the city banned tin-canning, the jobless had nothing to live on. Something had to be done. On 20 May 1938, some 1200 men occupied three Vancouver buildings: the Georgia Hotel, the Vancouver Art Gallery and the post office. Ten days later, the hotel occupants left to join the other two buildings. Then on Sunday, 19 June, police moved to the two buildings with an ultimatum of voluntary evacuation or forced eviction. The result was "Bloody Sunday."

PAT FOLEY: They wouldn't give us any work. Ah, we says, to hell with this, we're going to make 'em give us work.

STEVE BRODIE: The picture at the time was just a complete falling apart of everything that every kid my age had been taught to expect of the system. You could walk into a hundred houses in south Vancouver or the east end of Vancouver and on the kitchen wall you'd see a picture cut out of the newspaper of His Royal Highness, the Prince of Wales, walking through the mud between cottages in Wales where he had been down to visit the unemployed miners. And the caption on the picture was, quoting him apparently, "Something must be done." But most of the people who had his picture up on the wall interpreted that as "Something will be done." And you'd be surprised how much Edward Albert Christian George Andrew Patrick David Windsor had to do with keeping the people in hope, in spite of all their despair.

HAROLD WINCH: The single unemployed, they either had to beg or go hungry. There was no place to stay, so they slept in our own CCF halls, they slept underneath the bridges, like the Cambie Street bridge, the Georgia Viaduct. They slept out in the parks under the trees, they threw up makeshift shelters of any kind out of anything, and that was the situation. The people of Vancouver were sympathetic to the unemployed, because so many were either unemployed themselves or they had relatives or friends who were unemployed.

PAT FOLEY: There was no sign of relief of any description at that time. There was men sixty-five years of age on the tramp! We helped them on to the boxcars. Now, there was twenty-eight of us in the group that started the unemployment movement at that time. We had too many promises and we were sick and tired of going from one place to another.

HAROLD WINCH: The situation reached the point where something had to be done, because they didn't have anything to eat. There was nowhere to go, and they had to have something. They had to force the government's hand.

STEVE BRODIE: Marching and shouting had outlived its usefulness. Begging with tin cans on the streets, which was another thing that we had done for years, had pretty well outlived its usefulness. So, on the night of the eighteenth of May 1938, the active members of the committee met. And then I came up with the idea that I already had in mind and I was able to convince them that it was possible, because I already had paced it out and arranged some times where we could do this in a pretty sudden move.

HAROLD WINCH: So they evolved, in secret, a manoeuvre to try to force the government's hand, and that was to sit down in three places.

STEVE BRODIE: The tactic was, whatever we do, we make sure that there is no excuse for an attack that the public won't understand is nothing but an attack. The minute we're told that we're breaking the law, submit to arrest and demand to be arrested and tried before a magistrate.

Well, the next day it went off like clockwork. Division One set off at the exact time to arrive at the post office right at two o'clock; and we just cleared Cordova Street when right on time, Division Two, who had marched from the Orange Hall up another street entirely, came down Powell. They fell right in behind us, and I don't suppose there was a gap of twenty feet. And when we got to the post office, it just took one word, "in we go," and we were in. The reaction immediately was to call all the policemen in the downtown area down to the post office. Georgia Street was left wide open, so from away out on east Georgia Street from the Croatian Hall and the Ukrainian Hall, along marched the other two divisions. And they had no trouble taking the Georgia Hotel. And another division went on and took the art gallery. Then the fifth division marched in every known direction, around and around and around, and caused all kinds of trouble and excitement because nobody knew where they were going to land. But they weren't going anywhere, they were just a diversion group.

In the meantime, the response immediately was good. "At last you've done something that will show them. You've taken a federal building." It's surprising how soon the idea caught on, one group's got a federal building, one's got a private hotel and the other's got a provincial building, the art gallery.

PAT FOLEY: I was in the Georgia Hotel first of all, and we wouldn't leave the hotel. They gave us six hundred dollars to leave the hotel. Six hundred dollars! So we took the six hundred dollars and then we doubled up in the art gallery. We all went up to the art gallery and piled in there.

> *Although this paper is written, for the most part, in a light and humorous vein to relieve the strain upon the nerves felt by the boys in the Art Gallery and post office, please do not think that we do not fully realize the gravity of the situation we are facing. We were forced to use this unusual method of bringing our case before you, the jury, when all constitutional means had been exhausted and the government and local authorities refused to act.*
> — *Post Office "Sitdowners" Gazette*, Vol. I, No. 1

BILL CROSS: Many of the men that went on that march, I must admit, did not know they were going into various buildings, public buildings, to take over. However, having got into the buildings, it was carefully explained to them why we had gone in, what we planned to do. We planned to stay there until the government took action; there would be massive publicity as a result of what we were doing, there would be massive public support. And there were very, very few of the original bunch that started on those marches that left those buildings.

The government was angry. Very angry. But there was laughter amongst the populace, laughter at the gall . . . support. I was in the art gallery, I wasn't in the post office, but we used to have interchange, you know, with our boys. You went out for a period of time from each place. The public were greatly inconvenienced, but took their inconvenience and said to the men, "Stay with it, stay with it, stay with it." It was massive public support.

PAT FOLEY: We had all kinds of stuff come in to us. All kinds of stuff. The people were very sympathetic and they were always helping in every way they could.

BOBBY JACKSON: We had a proper soliciting sheet signed by the committee of the organization and we used to present it. In this sense, businesses were very generous, really. We collected a hell of a pile of boxes of radishes and lettuce. And then we went out to the cold storage place on the dock at New Westminster and we picked up a half a ton of fish, I think it was. Frozen fish which they gave us. And then we carried on from there and went out into White Rock amongst the farmers, and I guess by the time we finished we must have had about two and a half tons of fish, vegetables, potatoes. We had a great trip. And all the food we used to get in this bulk sense, we used to take to the Ukrainian Labour Temple on east Pender and women and men, citizens of Vancouver, used to put together meals, and we used to deliver them to the post office.

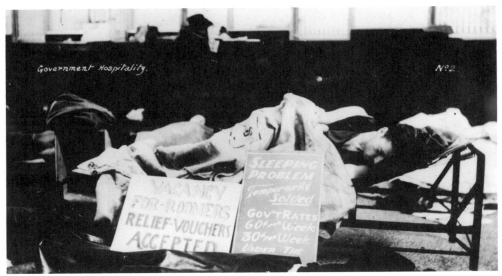

A sitdowner resting during the occupation of the Vancouver post office in 1938. Courtesy Provincial Archives of British Columbia / 55508

STEVE BRODIE: We were pretty well alone after our first request for an arrest if we were breaking the law. Foster, the chief of police, just quietly backed away from that one and let it go, because the crowds outside were growing and growing and growing. "Well, let's not do anything now," he said, "and I'll call the attorney-general," which he evidently did. And he came back with a proposition that we would be allowed to stay in with permission. Well then, that went on day after day after day.

On the night of the twenty-third, a *Winnipeg Free Press* reporter asked me, "Did you mean it when you were talking to the men the other night there and said that you were going to have a twenty-fourth of May sports day?" I'd forgotten about it, so I said, "Oh yeah, we got a committee right now." So he put that on the press that night. "The bastards are so defiant, they're going to put on a sports day." We had egg-and-spoon races, and we invited the mayor, who didn't come. It was an hilarious event, anyhow, and we told them that we'd invite them all back for the Christmas tree. In other words, we were getting the message across that we were there to stay until some definite action came about.

BOBBY JACKSON: The general demand was "work and wages"; that was the basic demand. But the immediate demand was to get some relief.

STEVE BRODIE: There was four or five times that either mounted police or city police made it their business to come in and talk to us, and they always got the same offer. "If we're breaking the law, arrest us. Take us before the courts and we'll take our punishment." That's the last thing they wanted. And so it drifted on until Sunday, Father's Day. We had announced on the Saturday that while we held onto the art gallery and the post office, we were going to send a delegation of at least five hundred over to Victoria.

BOBBY JACKSON: That morning of the eviction in the post office, that whole block on Cordova Street in front of the old police station was just full of police, just absolutely full. It was solid. And on seeing that, we realized what was going to happen. So we rushed to the post office and told them what we had seen, but in the process of rushing, we were stopped by the police at the corner of Gore and Hastings. And this cop asked the driver to get out. And somehow or other, it was one of the strangest things, instead of getting out, he just took off. And, of course, that was it. They chased us, and that's how we warned the post office at that period.

STEVE BRODIE: So I detailed one man to sneak over by devious routes to the art gallery and warn them to prepare for an attack.

PAT FOLEY: They give us, I think, ten minutes to get out. But anyway, we just sung and played the accordion and stayed on. We were singing "Hold the Fort," "Hold the fort for we are coming," you know, the old song, "union men be strong."

STEVE BRODIE: The singing went on that morning up until the postmaster led out Colonel Hill of the RCMP, who read what he said was a proclamation from the cabinet in Ottawa telling us that we must vacate the building or he would use necessary force to clear the building. And I said, "Colonel Hill, just to make sure that we all know what we're doing, I'm going to speak to the men." And I said, "Does every man here now understand that he has surrendered to the law and he is willing to take his punishment from a magistrate, he now considers himself under arrest?" "Yes." "Is there anybody here that doesn't understand this?" And there was dead silence. And I said, "Colonel Hill, you have approximately eight hundred prisoners." "I have no instructions about an arrest." Well, I said, "There's no use in talking to you anymore." So we just waited for the tear gas to come, and it came.

With the bouncing of the first tear gas bomb, every window came down, crash! Meantime, there were four men at each end of that L-shaped lobby with gas masks and well-loaded whips. They don't put down what they claim are riots with horse quirts, you know, they use wire wrapped with leather, good heavy cable wire. And they came smashing through from both ends of the lobby, and quite naturally, there was a mad rush for the four available doors.

HAROLD WINCH: That's when the riot started, that's when the riot started! And the men dashing down Hastings or Granville just went wild. And that's when all the damage was done to the windows up as far as Birks and down as far as Woodwards, at that time, running into, they estimate, around fifty thousand dollars. The men coming out had to run the gauntlet. That's when the riot started; that's when the men went wild. They were wild with tear gas and they were getting beaten up! And in particular, the police were looking for Steve Brodie. And they got him too.

STEVE BRODIE: They recognized me and they really went to work on me. They whipped me pretty good in the corner by the door and finally they grabbed me and dragged me bodily out by the heels. And then they got me over in the gutter and it was absolutely ridiculous. There's a picture in, I think, the *Province* of that the next day. And you can count ten or fifteen of them and one of me. I'm down in the gutter with a belly full of tear gas and bleeding, bruised, and they're gathered around beating me.

PAT FOLEY: I didn't see any beatings at the art gallery, but they didn't have to beat up at the art gallery. There was so much gas that they were all gassed out, you know. I was the last one to come out because I was wise to the gas. I knew what to do. I had the wet towel over my face, laying down very low. So from then on I was fine and dandy because I wasn't gassed, but there was a hell of a lot of the young fellows all gassed. They started falling by the wayside on the road to the Ukrainian Temple, and the trucks and cars was picking them up. They were all stretched out in the yard of the Ukrainian Temple.

HAROLD WINCH: One hundred single unemployed were hurt, thirty-eight single unemployed were hospitalized, twenty-three of the single unemployed were arrested, taken up to the city jail. Well, of course, not only do we now have the situation of the single unemployed being concerned, but this knowledge is spreading all over the city. And so people are pouring in, not to the art gallery and the post office (they've been cleared), but up to the city jail where these twenty-three men are incarcerated. At one time there, I imagine we must have had over two thousand people just jammed in front of that jail. And the tempers were very, very high — they were going to go in and they were going to release those twenty-three unemployed.

PAT FOLEY: We had the whole of Vancouver down there backing us, yelling and howling and singing from the outside. We had them all howling and singing in there, down around the police station.

HAROLD WINCH: Well, I had been inside the city jail and I knew the police were there, and they were ready for action. They were there, they were ready, all armed. So I jumped up on top of a car and I told the people, I says, "Look, it's no use going in there, you can't use this, nor your voice against those riot guns and everything else. It just can't be done!"

Just while we were in front of the police station and I was up on this car, this man takes this empty canister for the tear gas and he hurls it and hits one of the constables in the groin! So the constable straightens up and moves in to arrest the man that had thrown the canister, and just as he was doing that, a woman went to spit in his face. He threw up his hand, and the crowd thought that he had stuck the woman. And then the roar went up.

It looked then as though we were really in for it, that they were just going to sweep into the police station. So I just reached down and I got the woman's hand and brought her up on top of the car. And she said that she was not hurt, that she had not been hit. So that quietened them down and they agreed to go up to the Powell Street grounds, which is only a block away. And there we'd have speakers, Dr. Lyle Telford and Arnold Webster and various speakers.

By the time we got there, people from Vancouver were gathering. There must have been all of six thousand people there in Powell Street, and we all addressed them. There was motions passed demanding the immediate resignation of Pattullo and the Liberal government, et cetera, et cetera, which you could expect. And then it was decided that they would send a delegation over to Victoria.

BILL CROSS: Now we planned a committee to go over to Victoria on the actual evening of the Sunday that we were thrown out. The result of us being thrown out on that Sunday morning caused a demonstration in Vancouver, the like of which Vancouver has never seen and is quite unlikely to ever see again. Those of you who know the area around Granville and Hastings will recognize the fact that old Pier D sat at the foot of Granville Street in those days, and the ferries used to leave from Pier D. Now there was a mass of humanity that you couldn't crack through any way at all, from the interior of Pier D right up Granville Street to Hastings Street. And I mean packed. You couldn't move.

HAROLD WINCH: There were thousands there, and the men were going to take over the post office. They were going to go right back in and throw out the RCMP and take over, clear all the police out. So this time, instead of climbing up on a car, I climbed up on a lamp standard. And they listened to me!

Now, it's not only the unemployed that were there, there were thousands of Vancouver citizens. I tried to explain, all that can happen is that we can have a hell of a lot of people injured and killed! We've got a hundred going over to Victoria; the sensible thing to do is to be quiet now, to be reasonable and wait and see what happens. I don't know how it ever happened to this day, but they did, for the second time, what I asked them to do. The men marched away down Hastings Street towards their hall, and the Vancouver residents dispersed to their homes. And that was the day. That was Sunday the nineteenth.

STEVE BRODIE: The delegation that went to Victoria got nowhere. Nowhere at all.

PAT FOLEY: Well, of course, the war made a big change. The last meeting of the unemployed organization was held in 1942. And there was only fifteen at the meeting, so we closed it up. [People] learned a big lesson from Vancouver and the hungry Thirties, I'm telling you. And that is why the unemployed is getting a handout today, all over Canada! They learned a big lesson from Vancouver, I'm telling you that.

STEVE BRODIE: They've been very lucky. We're old men now, and the young guys don't believe it ever happened.

PART IV: ON LAND, OVER WATER AND THROUGH THE AIR

The Georgina Point Lighthouse on Active Pass, Mayne Island. Courtesy Provincial Archives of British Columbia / 11781

DAYS OF STEAM: THE RAILWAYS

*B*y 1900 railways were a key link in British Columbia's transportation network. The main line of the Canadian Pacific Railway had been in operation since 1886, and the Esquimalt and Nanaimo Railway served Vancouver Island. Before World War I, two new transcontinental lines — the Canadian Northern Pacific and the Grand Trunk Pacific — were built through British Columbia. In addition, the Kettle Valley Railway was built, completing the CPR's southern route from the Kootenays to the coast, and a start was made on the Pacific Great Eastern Railway from the south coast of B. C. to the Cariboo.

Railroading was, and continues to be, a tough life. In the years of steam power the work was long, uncomfortable, often backbreaking and sometimes dangerous. There were always uncertainties, particularly in wintertime, when snow and avalanches made keeping the trains moving problematic. In spring there could be floods or washouts, with a real danger of wrecks or derailments; and in the summer there was the chance of fire.

— Robert D. Turner

The Glacier Slide

Edited by Robert D. Turner

*T*he CPR line over Rogers Pass was one of the toughest sections of mountain railroad in North America. From the time of the railway's completion in 1885 until the line over the pass was eliminated by the Connaught Tunnel in 1916, it was a constant wintertime threat to the crews. In the first few years after the line was opened over Rogers Pass, thirty-one snowsheds were built between the railway's second crossing of the Illecillewaet River west of the summit and Bear Creek just a few miles to the east. The introduction of the rotary snowplow (or sometimes snowplough) also helped keep the line open. However, the rotaries were not the final answer to the problems of Rogers Pass, as the line was continually blocked by the winter storms and slides.

On 4 March 1910, a large slide came down over the tracks at the foot of Avalanche Mountain, and a rotary crew was called out to clear the line. En route to the slide, they picked up a crew of labourers to clear rock and timber from the debris. Then, near midnight as the men were working at the slide, a second slide came down from the other side of the pass without warning. The entire train and sixty-two men were buried in an instant. The incredible story of this slide follows, told by the only man who survived its direct impact: William "Bill" LaChance.

BILL LACHANCE: There were sixty-four men killed that night. Everybody that was there got killed. There was nobody left. [The actual number killed appears to be sixty-two. Fifty-eight bodies were recovered soon after the slide and four more were found after the snow melted in the spring.]

I was firing up there, then. I was on the helper engine; we lived at Rogers Pass and worked up and down the hill to help trains up. It was a pretty bad place for slides; some of them pretty bad. My engine was ready to go out and assist a train up the hill, and when we went down to the roundhouse to book out, they told us: "That is changed. There's slides down, and the trains that are up there are tied up, and this engine has got to take the snow plow and go up and clear out them snowslides."

So we hitched onto this rotary plow and away we went up the hill. We passed the passenger train at Glacier. Well, the slide was four miles farther, and we had an order from the dispatcher saying that there would be no trains going past Glacier until we came back.

So we went up there. We had picked up all the crews that were along the road, wintering in outfit cars. We took their sleeping cars and their cooking cars and we took the whole lot up. There was, oh, fifty-five men or so. We bucked right into the snowslides. It had run down and filled the cut, oh, I'd say, maybe fourteen feet high. That had just smoothed right over, but it was a messy place because it was full of timber. It had cleaned the hill right off and it must have run for over a mile down the hill. The rotary would clean it out, but then they'd come to logs. So then we'd back up, and all these men there with shovels, they'd jump down in that hole that we made — that tunnel in there — and pull out this timber. The timber would break the blades off of the rotary, you see.

So this time we'd backed up, and they were all down in there working. Apparently everybody was down in that hole. We just backed far enough for them to go down and work. It was along about eleven o'clock at night on March fourth, 1910.

The rotary had a big boiler and she had two fire-doors on her, but you always fired through one. But then, as we were just standing there, I opened the two doors and was throwing in coal. The engineer was standing there with his back to the wind, and his window was opened. I leaned over and got a shovelful of coal, and just as I brought my eyes back, the flame just come out of that fire from those

After the disastrous Rogers Pass snowslide of 4 and 5 March 1910, which buried a rotary crew of sixty-two men, another rotary crew begins to clear away the snow. Photograph by Byron Harmon, courtesy Canadian Pacific Corporate Archives / 19268

two doors, just a regular big flame. My goodness! I couldn't think why it had. The boiler — sometimes perhaps a flue or something would burst and it will blow steam all out, but this was just flame that came out, and no noise at all.

Of course, it was only a fraction of a second until the snow came in across the gangway, and I was right there. Well, it hit me — and how! It took me right out of the gangway and up through the top of that tunnel we had made. I knew it was a snowslide; right then I knew what it was, so I just grabbed my face with my hands. . . .

Well, then the snow got a hold of me and what it didn't do to me. Why, it done everything. It pulled me out twice my length, the way it felt, and then it just doubled me all up and rolled me. I was trying to keep rolling up in a ball to go with the snow. It caught this leg and just turned it around, and it would roll me up and stretch me out and double me up. Then the pressure come on, oh, just like as if there were tons on top of me.

Now, all the time I am in that I don't get one breath, because the snow was just packed right tight to my face. Then this pressure come on, and things kind of stopped. It just started and it seemed like as it was boiling, and it brought me up out of that heavy pressure. I had about, I suppose, a foot of snow on top of my face. When I threw my hands out, why, I had fresh air up there. I dug myself out and I thought this leg, my right leg, was broken.

Well, it must have all happened pretty fast for the engine, because after I got out I couldn't hear the engine. The engine should have been blowing a lot of steam, but there was no sound there. Everything was just dead.

There I was. I'd lost my hat and my gloves were full of snow — we had just little fine gloves, for shovelling — and I took them off and threw them away. My hair was all wet and my mouth was full of blood, and when I spit on the snow, there was a great big dark spot on the snow. I licked my lips and I spit again, and there was another big spot of blood, and I thought I'd been hurt inside and I was afraid to put my hands inside of my overalls for fear I'd find my guts laying there. That's the truth. That's just the way I felt.

Well, at first, I wasn't so bad. I pulled myself out of the snow and I got up and I stood up on my left leg. I dragged this other one up and I thought, I'll try it, and try and get back to where that engine is and maybe I'll save the engineer. I just touched the toe of that foot to the snow — and the snow was soft, too, and it just turned, and that knee went right plump down into the snow sideways. Well, that was that. So I put the right leg over the left leg and I tried to work myself back up to where it was, pushing with my hands. It was kind of level there, so I was making headway, but when I came to where it was steeper, why, I was just pushing snow down.

Well, I figured it out and thought how this would be. Everybody's gone by this time. There's no sound, there's nothing. I had hollered two or three times, but then I was getting kind of hoarse, and my left shoulder was knocked out and that went stiff.

Everybody's gone. If there was anybody there, they'd holler, the same as I did. This was all out there in front of me, and there wasn't a sign of life you could see on the snow. I had the order in my pocket — the engineer had passed it to me after he read it — that there would be no train come up the hill until we went back to the Glacier.

Well, I thought, here it is about eleven o'clock at night and it's cold; and the clothes I had on wouldn't wad a gun, just a pair of pant-overalls. I thought, it's going to be pretty cold here. I was getting kind of cold and so I thought, everybody's gone; everybody's passed out, because anybody [that] was in that slide never got a breath of air after they got in it. That snow was just the same as if you took and put your face down into a bag of flour and tried to breathe. That's what the snow was like.

I thought, now, there will be nobody come here till after daylight when they see what's going on, because they think everybody's working here and we haven't went back. But as it happened, Johnny Anderson, the road foreman, come down on the engine just as we backed up, and he spoke to us there, sociably like, and then he went out and away. He had all these men under him there: he was the road foreman. But he went down the track a mile to a telephone to phone them at Glacier to tell them how he was getting along. Then after he was down there, he was a long time down there, he walked that mile down and back and talked there — there was a watchman's shack down there — then he came back up.

Well, that slide just came down as he left. So I was on the snow all this time, and he came up. This first slide had come down from one side and filled the cut; then this slide came down from the other side where we were working there, one slide right on top of the other. So I laid there and I couldn't holler very loud anymore; I was hoarse. I sat there and I thought, this is it. I won't stand this cold here with no clothes on; I won't stand it.

My left leg began to get sore. I didn't know if there was anything wrong with it. I had stood up on it; it was pretty good, and I laid there. Well, it seemed like it was going to be pretty tough that night, if I pulled through it. However, I had to sit there and say my prayers. That's all there was to do.

By gosh, I see a lantern, you know, a brakeman's lantern, coming up along there, right along the edge of the slide. By gosh, as soon as I seen that I hollered, and it stopped and looked. I hollered again, and "Who is that's hollering?" he said. And by gosh, it was Johnny Anderson, the road foreman. I said "It's Bill LaChance." Oh, he come up and he says, "Bill, where are they all?"

I said, "They're all gone. A man never got a breath of air after he got in and that snow hit them. There's nobody in sight, and I've been here quite a little while."

"Well," he said, "It was a dry slide." And Johnny was standing there in the slide up to pretty near his waist with the loose snow. "Can I carry you off?"

"Why," I said, "you'd do well to walk off. You can't carry me with this snow, and I'm no help."

Well, he said, "I'll give you my mackinaw coat," and he took his mackinaw coat off and give it to me to keep me warm and away he went, back down to this telephone shack to tell them what had happened down at Glacier. So he was excited; everybody was excited, and he couldn't make them understand what was the matter so he walked the four miles to Glacier to tell them what was wrong.

But he got the cook out of one of the outfit cars and this watchman from the shack down there a mile, and he sent them up to take some blankets and put them on me in the snow so I wouldn't freeze to death. Well, they came up with the blanket — a Chinaman, the cook, and this watchman — and they wanted to cover me up. Well, I said, "There's two slides come down now and I've been in one of them. If another slide comes down, I don't want to be rolled up in a blanket. Now," I said, "you get me on that blanket and pull me out of here."

So I hooked that arm over the blanket, and there was one on each corner of it and they were doing very good. My jaws were working good; I could hang onto the blanket too with that, so they pulled me off and they got me down to where the outfit cars were, off of the slide.

There was a dance in Revelstoke that night, and when the news got down about the slide, well, they rung the fire bell. They took all them boys from the dancehall and everybody they could get. They put them on cars and they shot them up to Glacier to get the men out of the snow. By the time they got me down there to where the outfit cars were, why, these fellows had come from Revelstoke. They started crowding around there and they picked me up and put me in one of the sleeping cars. They piled on blankets and blankets.

Then somebody said, "There's another slide coming," and away they all went, beat it, and they left me there. The doors on the car were wide open, and I was sleeping right there. The blankets got so heavy and they were pulling my toes down and hurting my legs, so I pushed them all off and it got cold in there.

But anyway, the cook had gone and got a cup of tea and brought it to me. And I said to the watchman, "Look at my leg and see if it's hurt." He pulled up my overalls and he got sick.

I said, "Is it bleeding?"

He said, "Something awful."

I said, "Is the blood flowing out or is it shooting out like that?" I wondered if an artery was cut, you see.

"Oh," he says, "it's awful."

I thought, I don't know, I think time's up pretty good there. The bone was cut right in there, in the shin.

Anyway, he went away and left me there, and nobody turned up till daylight. Then they all crowded back up around there and they got me out of this sleeping car, and they took me down and put me in an express car to Glacier. They had a doctor there, Dr. Hamilton. He come in and he took my shoulder and set it back in. They couldn't do very much for that leg, because they didn't have any bandages. Somebody said, "What will you have? Would you have a drink of brandy," he said, "or would you have a cup of tea?"

Well, I said, "I'll have a drink of brandy," so they brought me in a cup of tea.

Now I'm all ready to go to town, so they take a rotary and the superintendent's car; and they put the rotary out ahead, so if any slides come down, why, they'd clean them out as they went down to Revelstoke. But they also sent a message down over the wire that Bill LaChance was the only man that was alive and they didn't expect him to live till he got to Revelstoke.

Bill LaChance was placed in hospital in Revelstoke and, after a long convalescence, recovered. For a few years he continued to work out of Revelstoke, but eventually moved to the coast, where he worked as a steam engineer with the forest industry.

The great slide had claimed sixty-two lives. It was the worst in the history of the railway and was a significant factor in the CPR building the Connaught Tunnel to eliminate the treacherous line over Rogers Pass. The old right-of-way still exists; a hiking trail through Glacier National Park.

BILL LACHANCE: This is what they told me: that the men down in that cut, that whatever they were doing, that's the way they found them. One fellow was standing there holding a torch, another fellow rolling a cigarette. They didn't last long. They never got a breath, and that I know.

Post Office on Wheels

Edited by Robert D. Turner

Nearly all lines operated by the major railways in the province carried mail on the passenger trains. Often the mail was carried in a car equipped as a railway post office, or RPO. Mail was picked up from stations along the line and sorted by post office employees while the train moved on to the next town. This system provided a regular, reliable service that continued in many areas until after World War II. With improved roads, elimination

The cab interior of a CPR *5900 series steam locomotive was a maze of plumbing and gauges. The fireman (left) controls the air supply to the fire and the water level in the boiler. The engineer (right) controls the throttle, valve motion and air brakes. Courtesy Canadian Pacific Corporate Archives / 21444*

of branch line passenger services and centralization of the post office system, the RPOs were phased out.

A. L. Robinson worked on the first RPO eastbound over the Grand Trunk Pacific from Prince Rupert to Prince George in 1914. After two years he moved to Vancouver Island and served on the RPOs on the Esquimalt and Nanaimo Railway until his retirement in 1954.

A. L. ROBINSON: I was on the first train going east out of Prince Rupert to Prince George. When I got to Prince George, I turned over the mail to the Edmonton crew; their run was from Prince George to Edmonton. It was twenty-two and a half hours on shift by yourself, working all the time; no sleep. Sore feet; you're standing up getting bounced around all day long. It's when you derailed you get into trouble. I was off the track one night for a thousand yards before anybody knew it. Before I could get a hold of the emergency cord and pull it down. That was in the Bulkley Valley around Burns Lake somewhere. My car was the only one that was off, but I had six cars of fish ahead of me — frozen halibut from Rupert going east. The engineer didn't know I was off and he just kept on going.

The first thing we'd do would be load the mail car at the Prince Rupert station. Out of Prince Rupert you'd get Inverness, that would be the first one, the cannery. And then Haysport, and the first place of any importance was Terrace. Bulkley, Burns lake, François Lake, Vanderhoof, then the car jumped to Prince George. There were small places in between. At some of them we took the mail off on the fly. We didn't stop. The bags were hanging on the posts. The arm rips the bag off the post, and you grab it before it falls down. That's what we call a catch post station. Up there we had twenty-four of them, and they were all at nighttime. The only way you would know they were there was a little hay burner lantern hanging on the post and you'd have to be looking out. When I made the first trip, I didn't know that any of them worked, because nobody had been along with me to show me. The engineer didn't know where they were. So I got off and I said, "For God sake, when you pick up that mail bag with your headlight, give me a couple of toots." The section man gave me a grubby piece of paper saying which side to the track and how many poles each pickup was west of the station. Well, hell, how could you count poles at nighttime? Bang, you throw one off and take one on at the same time. Sometimes you didn't get it.

If you missed one, you knock it off maybe. Just put in a report: No mail received from so and so, for such and such a reason. I always used to get away with it in the wintertime, because we used to say we couldn't see the post for snow and steam, which was quite true in lots of cases. The snowplow would be plowing ahead, so with the snow flying past the door, and steam as well, you couldn't see when you were at the post. It must have been damned annoying for the post-master. Some of them came as much as three or four miles in snowshoes to hang the flag up and stand there waiting for his, and the train goes by. I can just imagine what he'd say.

Whenever we had a breakdown, like a washout or a slide, it was always in the bush where there was no town. You couldn't go and buy anything, because there weren't any shops. And we used to carry a few canned goods for emergencies for maybe a couple of meals. But not enough for three days. Hell, I went out and shot rabbits and made a rabbit stew to feed the whole bunch of us, train crew and ourselves, because nobody had any food.

The CPR Motor Car on Rails

Edited by Peter Chapman

When train service in the Lardeau-Duncan area was curtailed in the 1930s, the CPR provided service with a gasoline-powered truck that ran on flanged railway wheels. It was officially known as Motor Car 600 and affectionately called the Noble 600. It was operated by various people in the valley over the years and provided a vital service.

MAITLAND HARRISON: In the Thirties the CPR didn't run a passenger service on the train any more because it didn't pay. They had a motor car on the track with a couple of trailers behind it. They looked after the passenger service with that on Saturdays. The boat came up every Saturday from Kaslo. They'd go up to Lardeau, put the trains on the track, run that thirty-four miles up to Gerrard, and back and out they went. That was our weekly service. In the old days we used to have quite the social gatherings. They'd have dances one week at Argenta, then the next week at Lardeau, Howser, sometimes even Johnsons Landing. We had a dance at Johnsons Landing once, and a whole bunch of us went down on the CPR motor car. It being a little sidetrack, the grass was growing high on the line. It was all around the wheels and, by gosh, we smelled fire. We were halfway down to Lardeau, and all this wild hay got in the wheels and caught fire. My wife and I were sitting right on the gas tank. There were flames all around us. We all jumped out and put the fire out and went on. Oh boy!

ARCHIE GREENLAW: I ran the "Six Hundred," which was a Model B Ford truck with a track car. We used to handle as much as forty tons of freight. It had a four-cylinder Ford truck engine. Everything was CPR. The "Six Hundred" ran once a week. It was actually a contract. You took all the revenue received from the tickets and express and you honoured any tickets that CPR issued, and they refunded that portion from Lardeau to Gerrard. I made the run on Tuesdays. We left Lardeau in the morning at six o'clock and as a rule made no stops, because the trip was from the Gerrard end. If there was a passenger, we stopped, but that was just a flag stop. The regular run started at Gerrard and then to Poplar Creek, Gold Hill, Bosworth, Howser Station, Marblehead, Meadow Creek, Cooper Creek and Lardeau. The boat came in around one o'clock, and after loading, it might be four o'clock before we got away again and made our regular stops on the way back, Cooper Creek, Meadow Creek, Howser and so forth north. Very often there'd be passengers to go up in the morning, for instance to Gold Hill. Doc Wilkinson was a

The CPR's M600, a four-cylinder gas-powered Model B Ford motor truck that ran on flanged wheels, pulling a track car, 1930. This truck replaced the passenger train on the Lardeau–Gerrard run. Courtesy Vancouver Public Library / 198

dentist and he was at Gold Hill. They'd have the day to stay and get dental work done and go back to Lardeau. Of course, we ran specials. You'd get a lot of specials to Meadow Creek. There was a rate for each place. If you made a special trip to Meadow Creek, you might have to travel twenty-five miles to Gerrard to turn around. We used to turn it on a jack mounted underneath, centred on the frame. I'd throw down a block, jack it up and swing it around, and drop it back on the rails again. That took ten minutes. There were a lot of people going through mining and then firefighting.

Teddy Evans had a flower bulb farm at Bosworth. He used to ship to Italy and all over the world. I used to haul express for him. They were all express. During the Second War, things went haywire. I'd see him on the days of my regular trips. He used to travel with me to the Loguses and get his mail, go to Poplar Creek and go back to Loguses and wait. I used to take him back to Bosworth at night. I could carry eight in the cab but I have carried as many as forty firefighters, because we had cars behind. The latest I think the "M Six Hundred" ever operated was Christmas. I used to plow a little bit of snow, but not a great deal. The flatdeck car in the front pushed snow. I had slides that I could drop down and wipe the rails. But when you got to a foot of snow or so, you had to use the plow. The CPR trains ran all winter and kept the track open.

During the winter, it was difficult to keep the rail line open from Lardeau to Gerrard. When the rail line was closed, people usually managed quite well. Being used to the isolation of the valley, they had plenty of food and a good supply of wood for heat.

CECIL PANGBURN: All the snow slides were down for three miles from Lardeau. It was just plugged solid. Well, the CPR went in there and tried to open up. Telegrams were going to Ottawa and Montreal that people were starving to death up in the Lardeau. So they got us to go up with a cat. We got off the *Moyie* at Argenta and got a set of sleighs from Johnny Galas and loaded on a bunch of groceries and mail and went up to Howser. When we got there, we changed sleighs and reloaded and went on down to the track. There was about four or five feet of snow on the trail. We got to Gold Hill. We had the policeman and a big shot from the CPR going up with us to see how bad these people were. We went in to see Mrs. Rear. "Oh," Mrs. Rear says to them, "if I'd known you were going to be here for supper, I'd have got a whole lot more cooked for you." The CPR man says, "It doesn't sound like anybody is starving to death here." We started up to Poplar and unloaded more stuff. We kept going until twenty-four-mile we were beat. The cat was floundering. We went back to Poplar and stayed there all night. We were a whole week up there before we got back. The train caught up to us. I made about seventy dollars on that trip. I understand the CPR made five dollars taking the freight in there and it cost them four thousand in expenses. That was the Depression time.

MAITLAND HARRISON: There's about six slides along the railway from Lardeau until you get to the head of the lake. The train would be held up for two or three days. The engine had a snowplow and they'd push through the slide. It was fifty or sixty feet deep, full of rocks and timber. My wife went down one day, and they ran into a few slides. It took twenty-four hours to get to Nelson because of the slides.

In 1935 the Canadian Pacific Railway applied to the Board of Railway Commissioners to tear up the Lardeau Valley rail line. The track had fallen into disrepair, and the CPR wished to be free of the burden of its maintenance. Activity in the valley had decreased slowly over the years. In 1935 George McInnis employed a score of men logging in the upper Duncan and in his mill at Howser; a dozen families raised beef and vegetables for sale along the rail line. Marble was shipped from the quarry at Marblehead, though the finishing was now done in Edmonton, and poles continued to flow out of the valley bottom. All in all, it offered the CPR scant opportunities for turning a profit; but to the people of the valley, the rail line was too important to give up without a fight.

MAITLAND HARRISON: In the 1930s the CPR wanted to pull their track up. The railroad commission came in, and we all went down to Nelson and had Mr. Wragge, our lawyer, appear in front of the commission. We gave an account of how much timber and marble was being shipped and one thing and another. And the commission decided that there was enough to keep the railway and they wouldn't let the CPR take it out. It was during this last war that the rail was taken up. The story was they needed the steel for the war, which wasn't true because the steel stayed there all the time. But they took the rails up, and the government took it over as a road. We were all away; there was no one there to fight it.

NAVIGATING THE COAST

With the completion of the Canadian Pacific Railway, what had been a small settlement huddled around several sawmills became Vancouver, end point on the transcontinental railway.

As Vancouver grew, so did the hinterland surrounding it. The lumber industry soon exhausted timber available along nearby shores and logging operations moved up the coast. Similarly, with a growing market for salmon both domestically and in Europe, canneries were being constructed near spawning streams and rivers all the way north to the Nass River. Immigrants coming to Vancouver and British Columbia looking for land to homestead set their sights farther and farther up the coast for available land.

Serving the shipping needs of these booming new communities was the Canadian Pacific Navigation Company, formed in 1883. Later, in 1901, the Canadian Pacific Railway bought the CPNC and established the CPR's B. C. Coast Service.

The CPNC service in the late 1880s largely ignored the hand loggers and fish packers of the mid-coast region. The demand for a new coastal steamship service was high; in 1889 a small group of Vancouver businessmen formed the Union Steamship Company of British Columbia.

— Peter Chapman

Swift Water: Upriver by Canoe and Steamboat

Edited by Allen Specht

The first permanent white settlement in the Skeena country was the Hudson's Bay Company post of Fort Simpson (later Port Simpson) established in 1832, but located forty miles (64 km) north of the mouth of the Skeena and so not exclusively part of the Skeena system. No trading posts were required farther inland for several decades, because the Skeena Indians handled the exchange of fur with the interior Indians. The importance of the river route is indicated by the fact that the Indians who occupied Kitselas Canyon, the main obstacle on the river, were able to control movement up and down the river to their economic advantage. The first large group of white men to penetrate the interior ran into this obstacle. They were a party hired to bring supplies for the construction of the Western Union Telegraph Company line, which was being built through central British Columbia to Alaska. The commissary clerk, Charles F. Morison, tells of the experience in his diary. This takes place in July 1866:

> *Naturally the* Mumford *[steamboat] proved a dismal failure in the shoal and turbulent water of the Skeena. . . . Following her failure to negotiate the Skeena it was necessary to contract for a large flotilla of native canoes; these were obtained from Chief Paul Legaic of Metlakatla. The canoes, with a capacity of 2 tons and over, were manned by many natives and 35 white men.*
>
> *Our flotilla finally arrived below the mouth of Kitselas Canyon — one of the most dangerous navigable portions of white water in North America. Captain Butler decided to make camp and tackle this turbulent canyon next morning. After supper, a small canoe came down river carrying an envoy from Kithorn, Kitselas Chief, bearing this message: "If we attempted to pass through the canyon the Indians would heave rocks upon us and sink our canoes." They were under the impression that we were a great fur trading company and would ruin their trade with the up-river Indians, whom they did not allow to pass through the canyon to the coast. Following a present of pigtail tobacco and a fill up of bacon and beans, Captain Butler informed the messenger that we were not a trading company but consisted of a working company, and far from interfering with their trade, would employ them thereby giving them a source of cash revenue. Incidentally the captain had the arms-chest opened containing a great display of Colts, repeating rifles, Sharp's carbines, and revolvers. The messenger's eyes grew wide at the sight of the arsenal. The Captain then told him he was going through the canyon in any case, and when he said a thing he meant it!*
>
> *We proceeded early next morning and reached the canyon proper. This canyon is one mile and a quarter in length. Both sides were lined with large Indian lodges, with approximately 500 inhabitants. The rock bluffs were lined with Indians far above us; they rushed down, but instead of smashing us, tackled our tow lines and drew us through the canyon in triumph, accompanied with much shouting and yelling. It took the entire day to get the whole flotilla through the canyon.*
>
> — CHARLES F. MORISON, *Diary*

John Morison is the son of Charles Morison, whose diary was quoted above. He travelled frequently on Indian canoes in his youth.

JOHN MORISON: I'd like to tell about the type of canoes they had. They were made from big cedar trees on the Queen Charlotte Islands. And they ran anywhere from thirty to maybe sixty feet. But the average canoe carried a skipper and four men, like deck hands, and five passengers as a rule. So you can imagine they were quite a size. And they carried two tons dead-weight freight besides. . . .

Hauling a canoe through Kitselas Canyon on the Skeena River. Courtesy Provincial Archives of British Columbia / 85750

After you got past a place called Graveyard Point on the Skeena, you started all this towing business. Three of the crew would get out and they hitched themselves on with a little lead to the mainline from the canoe, and one man stayed in the bow. He was a bowman — they used to call him Captain Nose. And the captain was up — you know, they had a great big high stern on them. He handled a huge "sweep" — oh, must have been fifteen or twenty feet long — a great thing that was hung on a crosspiece, sort of balanced. And he worked that thing back and forth to keep her from broaching-to in the current — a fierce current in most places, you know. Well, when they arrived at a certain part that was too difficult for the men towing to get along, they pulled the canoe into the beach and they all got aboard to cross the river to the other side, then, and everybody paddled. I paddled too.

Then there was a lot of poling to do. Some parts of the river weren't too swift. The crew got aboard, and you all had poles about ten feet long and you'd stick it down and push — push. And get it along that way.

Well, I think we were probably twelve days getting to Hazelton, and anchor ice was forming on the bottom, and slush was coming down the river. On some places we had fairly decent camps, like Meanskinish, like Kitselas Canyon, Kitwanga and places like that where they had missionaries stationed and houses to go into. But all along the lower river, it was just miserable . . . when we made camp at night it rained all the time, and they would cut hemlock and cedar.

The canyon [Kitselas], really, from the mouth to the top, is a mile and a quarter long and it's a box canyon. But parts of it where it

jutted out a bit, they could catch the eddies. There was no way of
them walking the canoe — damn box canyon, you see. And they'd
jump from one side of the canyon to the other until they got near the
head where it flattened out a bit, and then they could get a line out
and pull us around. But it took hours to do. And you couldn't do it in
high water. They were really marvellous, the way they navigated it.

They were from all along the river. Some were from Hazelton and
these other villages lower down. And some of the best were from
round about Terrace — they call it Kitselas — and then some of the
Port Simpson Indians were wonderful, too. They carried two tons of
freight and they got a hundred dollars for it, to divide among a five-
man canoe.

You could go down in a couple of days. If there was a fair wind
blowing from aft, behind you, they put up what they call a Stikine
sail. They had a great big mast and a thwart in front. They'd step the
mast and they'd put up a sail on each side, and with this wind blowing
behind you, they were making thirty miles an hour.

In 1891 the first stern-wheeler successfully negotiated the river up to Hazelton.
After that steamboats dominated the river trade, though they could only function
during the summer months, because in winter the water became too shallow and
heavily iced.

John Morison later worked on the stern-wheelers, which were as much at risk in
the dangerous Kitselas Canyon as canoes.

JOHN MORISON: I was with that old boy, Captain Bonser, and he was a marvellous
skipper and very reckless and daredevil. And when other boats would
be tied up, we'd be pulling along there. He knew every rock in the
river. He was a very wiry little fellow and active as a cat. . . .

We got so used to it [Kitselas Canyon] that we didn't think anything
of it. But the passengers were given permission to ride through the
canyon at their own risk — this was after the *Mount Royal* was lost —
otherwise they could walk over the portage. . . .

But I remember one day going up there, and no other boat would
look at it except ol' Bonser. And he let a holler out of him just at
daylight. He says, "We're going through that canyon today, but every
passenger get off." So they all trooped ashore. We had to stay. My job
was carrying one of these cork fenders around, slip it in between
rocks.

We got up to this Ringbolt Island, an' there's a right-angle turn at
the top of it, and there's a ringbolt in the rocks there for what they
call the "breast line" so as to pull 'er around this awful current running at high water. We just went from side to side, bouncing on these
great big boils. . . . And the Indians — they were all Indian deck
hands, white men couldn't stick it — were standing waiting there with
the heaving line, and when she touched the rocks there was a little
footing, and they went up like goats. They were supposed to take the

The steamboat Hazelton *turning around the current at Ringbolt Island in Kitselas Canyon on the Skeena River. The ringbolt sunk into rock is visible in the foreground. Courtesy Provincial Archives of British Columbia / 62235*

cable with just the smooth end of it, put it through the ringbolt, take a kind of half hitch and whip it with a piece of cord. Well, this day they made a mistake and put a hook in this ringbolt. Well, we started up and were just making the turn when the line fouled on the capstan. They did that sometimes; the coils got mixed up. And he gave a toot for them to let go on the rocks. Well, they couldn't. It was just like an iron hand.

I remember one of the Foley boats up ahead of us; they started lowering two of their boats, 'cause she started to lay right over. And I remember the wood was piled on the working deck, it slid right off into the river; it showed how far she went. And I was standing up just below the wheelhouse, and the ol' skipper hollered at the mate — the mate had an ax, was chopping away. He says, "Send this young fellow up a heaving line." He threw it up to me. And the ol' man looked down at me and said, "Now, when I say throw that line, you heave it, throw it to those deck hands so they can get another line into that ringbolt. And God help you if you miss." I hit the mark. Yeah. If we hadn't had a solid cargo like sugar and flour and things, we would have rolled right over.

Those boats were anywhere from 120 to 130 feet long. And they had the main deck, down below where all the cargo was stowed — the engine room was down there, the galley for cooking and the great big boiler that carried 210 pounds pressure and fed them with cord-wood. And then on the next deck was the passenger deck, where the staterooms were, the dining room, the smoking room and the ladies cabin. We had a licence to carry 150 passengers. So they weren't very small boats. And then up on top of that, they call that deck the "texas," and that's where our quarters were, supposed to be officers, you see. And then on top of that again was the captain's cabin and the wheelhouse. Very lofty and painted snow white. Very beautiful ships, you know. . . . The funnels were black. . . .

Our last trip used to be the twentieth of October, and then they had until the first week in May. A long time. Everybody was packing their baggage and saying where they were going that day and won-dering if they could keep going right on to Telkwa and Aldermere — those places — no Smithers then. But the greatest crowd was the population of Hazelton waiting on the bank. There used to be enor-mous crowds! Especially the first boat in the spring. They all wanted to buy oranges and fresh fruit, stuff like that, flour. And all kinds of eulachon grease for the upriver Indians.

Passengers and Freight of Every Description

Edited by Peter Chapman

The Union Steamship Company ran both regularly scheduled freight and passenger service and charters. The fleet covered the entire Inside Passage from the heads of inlets to the outer islands. Ore was hauled from Surf Inlet Mine on Prince Royal Island. Canned salmon was packed from the head of Dean Channel.

JOHN PARK: I joined the *Venture* in September 1911, and the first winter we were on a two-weekly schedule. We took in all the ports all the way up and our first trip we left Port Hardy at about midnight, and Boden was first mate with me. Boden took over. By and by, he called me and said, "There's a ship ashore here at Noble Island." So we stopped, and it was the *Princess Beatrice* ashore on Noble Island. And it was the fall of the year, and she had about two hundred passengers aboard, so we waited until morning and took them all aboard. The captain said to me, "Take them back to Hardy Bay." I said, "What the heck's the use of taking them back to Hardy Bay? They'll all starve there." I took them back to Alert Bay, and the CPR sent another ship up to take them from there.

FRED SMITH: We went all over the coast. We carried heavy stuff on the freighters. Reels of wire to the logging camps. You couldn't handle them in anything else but a freighter. And donkey engines and anything else that was going. And we packed salmon. The Union Company pioneered the coast pretty good.

JOHN MUIR: I went from the *Cowichan*. Captain Smith was chief officer on with Captain Grey on the *Coquitlam,* the freighter, and that's where I got my idea of this coast. She was into every creek and river that was around here, with general cargo, lumber, coal. Spread the coal down for the lumber to go on top.

JOHN PARK: Captain Cockle took sick, and one man that had been in the CPR came with us as captain of the old *Capilano,* and we were going into what we called Salmon River in those days; it's Kelsey Bay now. And I said to him we always made a starboard landing. "Oh," he says, "I can make a port landing." And she went and struck the dock head on, and twenty tons of dynamite in her bow. And he turned around and made a starboard landing. We used to carry quite a bit of dynamite. There's a place over in Victoria we used to go for dynamite, and another place not far from Ladysmith.

When the salmon-fishing season opened on the coast, business picked up for the Union boats. Each year a great migration took place as the canneries prepared for

Indian families and their belongings on the deck of the Union Steamship Company's Venture, *on their way to a fish cannery for seasonal work, 1923. Courtesy Vancouver City Archives*

the months of salmon packing. Chinese labourers were brought up the coast from Vancouver. Native people moved from their upcoast villages to nearby canneries. Tin plate was shipped to the canneries, and in the early spring, seated on the cold cannery floors, Chinese men sat cutting out the tin cans for the salmon, like cookies out of cookie dough, and soldered them together.

With fall, the migration of the workers reversed. Native people returned to their winter villages, Chinese cannery workers returned to Vancouver and the winter caretaker was once again left alone until the cycle began once more the following spring.

FRED SMITH: The Chinamen used to go up in the spring and make the cans. They'd cut the shapes out of tin that came from tin plate and they made the cans on the cannery floor in the spring of the year. It was a damn cold job. There was a lot of leaky cans, too, because they were handmade. Then the American Can Company became interested and they shipped cans already made. They found that wasn't too profitable, so they shipped them collapsed cans, or reformed cans. They made machinery and shipped it to the canneries for reforming the can again after it had been flattened. They could ship it over in a case and make it more economical. They owned the cannery machines and they serviced them themselves. They had experts that went around and did anything that needed doing on these machines. They were rented.

WILLIAM VENINI: We used to take all types of freight up and down the coast. We'd
take up passengers and freight to all the logging camps. The *Capilano*
was mostly freight. We'd leave Vancouver loaded with coal and we'd
sell it on the way up and bring back salmon shooks; we'd pick up the
empty boxes, and they'd put them together up there, and then we'd
load it with salmon and bring it back down again.

FRED SMITH: There was thirty canneries between Prince Rupert and Vancouver, but
they were small canneries . . . one line. After they started amalgamat-
ing them, they done away with quite a few of them. There was a lot of
canned salmon shipped. Union Company carried hundreds of tons
of canned salmon down the coast, and in those days it was packed in
wooden boxes, and there're ninety-six half-pound cans in a box.

WILLIAM McCOMBE: The *Cardena* had started out with two classes and then it ended
up practically with one class, except for the Chinamen and Indian
cannery workers. They travelled second class, but bunks had to be
built up for them. Then after they were up at the canneries, you took
all that down until they were ready to bring them, the workers, back
again to Vancouver. All you had to do was put the stanchions in, put
the bed ends in, and then the Chinamen brought their own donkey's
breakfast, we used to call it. Little straw mattresses. You might as well
carry a bag of straw. But, nevertheless, he was charged second-class
fare for it. Pretty grim, pretty, pretty grim. They exploited these
people. They let the contract out to a Chinese contractor, and then he
collected all these guys and then he just paid them what he thinks.
Now, the owners didn't care what he pays him, as long as he's got to
do it. It's up to that Chinaman to keep that cannery supplied with
Chinamen.

JOHN PARK: Bell-Irving used to make a trip once a year with us. Mr. Bell-Irving was
the manager of their outfit. The manager for B. C. Packers and Bell-
Irving used to make a trip once a year with us around to all the
canneries.

    We called into Rivers Inlet, Safety Cove, Namu, Bella Coola,
Kimsquit and Bella Bella, and all the ports up north, twelve canneries
on the Skeena, Port Simpson, Prince Rupert, four canneries in the
Nass River and an Indian village there, and up to Anyox; and at
Anyox we started south again, called into Vancouver and on down to
Victoria.

When the *Comox* slipped out of Vancouver harbour in 1892 on its first run to
coastal logging camps, a long and vital association between the logging industry
and the Union Steamship Company began. Loggers were among the most colourful passengers carried by the Union boats, and also the most loyal. In the days of
hand and donkey logging, there were dozens of ports of call for the *Comox* and its
later replacements, and a great affinity grew between the loggers and the ships that
served them. Along the waterfront, near the Union Steamship dock in Gastown,
establishments entertained the loggers when they returned from the logging
camps, their time cheques in hand. As if on a pendulum, the men of the logging

camps swung between the coastal logging camps and Vancouver. The vital link between the two was invariably a Union Steamship boat.

FRED SMITH: We started going in the early days around Knight and Kingcome Inlet and Surge Narrows and the Yuclataws and Iron Rapids. It was pretty near all hand loggers. They'd pack a jack and fall a tree and jack it into the water and go down there and lop it, saw it up and tow it, in many cases a rowboat, tow it until they hit some sheltered little nook and leave it until they had enough to go in with some more on a boom. They'd make a swifter of logs and pray to God that the tugboat wouldn't lose them getting down, and if they were lost, well, that was their season's work. They had no money. They couldn't insure their booms.

WILLIAM VENINI: We used to take a lot of funny guys up there, too, gamblers. They'd say they were going up to take a job in the lumber camps, and I'd notice their hands would be nice and smooth. I told three of them, "You never did much work with those hands." But there was nothing we could do about it, but there was an awful lot of shenanigans going on.

In 1901 the *Cassiar* was added to the logging camp service. It was originally the *J. R. McDonald.* It soon became known as "the loggers special."

FRED SMITH: In those days, labour agencies were around in Vancouver. They shipped men to the logging camps. They'd work so long and then they'd get laid off. They'd come down, then Tommy Roberts's helpers would meet them when the *Cassiar* came in and take them up to the hotel, and he'd cash their cheque and keep them there and give them room, booze; and then he'd go to the labour agencies and find out where there was men wanted and he'd tell them their money was gone, they had to get back to work again. So he'd get them aboard. There was a ship the Union Company had that done most all the logging run and it was called the *Cassiar.* They thought she was a palace because they could wear their cork shoes on the *Cassiar.* They couldn't on any of the other ships. They'd even go to bed in their cork shoes. I was aboard her for a little while; she was an old American steam schooner.

Loggers were good men when they were sober and good workers. They worked in all weather in a pair of tin pants, they called them. Buy a new pair and take them to a stump and chop the legs off about halfway up their leg with an ax. They'd wear those pants until they were so stiff with gum they could stand them up themselves. And a suit of Stanfield's underwear. It didn't matter if it was raining, pouring; they never wore a coat or anything. They worked in that union suit, combination Stanfield's heavy underwear.

JOHN MUIR: Lots of money came out of there, all that logging, you know. And then it happened that this MacMillan and them formed this business on the island. There was nothing but hand logging going on on the mainland at the seashore. Put those chutes down and put a barrel or two of grease on them and shoot the logs in, and half a dozen men or two or three men would form a boom in no time that way. There was a lot of money up there. Those loggers used to come down with pretty good pay. The ordinary logger, you know, he'd be up again the next week, get into this famous Tom Roberts's. They'd soon get their pockets emptied there.

WILLIAM VENINI: I joined the Union Steamship Company in 1910. I shipped out on the *Cassiar,* which was called the loggers boat, running north as far as Alert Bay and way points. We did quite a business with the loggers, taking them up the coast and bringing them back, looking after them all the time they were on the boat. They were drunk most of the time. And we'd bring them into Vancouver; we'd turn them over to Tommy Roberts of the Grand Hotel. He looked after them till he got rid of all their money and then he'd give me the money to take them back up again, pay their fare back up the coast. That kept going on and on and on, week in, week out. They didn't care, they just threw the money away anyway, and the *Cassiar* was the boat that seems to be making the most money for the Union Steamship Company. All the loggers knew was the *Cassiar,* CPR and Tommy Roberts. They had a little poem:

> Vancouver
> CPR
> Tommy Roberts
> *Cassiar*

That's all they knew. Tommy Roberts was quite a gambler. He had a great big diamond ring and he was playing poker up behind the St. Paul's Hospital, and there a man broke in and held them all up. He tried to take Tommy Roberts's ring. He shot him. That was the end of Tommy Roberts.

FRED SMITH: I remember the night he was shot. Tommy Roberts had a hotel in Gastown called the Grand. In those days the loggers all worked up the coast. They came out here to work logging camps from Sweden and Finland. They knew three words of English — CPR, *Cassiar* and Tommy Roberts. The CPR brought them out here from Montreal, and Tommy Roberts's runners met them when they got off the train, give them a cheap bottle of whiskey and shipped them on the *Cassiar* up to the logging camps. They worked up there in the logging camps for a few weeks; they'd fire them, and they'd come back down to Vancouver on the *Cassiar,* because that was the only boat that called into these camps. Tommy Roberts's runners would meet them and take them up to the hotel until they'd spent their stake that they'd made, give them another bottle of whiskey and ship them back on the *Cassiar* to another camp. They worked hand in glove with the logging agencies.

WILLIAM McCOMBE: I went on the *Cowichan* around to logging camps. We didn't go across Queen Charlotte Sound. Just went up to the logging down on the lower end here. We called them "the jungles." It was purely the jungle you were working in. You had no lights, no nothing, you know. You got to know the point and that was the point you turned at. If you didn't see that point, well, you didn't know where you were. There were no lights to show you. The coast wasn't in any way organized in those days. A logger would hang a light up, and then the authorities used to make him take it down because it wasn't listed. I think the term "jungle" comes from the towboat men. You know, loggers could go up drunk, you throw them off drunk; they would take them just as well. That was our income. We knew where they were going. The pursers had to see that they got ashore, drunk or sober.

Navigating by Whistle and Echo

Edited by Peter Chapman

Running into small logging camps and out-of-the-way canneries, the navigators of the Union fleet had to devise special methods for finding their way. One master used to draw the outlines of the mountains in his logbook. Even on a dark night, the mountains were often visible against the night sky. Two techniques were employed on almost all the coastal vessels. Exact logbooks were kept. Each course was run for a specific length of time, then a change was made. Each course change was carefully noted. If the speed of the ship was constant, the same course and time could be used over and over again with confidence. When the speed of the ship changed, this method was not as accurate.

The other main technique for navigating involved the use of the ship's whistle. A short blast was given on the horn, and the time for an echo to return from the shore was carefully counted. The length of time it took the echo to return indicated how far off shore the ship was.

It wasn't until the end of World War II that radar was available for commercial ships on the coast. This was a most welcome aid, especially as diesel engines became more and more common and their noise interfered with the navigator's ability to hear the echo.

JOHN PARK: It was all navigation by the whistle in those days, and the sound was supposed to travel five and a half seconds to the mile. If you got the echo back in eleven seconds, then you were a mile off. Five and a half seconds to go ashore and five and a half seconds to come back. But I always used the twelve seconds. I got her back in three seconds, I'm a quarter-mile off; six seconds, half a mile off. That's how we navigated in those days. There was no TV nor anything else then.

FRED SMITH: The Union Steamship Company had some fine men. There was no radar and there was very little aids to navigation, such as markers and lighthouses, and many ships have no searchlights. The ships that did have searchlights had the old carbon searchlights, and it would fail just when you needed it. They navigated in thick weather by blowing the whistle and counting the seconds that the echoes came back in. They could navigate in pretty bad weather. Snow was the biggest bugbear because snow deadened the sound coming back. They'd go full speed in fog. They relied quite a bit on the man down below maintaining the revolutions and keeping up the speed, so they knew what they were doing. If you started to lose time, then they were lost. It could happen by some defect in the machinery that you couldn't keep the speed up, and it could happen by difference in the tidal currents. Of course, that was up to the skipper to allow for. They had good navigators in all the companies, but I will say, for the little hazardous holes and corners that the Union Company went into, they had some of the very best. You had to go in because there were people there. You had to maintain service to them. Up in what we called the jungles, up in around Kingcome and Knight inlets, there were some pretty hazardous holes to get in and out of.

JOHN MUIR: Lighthouses up the coast, like Pine Island, were just marvellous. They would hear a ship's whistle if it was fog and maybe they had the whistle going before ever you got up to it. The lighthouses were well looked after in that respect. You usually heave a sigh of relief: "There's the whistle." The man in the bow may have heard it, or the skipper himself. "There's a horn so many points on the bow."

I remember one captain, Andy Johnstone. He says to this young fellow in the bow, "Now, look out for a buoy." We'd just come in in the fog from the Nass River. We were going in amongst the shoals of the Skeena River, and there's a buoy which marks a certain patch up there; and you know, we just went slowly up, as he had shouted about the buoy, and edged along past it. The buoy is only a small one, no signal on it. That shows you how well they navigate.

I used to marvel at some of the elderly men that were masters and the places they would go through in daylight in clear weather. It was the same in the dark.

There was one minister at Vananda. This minister used to put his lamp outside just the same as if he was a government light. Mrs. Thompson in Whaletown had the job of putting a light on certain rocks if you were going from Whaletown to Manson's Landing. You could go through that way if this light was on. Sometimes you'd be so close to the beach, the ship's lights would shine on the beach.

Going into some places in the wintertime, there'd just be a watchman and maybe his wife looking after the cannery. If he slept in, the ship's whistle would usually waken him up. The dog was a great friend. As soon as it heard the whistle, the dog started barking, and the watchman would know the ship was coming.

You had marvellous engineers, and they always took a pride in having their engines that you could just touch and she'd stop. Oh, they were great engineers on this kind of work, making lots of landings and that. They took a pride in having whistles that a man on the bridge could give a little toot and get this toot back off of this point, off a log, off a fishing boat; yes, that's a fact. I've got echoes off a log. I've got some peculiar echoes. You could follow an echo when it hit the point, but if you were a stranger, it would be different. You visualize this point and then the next. Up on the hill the sound would go right over. It would be quite a bit away. You knew you were on the proper side of the channel by the difference in the two echoes. You knew you were in the middle of the channel and you were all right.

Some people don't understand navigating with the echoes. If you were going along a narrow channel and you heard a fellow blowing his whistle, you knew it was a ship's whistle 'cause there was nothing else there. You made sure you were on your own side of the channel. Toot your whistle. You got maybe three seconds on that side and only one second back here. Well, you knew you were closer here and on the wrong side of the channel, so you tell the man at the wheel starboard so many degrees. You get back onto your own side on a foggy night.

One time I was mate with Captain Findlay, old-time square-rigger skipper. Good seaman. We were going down the channel from Lowe Inlet and out in the open, Wright Sound, where Surf Inlet's down that way and Kitimat's way up here. There was a boat blowing, then the next thing I heard was the bells going. This was the CNR boat coming north and he must have been going full speed in that fog. He knew he was in open water. We had our vessel going, too. Well, you could hear the bells from the bridge on this CNR boat, I think it was the *Prince Rupert,* signalling down to go astern. He never touched us. He came right up. His engines were going astern, but still he was going ahead.

I've seen Americans come down with some lights. They would blind you with all the lights they had on their deck, and you would have every light practically out. Sometimes going through channels you put all your navigation lights out, the red, the masthead, because it was throwing shadows, kind of blind you. Anything that a seaman does for safety is all right.

ROBERT NAUGHTY: They were all pretty good skippers or they wouldn't have been there. They didn't have the equipment that they have today. CPR were in the same thing. They were running their boats full speed and no radar. The Victoria run and the Skagway run, and these guys did a marvellous job.

The skipper used to take the whistle in the Grenville Channel. He wanted an echo back from each side at the same time so he's in the middle, or maybe he wanted to favour the starboard shore. Then he'd move over a little and get that echo quicker than the other one.

The diesel engine was kind of hard. 'Cause of the noise of them diesel engines, you couldn't hear the echo hardly, unless you stopped here. And you daren't stop. But steamboats were quiet. You wouldn't hear a sound, only the throb of the engines under your feet. You get a sharp, clear echo. On the diesels, if you were pretty near to Egg Island and I thought I should be at Egg Island in so many minutes, you'd come up and stop here and you might hear the sound like an old cow, the lighthouse, and then full ahead again. It was pretty hard to tell your distance off. You ran pretty well the same courses, the same times with the same tides. You kept very strict logbooks. You'd notate: "Pine Island was a little close tonight," or "a little wide." You'd make little notations and try to correct them every trip until you got it pretty well.

WILLIAM McCOMBE: It's not as easy to navigate by the whistle on a diesel boat. You've got this chug, chug, chug, chug. You have that coming in with your count, but the air whistle hits the beach the same as a steam whistle, although it's different sound. A steam engine had no sound. It was quiet. There was no noise up the funnel unless she had a whistle leaking somewhere. It becomes like second nature to you.

When the miners and loggers located their camps, they often did not consider accessibility for the steamboats that called to bring them supplies and mail. Drumlummon Inlet was just such a place. It was the location of a mining camp south of Kitimat on Douglas Channel.

JOHN MUIR: Captain Grey was taking the *Coquitlam* into Drumlummon Inlet, narrow entrance, big bluff. The tide used to rush into that inlet, a long inlet. When the tide is running out, it would rush something like Seymour Narrows, and they didn't want the boats going in there. They had a big float moored outside, and Captain Grey was going in there with the *Coquitlam* to this float and he had to cross this tidal water and he just slashed on the big cliff and on this side here, and we sprung some rivets. Well, we had to get out of there in a hurry.

FRED SMITH: Jock Muir was the mate of her, and I told Jock, I said, "There's something wrong." I said, "She's acting very funny." And Jock took the hatch covers off or he got them taken off and, God, we had five feet of water in the hold, and she was making water pretty fast. We were in the Grenville Channel then, so the skipper decided to put her on the beach at Lowe Inlet. Instead of taking the beach at an angle, he ran straight onto the beach, and she didn't leave the water aft where she was holed.

JOHN MUIR: I remember taking soundings with a sounding lead all the way to Lowe Inlet. She just made it. We got into Lowe Inlet and we ran her up past the cannery that used to be there, and there's a nice beach, and we put her on the beach. Our engineers and the mate and myself, we got hammer and tongs and things. We had to dig through the coal in the cargo to get down to the bilge, where she had hit, and we fixed up those rivets and got them screwed up and we made our trip away up to the Nass River, calling at different places. I don't think she would have gone very much farther than Lowe Inlet without sinking 'cause she had a lot of cargo in her at the time and the water was coming up.

FRED SMITH: She was an old-fashioned boat. She'd been built here. She was sheathed with timbers — planks about four inches thick, and we had to cut through that to get to the skin of the ship. We only had a blunt old ax, but we had a deck hand that had been a logger and he made a marvellous job. He chiselled this timber off until we could get at the skin of the ship, and then we took a plate off the stoke hold and marked her where the rivets were in the side, the rivets we were going to take out and put bolts in. We only had a ratchet drill to drill the plate with and we drilled five-eighth holes in this plate; and we put a plaster of white lead putty on the skin of the ship and put that plate on, knocked the rivets out, and put bolts into place, tightened 'em up, and she was tight as a bottle. We were in water, but we could get at this hole in the hull not too bad. We banked the sand up. The tide wasn't coming in. We had done a good job, but all to no account.

Coming across Queen Charlotte Sound on the way down, she lost the wheel [propeller], and we had to go into Alert Bay where the Indian School is. There's a beach there. We beached her, and they sent to Vancouver and they got a propeller sent up. They sent a propeller for the sister ship, and the key wasn't big enough on that one. It hadn't been cut as big as the key that we had. So we had to file the keyway out. It was quite a job. And hauling that propeller up with chain blocks and trying her on, but we didn't get her right. The tide started to come in. We had to pull out. Everytime we'd go astern, she'd move a little bit on the tailshaft. We had to wait until we got to the cannery and we put her on the beach, and of course, you know how they used to throw all the heads and the fish guts in the drink. You had to wade through that up to your waist to take the wheel off and file the keyway a bit more so we could get her right. It wasn't a bad job. It's things like that you run up against, but it was quite an experience. We were out about three or four weeks. My wife had a baby, her first, while I was away. I was hoping to be home, but I wasn't.

Collisions and sinkings were rare during the Union Steamship Company's seventy-year history. The first major accident involving loss of life occurred on 12 July 1906, when the CPR steamer *Princess Victoria* and the Union Steamship Company tug *Chehalis* collided in the First Narrows, causing the *Chehalis* to sink.

The Union Steamship Company's Cardena *in for repairs at Burrard Dry Dock in Vancouver. Courtesy Vancouver City Archives*

ADA DAWE: I can see that man on the deck of the *Empress* now. They got him on there quick so he wouldn't say much, 'cause it was a CPR boat that hit him, hit the *Chehalis. Princess Victoria.* And they were very much to blame. I didn't actually see the accident, but I saw them bring the men aboard the *Empress* to give first aid. I can see my father giving them first aid right now.

WILLIAM VENINI: I shipped on the *Cheslakee*. They cut her in half. She was too cranky. They put in thirty feet and called her the *Cheakamus.* The *Cheslakee* went down first at Vananda on her way over to Powell River. She shipped a lot of water and her freight doors were open. She turned around and just got back into Vananda and sunk straight down. Six lives were lost, and they took all the passengers ashore and got them clothing and food from the store there. That was the end of the old *Cheslakee.* After, they dug her up and gave her thirty feet. She struck Siwash Rock coming into Vancouver. That was 1913.

ROBERT NAUGHTY: The *Lady Cynthia* had a bow on her like a knife. The old *Cowichan* was coming south in thick fog, no radar. The *Cynthia* was making a special trip up to Powell River, Christmas trip [27 December 1925]. She was steaming pretty well out, and they thought they were clear and they could hear each other's whistles, but you can't depend on these whistles. They saw they were going to collide. The *Cynthia* went into the *Cowichan,* and by gosh, the skipper had enough sense to keep his nose in the *Cowichan* till they all jumped off the *Cowichan* onto the *Cynthia's* deck, and then as soon as they all jumped, he pulled out. He couldn't wait too long because of the weight. She might not have been able to pull out. Anyhow, he got them all aboard and then he pulled out. She went right down. I think she went down in eleven minutes. Didn't lose a soul. Both skippers in the Court of Inquiry were bawled out for too much speed, but high recommendation of the actions after the accident. Nothing happened. They were both good men. They'd been in the company for years.

JOHN MUIR: Well, the *Lady Cynthia* ran into the *Cowichan* and she's lying at the bottom up there just off Sechelt. Captain Boden and Captain Wilson were just the finest skippers in this coastal work here. Couldn't beat them.

The Life of a Lighthouse Keeper

Edited by Derek Reimer

There were three major lightstations constructed between 1885 and 1902 on the Gulf of Georgia coast of the Gulf Islands: East Point light (1887) in the southeast, Georgina Point lighthouse (1885) at Active Pass and the Porlier Pass lighthouses (1902) between Galiano and Valdes islands.

In the early days the name Georgeson was almost synonymous with these lighthouses, and for nearly sixty years various branches and descendants of the two original Georgeson brothers controlled the lighthouses of the Gulf Islands.

The earliest of the Gulf Islands lighthouses was built in 1885 at Georgina Point, the entrance to Active Pass. The first lightkeeper was Henry "Scotty" Georgeson.

MARY BACKLUND: My great-grandfather was Henry "Scotty" Georgeson, who was born in the Shetland Islands in 1835. He came out when he was very young on a hundred-foot sailing ship around the Horn.

He came to somewhere along the California coast in the very beginning and then went up the Fraser River looking for gold. While he was up there around Lillooet, he met this lovely Indian lady and consequently married her. She was a very fine person. He brought her back down here, and they wandered around quite a little bit, and he finally had a position as a lightkeeper at Sandheads at the mouth of the Fraser River.

Archie Georgeson was one of Henry Georgeson's grandchildren. He lived at Georgina Point with his grandfather between 1909 and 1922. He describes his grandfather and his life as a lightkeeper.

ARCHIE GEORGESON: He was just a happy-go-lucky Scotsman. He wasn't very tall but very wiry built, that's all. He wasn't what you'd call today a strong man, although he used to pack some awful loads. Because when he first came up here, he said when they went up the Fraser River they all had two hundred–pound packs. I think a man has to be pretty strong to pack two hundred pounds up some of them mountains; I don't think I'd want to do it, anyhow. He was all over the place at that time. He was young and full of energy, I suppose, like a lot of young men that came out here. He wanted to find something more suitable to himself. He always liked boats; he always wanted to be on a boat. He wanted to go places, because he was very good in the boat, and so was my father. He taught my father a lot of things that he should have known, which was very handy, and I think it went down into the rest of the family.

Later on he got a job on the Sandheads Lightship, which he had for two years, I think. Then he got the appointment [in 1885] as the first lightkeeper at Georgina Point.

Watercolour portrait of Henry Georgeson in 1925 by Col. L. G. Fawkes. Georgeson, born in Scotland in 1835, was the first lightkeeper at Georgina Point on Active Pass from 1885 to 1922. Courtesy Provincial Archives of British Columbia / pdp 199

I didn't like it when I first went to Georgina Point in 1909 for one simple reason: they had a steam foghorn at that time. I used to hate steam. I never had any use for it. It seemed to be so quiet, yet it was so loud. When the horn would blow, it used to scare the daylights out of me at times. But you get used to it after a while.

Of course, my grandfather wouldn't have anything to do with the foghorn at all. The only thing that he'd ever do in regards to the fog station was to come down and see that everything was clean. He was all eyes when he walked in, and if he found a little speck of dirt on anything, you had to clean everything. Everything had to be clean because he got the best name, I guess, of any lightkeeper on the coast.

He wasn't young then, but he was still very active. He was about eighty, but he was still just about as active as I am, running around. He always just more or less looked over things. If things didn't look good to him he'd just say: "Polish the brass and clean this up and clean that up and clean the windows." Everything had to be just so-so all the time.

But that's the life of a lighthouse. A lighthouse is not a place just to live in. Things are not made just to keep machinery in; they're made to keep clean. Everything had to be clean. He saw to the fact that everything was clean. I always admired anybody like that, you know, but when I was young I didn't like it too much because we had too many other things to do.

He had absolute control over the lighthouse at all times himself. He always looked after the light himself; nobody else did any of that. He always lit the lamp at sundown and put it out at sunrise every day. It was a little light when we first went to Georgina Point, but later the shades for the revolving part went around the light just to blank out the light through the glass. But the one they have now is a different rig altogether. In them days, up till 1920, Active Pass lighthouse was the most important lighthouse on the Canadian coast. Of course, today it isn't because ships go a different way. But in them days the ships used to come through here because this was the only Canadian fog station. Now they go around the bottom end of Saturna Island, and they have a fog station besides the one at Patos Island, U.S.A., right across from it, which makes a big difference.

The house and the lighthouse were both together — the lighthouse and the dwelling part of it. It's all in one unit, living quarters and everything. It had four bedrooms so there was lots of room; it had quite a large living room and quite a large kitchen.

The only thing that we ever figured that happened that was exciting at all was when the *Princess Adelaide* went ashore [13 October 1918]. I was running the foghorn that day. It was very funny the way it came up, you know. Of course, when you're in there, inside the building, you can't hear anything outside. You can't even hear a boat blow. So this day I was threading a pipe for a fellow on a boat, a friend of ours there. I said to him: "Run out and see if you can hear the *Princess Adelaide* coming." So he just went around the corner of the building just as the *Princess Adelaide* blew. She was so close in that he came tearing back all excited. He said: "She's right here on the beach!" Just like that, you know, all excited. I looked out the door, I was looking straight ahead, you know; I was working at this vise. I looked out as she went by, you could just see the outline of her going by right close into the lighthouse as she piled up on the rocks.

She had a hole in her, all right, but it didn't do that much damage. It ripped her propeller all to pieces and broke her rudder, I think, and a few little minor things, but not too much damage.

She was there for three days before they pulled her off, but that was great excitement for us because the next day it was quite clear and here she was stuck up right in front of the lighthouse like a great big city. For young people, you know, that's quite a thing. My brother towed all the lifeboats in and tied them up at the mooring. They all went ashore but the ones he tied up; the rest of the life-boats all went ashore on the beach. So they had to spend all that day pulling these lifeboats off the beach and taking them back out and anchoring them again, because if it blew they'd all smash up. But they got this big American tug up and they pulled her off — three tugs, four tugs.

It's pretty hard to say whose fault it was in one respect, because the master himself apparently wasn't on the bridge. The chief officer figured he had another minute and a half to go before he would have to call the master before they entered Active Pass, but he was a min-ute and a half faster than he figured. He was in on the lighthouse before he realized. Then, of course, they naturally said that the foghorn wasn't going, but they were away off on that, because the foghorn was going about ten hours before he came in there. But that's the only real excitement we ever had at that place.

The most recent of the major lightstations in the southern Gulf Islands is the double light at Porlier Pass. The first lightkeeper was Frank "Sticks" Allison, who served from 1904 to 1941. His wife was Matilda Georgeson, granddaughter of Henry Georgeson, the famous keeper of the Active Pass light. Allison's daughters, Devina and Frances, both became wives of subsequent keepers of the Porlier Pass lights. When they describe the lights, their father and their life at the lightstation, they are speaking out of a lifetime of familiarity.

DEVINA BAINES: There was no fog alarm or anything at Porlier Pass in the early years. Being an old sailor, my father was interested in boats and ships and everything. In the foggy weather, when he would hear the boats blowing out in the gulf or out in the channel, he'd get himself up on the top of the hill where the sound would travel, and get an old coal-oil tin and a stick, and he used to beat away on this tin can to show the boats as they came closer where the pass was. The captains soon got to know the sound of this tin can in the fog.

Eventually, they gave us a hand foghorn, and we used that until recently when they installed our new electric foghorn. The hand foghorn worked on a bellows deal. It was just a small box, about the size of a packing case like they used to put coal-oil tins in years ago. It had a handle on it and a horn out the front. The harder you moved the handle back and forth, the louder sound you got coming out of it. It had quite a different sound.

In those days we listened for boats to blow. As they got closer and they were wondering just where the pass was, then we would go out and blow the foghorn to them and listen. They would blow first, then we would listen and listen to their echo die out. When it died out across the pass and we couldn't hear it anymore, then we would answer with one long blast on our foghorn; just a nice long blast so that it would carry and re-echo and sound from across on Valdes, so that they could pick up where the sound was coming from. In that way we used to direct them either out or in through the pass. Then, if they were coming from Vancouver, coming through, when they got beyond Virago Point, we used to give them three little short blasts which said good-by to them, and they would answer. It was the same going the other way: when they went from Race Point, we would signal good-by to them. You soon got so that you picked out the whistles on the different boats and you could tell if it was the old *Qualicum,* the *Nitinat, Nanoose* or *Swell,* any of those old-time boats. They all sounded different.

FRANCES BROWN: When Daddy first came, in 1902, the lighthouses were the same buildings that are still standing today. The lamps were brass lamps, and they burnt coal oil. These lamps were filled in the morning, and the chimneys polished, and the wicks trimmed. Then in the afternoon, as the sun went down, the lights were lit and you stayed in each light tower for fifteen minutes or half an hour until it warmed up — it took quite a while — and waited until your wick burnt up and came to the height where it wasn't going to flare, and yet was going to be high enough to show through the magnifying or prismatic glasses that surrounded the lamp. Then you left it overnight, and it burned all night if things went well. If a draft came in, you ran into trouble and had to go down and relight your light. Those wicks were in operation in these lighthouses right up until my father retired in 1941.

We lost the *Peggy McNeill* out here. That has always been one of the mysteries of Porlier Pass. We don't know just what happened to her. She was towing two coal barges when she came out. It was quite a calm night, although it was a strong, strong tide, and Daddy and I watched her come down the inside shore there — this was around midnight — and then we went to bed. We didn't hear her go through the pass. Two days later her two scows were picked up off Gabriola Pass. There is no record of what happened to the *Peggy McNeill.* One of the bodies was picked up towards the north end of Valdes. The only presumption is that she got caught in the strong tiderip off Race Point here and was completely capsized and sank before the men had a chance to get off. The *Peggy McNeill* is just one of our mysteries.

There are quite huge whirlpools in Porlier Pass and there seems to be a drop-off. Fishermen could probably tell you more about that. I don't know too much about that, but there seems to be quite a deep hole off Race Point there in one spot.

If you don't know how to handle your boat, you can get caught in the whirlpools. But you never see any of the Indian folks getting into trouble out there in their canoes. They can go across at most any stage of the tide. They know exactly where to go and which way to catch the eddies. I wouldn't say the same for other people. We don't seem to be quite as good at knowing the tides as they are. It's not so important in these days, but in the old days they travelled more in rowboats. They had to watch the tides. At some stages of the tide, you just couldn't go through. Even today you can't go through on the strongest tides. A lot of the gas boats wait.

Yes, Porlier Pass is one of the bad little passes. It's a short pass, but it's a strong pass. I think we run about nine knots at the strongest tide, somewhere between six and nine, which is quite strong. We like to boast that we're the strongest of the two tiderips on the island.

FLYING WAS IN OUR BLOOD: EARLY AVIATION

A fter World War I, it was necessary for enthusiastic airmen to demonstrate the worth of their machines to the nonmilitary world. The British Columbia coast was ideal for this purpose. Previously accessible only by boat, it was opened anew by flying boats and floatplanes, which proved themselves not only valuable but virtually indispensable.

The Spirit of Adventure

Edited by Dennis Duffy and Carol Crane, commentary by David Parker

F ollowing World War I, Canada was left with a considerable number of usable aircraft. The British Government had donated eighty airplanes and fourteen flying boats to Canada, and the United States Navy, which had been training Canadians in the closing months of the war, turned over twelve HS–2L flying boats and twenty-five spare Liberty engines. Half of these machines — single-engine biplanes with seventy-four foot wingspan — were to serve in British Columbia. Having aircraft available, it was then necessary to decide how they would be used. Pilots returning home from the war were convinced that airplanes had proven their military worth and had great potential in the civilian world.

The Canadian Air Board established bases across Canada, and Vancouver's Jericho Beach was chosen as their West Coast base. In February 1920, temporary canvas hangars were erected.

Five HS–2Ls acquired a short time earlier from the U. S. Navy were assigned to Jericho and went into service quickly. In an era without airports, the ability to operate off water was vital. Coastal waters and lakes large enough to accommodate a flying boat with a landing speed of about fifty miles per hour could be used as a base. It was necessary, however, to haul the boat-hulled aircraft ashore periodically to ensure that the wooden hulls didn't become waterlogged. Performance could be drastically reduced if this were allowed to happen.

HAROLD DAVENPORT: The operative aircraft at the base were Curtiss HS–2L flying
boats that had been designed and built starting in 1916. The whole
boat would be built [assembled] at the base. The hull was wood and
the wings were substantially wood; the struts were wood, the spars
were wood, the ribs were wood, the hull was covered in wood. In
other words the aircraft itself was built out of wood, out of fabric and
out of steel — eight hundred pounds of round, high-tensile steel
flying wires.

DON MCLAREN: They were made of mahogany — mahogany planking on wood. We
called them flying cigar boxes.

GORDON BALLENTINE: I had my first airplane ride at Jericho Beach in an HS–2L. Do
you know what that is? That's a flying forest!

EARL MACLEOD: One thing that we started was a pigeon loft, so that in case of a forced
landing, we would be able to write a message, put it into a clip on the
leg of the pigeon, and the pigeon would fly home. We used female
pigeons with little ones at home, because we found that they were
much quicker in getting home to their brood than others would be.

HAROLD DAVENPORT: The birds were carried in a wicker basket that held about six,
and each bird had a tiny aluminum tube attached to one leg. When
necessary, the message was written on a small piece of very thin and
light paper, rolled, inserted into the tube and the birds released. We
had no radio at that time, and the pigeons were frequently used.

The farthest [pigeon] flight that I can recall was from Bella Coola,
and only one of the seven birds released made it back to Jericho
Beach. The following year we were told that several had taken refuge
at a farm in the Bella Coola valley. Hawks would attack the birds in
flight, driving survivors into cover on the ground and disorienting
them.

EARL MACLEOD: The pigeons proved to very useful for myself on one occasion. I
was flying over the south end of Texada Island and my engine cut
out. I was actually able to come to a stop right inside a tiny little safe
harbour. There was no communication to that part of British Columbia at that time. I put a message on the leg of the pigeon, and it got
home surprisingly quickly. And the part that we asked for — the
ignition part that had failed us — was brought to us within an hour
and a half by another plane from Jericho Beach.

HAROLD DAVENPORT: We did a great deal of photographic work. The camera was a
Fairchild K–2, a magnificent camera. It had an objective lens of ten to
twelve inches, and the films were quite big. We did vertical work and
oblique work; and I tell you, if you want a real cold job, it is to sit in
the front of the cockpit of an [HS–2L flying boat] doing vertical
photography. You're mapping a whole area; you follow predeter-
mined lines and overlap, and this carries on for hour after hour, you
see. At ten thousand feet you can get awfully cold — you know, it's
really cold.

The oblique photography usually was used to depict buildings of
some stature like the big sawmills or other big edifices of this type. We

In the front passenger cockpit, Howard Hines prepares a pigeon to carry a message being written by the pilot, Earl MacLeod. Courtesy Earl MacLeod

did quite a bit of this. The camera was a pretty heavy camera; it must have weighed thirty-five or forty pounds. And you'd find yourself with one leg over the front of the boat, holding this camera, with one leg locked around the thrust boom from the engine, trying to get the camera into position for the picture. And bumpy air: there were lots of times you left the aircraft altogether, momentarily. So later we tied a rope around ourselves and onto the airplane. We took a good many pictures, a lot of them on display yet all over the place. The camera was good, and the service off it was quite good. There wasn't a great deal of money in it, but all this helped, of course.

EARL MACLEOD: One employment of our aircraft that was peculiar to the Pacific coast, one that proved to be quite effective, was in dealing with an international narcotic trafficking problem that existed there. Vancouver was recognized as being a main distribution centre for smuggled consignments arriving by liners from the Orient. One method employed by the smugglers was for consignments packaged in watertight parcels to be dropped overboard at prearranged points between the open sea in Juan De Fuca Strait and Vancouver, and for these parcels to be picked up by waiting smuggler-ring speedboats. Customs officers aboard the liners had actually observed this happening without being able to do anything about it.

When I flew customs officer Harry DeGraves on the first customs patrol in 1921, we noticed that voracious sea gulls circling the liner vied with one another to investigate en masse [every] thing, large or small, dropped overboard, thereby ensuring that we could not fail to observe anything that might be jettisoned.

On one later occasion we in the aircraft were tested in respect to our effectiveness. A suspicious parcel was dropped overboard, and there was a speedboat in the vicinity! We landed, picked up a well-packaged parcel, which we examined expectantly on completion of our escort patrol. We found the parcel well sealed with many layers of waterproof wrapping, then several layers of other wrapping, with nothing inside — a well-prepared dummy!

Most of the aviation work that had been done in British Columbia up to 1924 was done in conjunction with the Air Board, then the Canadian Air Force and finally the Royal Canadian Air Force, which came into being 1 April 1924. The RCAF withdrew from patrol duties despite its success in this role. It felt that the HS–2Ls in use at the time were unsuitable. Ironically, when patrols were taken over by a commercial air service, the same type of machine was used. A few of the people who had been flying for the military until this time decided to strike out on their own. They wanted to form independent companies, and still make a living doing what they enjoyed most — flying. Don McLaren was one such person and he formed a company called Pacific Airways, in February 1925.

GORDON BALLENTINE: In December of 1927 I somehow convinced Don McLaren to hire me for ten dollars a week. This was absolutely great as far as I was concerned — this was the end of the rainbow. I don't know if you've ever wanted something like young guys wanted airplanes in those days. I was a crew man. This job was necessary because nobody thought to invent the water rudder to attach to a seaplane. We used to have to walk the wings on the water to steer the boat into the dock, by dipping one float or another. So I guess I was worth ten dollars a week for that.

DON McLAREN: The hemlock trees in [one] area became infested with hemlock looper. It's an inchworm that eats up the needles off the tree. An infestation of hemlock looper, if allowed to go on for a month or two, could completely destroy the whole stand. It was discovered, first of all, at Indian River at the head of Indian Arm. They knew there were also some in Stanley Park and they knew that something would have to be done. An entomologist, Professor Lofting, came to me one day and he said, "Do you think you could find some way of distributing dust from the aircraft to spread on the trees?" Calcium arsenate, it would be, which was lime mixed with arsenate of lead. I took a look at this stuff and I said, "Yes, we can do this."

The Boeing Company worked with us and they made what looked like packsaddles in the flying boat. We took the doors out and put big packsaddles out that came out over the edge of the hull. There were little trap doors on there, and all you had to do was pull the thing and the stuff fell out. We carried eight hundred pounds in a load, each four hundred, either side. I ran the first one to Indian River, and in the one day, we put down about a thousand pounds of dust on the trees there. Six days later, there wasn't a bug to be found anywhere.

So then, that gave them the idea we had to put nine tons on Stanley Park to cover it. So what did I do? I got a little scow out to the middle of the inlet, just east of Brockton Point. It was a nice little thing with a house on it. We put all the dust on the top of that in bags, and we had barrels of aviation gas. So I said, "All right, we'll start this thing at half-past four in the morning, because the dew is on the leaves; there'll be no wind, and in August we'll be sure there'll be no clouds or anything like that.

I got four pilots — three others and myself — from the base at Bute Street. We started off at half-past four in the morning, ran over to that scow, and by the time we got going, it was a little after five o'clock when we made our first formation flight. Well, my gosh, you know, by half-past eight, we had put down that nine tons of dust. They had about half an acre of tarpaulins laid out under the trees, and just one week later, it was ankle deep in these worms. There's never been another worm seen or heard of since that time in that area; the same at Indian River.

On being awarded the fisheries contract, Pacific Airways set up a base at Swanson Bay near Princess Royal Island. They operated from this location until they were purchased by Western Canada Airways in May 1928. Boeing flying boats replaced the HS–2L. Immediately after the purchase, McLaren became manager of the British Columbia operations of the new company and later, its successor, Canadian Airways.

DON MCLAREN: Swanson Bay was the location that we used because that's where the fishery inspector lived. He had his home there. His patrol boat was moored there. There was electricity there. They kept a little generator running but the old pulpmill was falling to pieces and was abandoned. It was a handy place. Also, it was out of the eye of the fishing fleets. They didn't know where you were, you see. They couldn't see you come and go, because you weren't anywhere near a cannery. This was the idea of Mr. Cameron, the inspector.

GORDON BALLENTINE: It was quite an operation. There was something like five aircraft at anchor there at one time.

I might say that the Boeing B1Es were closed in, had windows that cranked up and down, upholstered seats, and all sorts of fancy goods. In the Vickers Vedette and the HS–2L you sat out where God meant airplane drivers to sit: out in the noise and the wind. The Vickers Vedette had a horrible motion in rough air. We were, I suppose, spoiled a bit by the Boeing B1E, which was quite a tough, comfortable airplane. The RCAF used Vickers Vedettes for photography and patrols all over Canada very successfully, so there was basically nothing wrong with it if you liked open airplanes that flapped their wings.

MAURICE McGREGOR: Fisheries patrol was very interesting, because it was necessary to visit every little fiord, every little river mouth on the entire coast. Of course, the job was to apprehend poachers and so on. We carried a federal fisheries inspector in the aircraft. That was interesting indeed.

There is one interesting thing that I was instructed to do. When the pilchard fish didn't appear, there was very great concern on the part of the industry.

DON McLAREN: Pilchards were a very valuable asset on the coast. "California sardines," they called them. They were catching them to make fishmeal, and also they'd can them and sell them whole. They were beautiful things to eat. They'd come up here in tremendous droves, but you never knew where the hell they were half the time. They would disappear. One day there would be millions of them, and they'd go to fish them, you see; and then they went out again the next day, and they'd be gone. They couldn't find them anywhere.

MAURICE McGGREGOR: So the federal Department of Fisheries asked that we fly out over the Pacific to try and locate the pilchards. Initially, we made contact with the fishing fleet prior to its departure. I was piloting a Boeing B1E flying boat, which did not have radio. Therefore the fleet was informed that we would drop messages in bottles giving course to steer and distance to the pilchards. I was informed in advance of the departure time, course and cruising speed of the fleet and, therefore, had some idea of their track for interception purposes. I told the fleet captain that we would fly out a hundred miles into the Pacific and then make sweeps parallel to the coast and gradually work our way in. This was not easy, as the smoke from many forest fires mixed with fog caused poor visibility. We located the pilchards, then intercepted the fleet and dropped instructions in the bottles, which gave the course and distance to the pilchards. That is how the industry got its fish.

GORDON BALLENTINE: One of the tricks we learned was that if we flew close enough to the thickly timbered hillsides, the noise of our engines would be very largely absorbed, so we could go sneaking along and drop down on some poor innocent poacher.

WALTER GILBERT: The way we worked it was to park around one side of the long fiords or inlets. We made a sudden approach. You see, you couldn't hear an engine on the other side of a ridge — not until you popped over the ridge and there you were. We carried an aerial camera to gather evidence.

GORDON BALLENTINE: I had a fisheries inspector on board one time and we were sneaking along the ridge of a mountain, very close, and I saw this guy down with a net set right in the mouth of a creek — well inside of the boundary lines. We landed, taxied slowly up to him, and the fisheries inspector said, "You've never made an arrest this year. You'd better make this arrest." I didn't want to make an arrest; I was there to fly airplanes. But I got out; I actually tied the airplane up to the seiner while he was pulling in the net before he heard me. I got up on board his boat, and the skipper was standing by the winch with his back to me and that guy was seven feet tall if he was an inch. I finally had to tap him on the shoulder and say, "You're under arrest." He turned around and he was just as scared and shocked as I was.

You were just playing cops and robbers with an airplane. I guess ninety-nine per cent of the fishermen took being caught at poaching as a simple business risk. They would poach if they thought they could get away with it. Those who did poach seemed to take it as a simple business gamble. So, if you caught them, well, tough luck.

Crash Landing

Edited by Dennis Duffy and Carol Crane,
commentary by David Parker

*I*n the summer of 1928 the Pacific Airways fisheries patrol base at Swanson Bay lost two aircraft: a Boeing B1D and a Vickers Vedette. Ballentine was a crewman on the Vedette and recalls the incident:

GORDON BALLENTINE: This thing is very vivid in my memory although it happened fifty years ago. I was assigned to go over to the Queen Charlottes in the Vedette with a pilot called Neville Cumming and an air engineer called Alf Walker. We went up to Prince Rupert, overnighted there and started off the next morning for Queen Charlotte City. It was a grey sort of day. Once you could see beyond the islands, the grey sky and the grey sea started to blend. We were flying between two islands. All of a sudden we were in clouds, with nothing much better than a carpenter's level for instruments. I was in the front seat, sort of a round bathtub arrangement.

Anyway, we ran into this cloud, and I heard the power come off, and we started down. We were between two islands, and I assumed that we would simply break out over the ocean, which I'm sure is what the pilot assumed, too. But the first thing I saw were the tops of trees that looked about three hundred feet high — as far as I was concerned — and about ten feet below us. I might say that's a shocking experience. The pilot poured the coals to it then, and we started to climb. What manoeuvres we went through it's impossible to say, but every few moments I'd see the trees again. Eventually, we got above the trees and smacked into the top of the mountain.

This HS–2L flying boat made the first flight up the coast of British Columbia in 1923. Courtesy Earl MacLeod

The first thing I did was get out and stumble about fifty feet, you know, thinking of fire. The airplane was a pile of junk. The air-cooled engine was flat like a pancake and still running. The gravity fuel tank, with about three or four gallons of gas in it, was ruptured. The gas was steaming off this air-cooled engine, coming off in clouds of steam. Why the thing never blew, who can tell.

I had to go around the rear of the thing; it was like crawling through a barbed-wire fence, because it was just a bunch of splintered junk. I finally reached the cockpit. The pilot, Neville, was sitting with his head slumped down on his chest, blood running all over his face. Alf Walker, who was sitting on his right, looked as though his face was made of chopped liver. He was dead, as far as I was concerned. I was just reaching in to try to reach the switch [to reduce chances of explosion and fire] when Neville made a reflexive action and knocked the switch off with his hand and flopped his head down again. So, I decided he must be alive if he could do that. Alf was definitely dead; I was just as sure as I am sitting here.

In my bathtub front seat was the emergency gear, with axes and food and all that sort of stuff. So I crawled out through all this junk, went around to the front of the airplane again, and I couldn't get into my seat, it was such a tight fit. The top wing had come down and cut my seat in two and hadn't even touched me. Anyway, I dragged the stuff out, got the ax and started back to the cockpit. I got there, and the dead man was gone. He just wasn't there. I thought, well, God, he's going to be stumbling around the mountain out of his mind. So, I went back outside again, around to the front of the airplane. As I got around to the front, I met this apparition coming around the other side, his face a mess of blood, his hands all bloody. We stood and looked at each other and we both started to laugh. You know, a hysterical reaction. I was relatively undamaged, but Alf was a mess.

Turned out that what had happened was that he and Neville had both been hit in the back of the head by the struts from the engine when it came down. Their faces had been smashed through three-quarters of an inch of mahogany plywood — the instrument panel.

Anyway, Alf and I organized ourselves. Then we had to do something about the pilot who'd put us in this horrible position. Quite frankly, we didn't much care. (I became a pilot later and often wondered how close I came to making people think the same about me.) Anyway, we decided to get him out. We chopped a hole out right through the bottom of the hull and got him out that way, and stretched him out some few feet away from the airplane. Then we decided, "Well, the thing might still burn." So we dragged him another fifty feet and stretched him out again. He was a mess, and we didn't know whether he was going to last or not. And we didn't know where we were: whether we were on an island, the mainland or where. So Alf and I took turns wandering around the mountain.

About five that afternoon we finally saw a glimpse down through the hole in the clouds and we saw blue water. We didn't know what it was, whether it was a lake, ocean or what, but it was better than where we were. So we decided that was where we had to go. We still had this guy, who had refused to die; we still had to look after him. Alf and I decided to make a stretcher, boy-scout style. We managed to get a couple of poles. We were taking Neville's coat to use as the other half of the stretcher when he sort of came to and wanted to know what the hell was going on. We said, "We're going to carry you down the mountain." He said, "You're not. Where am I?" He said we weren't going to carry him; he was going to walk. And walk he did.

So the two of us supported Neville, and we stumbled downhill, something like coming down Grouse Mountain at midnight without a trail. About two in the morning, I think, we got to the beach and laid Neville out. We were pretty beat. We tried to light the standard three signal fires. We'd get one lit, and the tide would come in and put it out. We'd light another one, and the tide'd come in and put *it* out. We got the third one going, you know, really great boy-scout stuff. Alf and I sat up all night by the fire signalling s–o–s off shore. When daylight came, we found we were in a little bay with an island covering the whole mouth of it. So we were signalling to a vacant island all night.

We tossed a coin to see whether we'd go right or left; tossed another coin to see whether Alf would go, or I would go. The toss came that Alf would go, and he would go to the right. Alf came back in about two hours with his eyes all bugged out. He told me, "Some people will be coming along pretty soon to pick us up." He said he got down the beach about half a mile, and there was a launch at anchor in the bay. He'd yelled and shouted and whistled and thrown rocks at it but couldn't raise anybody, 'cause there was nobody in it. He went a little farther and came to a trail up the hill. Went up the trail about a hundred yards, and there was a telephone on a tree! So he cranked this thing, and if you can imagine Alf's feeling and the feeling of the people at the other end: you know, "Who am I?" and "Where am I?"

Well, it turned out that it was the beach site for a mining company, and that we were on Porcher Island. So they came down the hill and said they'd get a boat and come around and pick us up. They took us into Prince Rupert on this launch, and Alf and Neville into the hospital. And I took the glad news back to Don McLaren at Swanson Bay that he was short an airplane.

Barnstorming to Make a Dollar

Edited by Dennis Duffy and Carol Crane, commentary by David Parker

*I*n 1929 the Depression hit North America and flying enthusiasts were left struggling to find some way to make a living. Like their comrades all across the continent, pilots in British Columbia began to fly around the province, stopping at various towns and enticing people to go for a spin in an airplane. They would set up anywhere they felt they could attract a paying crowd. A farmer's field was ideal, and for a fee to the individual farmer, the pilots were able to provide joy rides for all who were able to pay. The usual location of these activities led to the term "barnstorming."

MAURICE MCGREGOR: In those days one had to do barnstorming. When I was operating in Victoria from Lansdowne airport, business was rather slack, so I decided to try and drum up business in Sidney. There was no airport there. So I flew over Sidney and selected a field, a farmer's field. That field was located on what today is the eastern boundary of the Victoria International Airport. It was just a green field. So I put on a show — aerobatics and all that sort of thing — to try and create a little excitement, and then dove down at the field. In consequence a lot of curious people would come out to see what was going on. They were unsuspecting clients, our customers! That's what barnstorming consisted of. You'd keep moving around trying to pick up a dollar here and a dollar there.

GORDON BALLENTINE: We used to barnstorm up and down the Fraser Valley with our little two-seater airplanes. Barnstorming was a favourite way of making a dollar in those days. You'd fly up to some farmer's field, take him and his family for a ride, and he'd let you use his field, and you'd carry whoever came along for whatever you could get. A lot of people got a lot of experience that way. Made a little money. We didn't have the traffic problem that there is today. There weren't that many airplanes around, so the likelihood of running into somebody else was pretty remote.

MAURICE McGREGOR: I flew in Ladner and then I came to Victoria and had students over here, gave them training, and then put on air displays of aerobatics and all that sort of thing. Periodically, then, I'd barnstorm out of James's Seed Farm at Duncan and teach some people up there, and then I'd fly over to Saltspring Island and we'd barnstorm from the golf course there — a small golf course. I used a Fleet powered with a Kinner engine, a biplane. I also used a Barling, which is a low-wing monoplane, and also a Gypsy Moth. In addition, when I was flying for Sprott-Shaw's school, I flew a Waco Ten. Sprott-Shaw school had an aviation division. They had one airplane, one antiquated old 1928 Waco Ten with a first-war engine in it, which I may say was always stopping, and one always had to find a field to land in. So I did barnstorming in that and I trained students in that in 1930. Barnstormed out of Courtenay, from a farmer's field that almost wasn't long enough. So that's the sort of thing that went on.

In some of these places the potential takeoff area was so restricted that, on some occasions, it'd be necessary to get a man to hold one wing, and then point the aircraft at the fence behind. Then you'd open up the engine, get the tail up and then the ply-rudder, heave on the wing, and the aircraft would be swung around. You'd have the engine wide open, almost heading towards the fence, and he'd let her go, so it was that marginal. But you know, in order to make a living you had to do that.

TED CRESSY: Every Saturday and Sunday we did barnstorming [at Lansdowne airfield]. It was five dollars a trip, that was for a full twenty minutes. Every now and again, in the summer particularly, if we had been a little on the slow side, we'd get a scale, a weighing scale that you would see outside the stores, [a] penny scale. And then you would fly [people] at a penny a pound. The passengers would come, stand on the scale — 150 pounds, all right, a dollar fifty and away you'd go for ten minutes.

MAURICE McGREGOR: If a person was light, then they got a reasonable rate. But on the other hand, you wouldn't stay in the air for long. At a cent a pound with a 150-pounder, you would just take off and do a quick circuit and [come] down again and get the next one.

JOE BERTALINO: They'd do parachute jumping or have a "cent-a-pound day" just to get the excitement going. If it wasn't for all that, we wouldn't have

Joe Bertalino flew this DH60X Cirrus Moth in about 1928. Courtesy Joe Bertalino

made it through. Everybody sort of helped each other out at that time.

MAURICE MCGREGOR: Economic conditions were terrible, and it was a very difficult thing to find people with enough money to either take lessons or to take a joy ride. Nevertheless, they often would reach for the last dime. I met a man just the other day in Victoria who reminded me of the first ride that he had in an airplane with me at Lansdowne Airport. That was a five-dollar ride for about ten minutes. When he returned home, his father chastised him for first of all taking the risk, and secondly, for spending his money so foolishly.

Joe Bertalino and his friend Humphrey Madden flew to Kamloops and set up a flying school there. On weekends they barnstormed throughout the area.

JOE BERTALINO: One Saturday we flew to Merritt. We just got over the town and we went right down low and, as we started, we'd go down the streets, and all the kids and people would start running down the streets, following us. We'd go back up over the town again and make a circle, and they all ran back again, and you could see they were all looking up and watching us. So we were looking for a place to land, trying to get something close to town, you see.

And then we saw this field. It wasn't very good, but we thought, well, we'll try it. We landed in it. It was all right. But we no sooner got down and here comes the kids on bikes, dogs, people on horseback, and everybody running up to the airplane, you know. And I got out and Madden got out. We were standing around there when everybody walked up. One old gentleman came along; he had an umbrella and he walked up and poked it in the wing, and he says, "Oh my God, that isn't solid!" Put a hole right through it! Of course, that just about drove me up the wall. And the dogs were fighting under the machine, and the kids were leaning their bikes against it. We finally got everybody away. It was quite a lot of excitement — oh, real excitement.

Sometimes we'd fly all day. We'd start in the morning; we'd go to a place and stay there. As long as there were people there, we'd keep flying. It was surprising, the people up there seemed to be able to get the money to fly. We'd make maybe three or four or five hundred dollars sometimes. That was a lot of money. If you made a couple of hundred dollars in a day, that was big money.

Then we'd be invited into town and have dinner with the officials, or somebody there would invite us for dinner. Oh, we used to have a lot of fun. We wore breeches, and these big boots, leather jackets and scarves around our neck, helmets and goggles — really dressed up. In those days it was really exciting. We had a lot of fun, and that was the best part of aviation.

MAURICE McGREGOR: The first air show we had in Vancouver was at Lulu Island in the summer of 1930, which was very small and very, you might say, amateurish. The usual display of loops and rolls and so on. Another stunt was to chase a car, which roared about the field, and drop bombs of flour on the car!

HAL WILSON: In 1931 things were very tough out at the Vancouver Airport. We had moved from the old Lulu Island field, and having moved to the new airport, there was no means of transportation [to the airport] and things were difficult. Students were infrequent, and people going out to the airport to see what was going on were infrequent. We wanted to make a few bucks, so we decided we should have an airshow. [In 1932] we started what was called the B. C. Air Tour. [We went to] Victoria to start off with, then back to Vancouver, then up to Penticton. We went on to Vernon, and then from Vernon we went to Kamloops. Then we finally finished up at Chilliwack, and that was the end of the tour. Everybody made a few dollars, enough to keep them eating for a couple of extra months, and that was it.

MAURICE McGREGOR: When the B. C. Air Tour of 1932 arrived in Victoria, there were, I think, about ten or twelve aircraft. Among the pilots were Hal Wilson, myself and Don Lawson. We were known as the three musketeers, as we did aerobatics in formation. We took off in formation and did the entire performance, including Hal Wilson flying inverted while in tight formation, and ended up with the Prince of Wales feathers.

HAL WILSON: First of all, we had to stay on the ground until the starting [time], because any airplanes taking off could be seen for several miles around. If people could see the airplanes flying, they wouldn't pay their money to go into the gates. So we had to stay on the ground until the starting time.

We started off by a formation of three, which consisted of a formation by the Aero Club of British Columbia. The leader flew upside-down, and the other two flew rightside-up and flew up the centre of the field. This was followed by a race or something of that sort. Then we had an event called "crazy flying," which Maurice McGregor was the chief executor of, on an Eaglerock.

MAURICE MCGREGOR: I also did an act called "crazy flying." This was to show how an airplane could be improperly flown at low level and almost crash, but not quite. The method was that the pilot — myself — would enter the aircraft disguised as a nervous senior citizen passenger. The official pilot would then walk away from the plane in response to a query; and suddenly, I would hit the throttle, and the airplane would start zigzagging beside the grandstand, and I would then pull it off the ground and stall it so that it almost crashed, but didn't. Then I would fly the plane on its side and drag the wing close to the ground, just to raise the dust and clip the clover heads, and charge at fences, always in complete control but with the appearance of impending disaster.

HAL WILSON: Then we had to get back again to an aerobatic display, which usually was done by myself. Finally, to wind the thing up, we had a race and then a parachute jump. While the race was on, the parachute jumper was climbing up to the heights so that he could jump out. I know in one place he finished up in the hospital. Not that he was badly hurt, but he landed on a cactus, and they spent half the evening with a pair of pliers, pulling out the spikes.

MAURICE MCGREGOR: On the occasion of that B. C. Air Tour there was a great uproar and many editorials in the press. No doubt, if they had television they would have had comment on the tube. Many people were complaining in letters to the editor that this should never be permitted again, that these airplanes in great numbers — we had twelve — should not be permitted in the area of Victoria or Gordon Head, because it was noted that the sparrows had disappeared. Undoubtedly, these airplanes had so upset the atmosphere that the birds deserted Victoria. But that's Victoria.

Bush Pilots

Edited by Dennis Duffy and Carol Crane,
commentary by David Parker

DON MCLAREN: The bush pilot came out of the other provinces — northern Manitoba, northern Ontario and northern Alberta. That was "the bush," because you were in the bush right away. All your prospecting was in the bush. They got the reputation of being bush pilots, flying into unorganized territory and unmapped territory and so on. We inherited that title [in British Columbia] because we were doing work of a similar nature.

Aircraft proved invaluable in the development of British Columbia's northern interior. They carried survey teams to chart the landscape. They ferried miners and prospectors in search of mineral wealth, and brought supplies to their claims. They brought remote settlements just a bit closer to civilization. And they could carry large payloads over previously impassable natural obstacles.

A new generation of "bush planes" — such as the Fairchild FC–2 and "71" series, the Fokker Universal, the Waco and the Norseman — started coming into service in the late 1920s and early 1930s, as did a variety of German Junkers aircraft. Many were designed specifically for the North American wilderness — rugged aircraft incorporating such features as heated, enclosed cockpits, improved freight capacity and high-mounted wings for easier loading of cargo. In addition, alternative undercarriages — wheels, skis or floats — were available, giving the aircraft landing ability regardless of season. However, in the beginning there were no navigational aids, no accurate maps and no organized search and rescue services. In this mountainous and inhospitable environment, the pilots were very much on their own.

DON MCLAREN: There was no such thing as navigation; you just went where you could see your way. There were no detailed maps. Anywhere in British Columbia and the north, you had to watch where you were going. Your prospector said he wants to go into some lake; he'd never been in there before but he wanted to reach this little lake. Well, you get off this lake and you went up and you saw a pass. You'd ask yourself: Can I go in through there without getting into the murk, and get out again, or shall I go around another way? You'd manoeuvre around and you'd find a way in there. But you had to make sure you knew your way out, too. You'd land in there and then you'd mark that on your sketch map. There were a lot of lakes you saw in there that weren't on the maps at all. [A prospector] might go in there and he might do a little panning in the gravel. Or he'd set up his camp, and you'd come back and get him a week later, two weeks later, something like that. He'd stake some claims in there and when he found some-

Pilot Gordon Ballentine landed a prospector at Woss Lake during the Zeballos gold rush. The aircraft is a Bellanca Pacemaker. Courtesy Gordon Ballentine

thing, you used to freight his stuff in there for him. That's the way we were doing things in northern British Columbia.

Certain parts of the country, like northwest of Prince George, were full of small ridges of mountains, and some of the lakes were at five thousand feet elevation. You had to be pretty careful about going into some of those without knowing your way out. The main thing, of course, was to have an airplane that had lots of power performance. You couldn't take an HS–2L into that part of the country. Boeings, Fokkers and Fairchilds were the only types for that north.

MAURICE McGREGOR: I had many forced landings. What one had to do in order to survive was to always anticipate an engine failure, and just what you would do when the engine stopped — whether you could land in a field, whether you could reach a lake if you were on floats, or how you could most effectively crash land in the trees. But you had to be thinking this way.

GORDON BALLENTINE: You looked at a lake, and only your own background and experience told you that you could get into the lake and get off again, or into a field and off again. Now, this meant that there was a good deal of trial and error. How do you know what's the shortest lake you can get out of until you've tried it? How do you know what's the biggest waves you can land in until you've tried it? Occasionally, you get pretty close to the edge. You never become one hundred–per cent efficient, because that means at some point you bust something in learning what the absolute maximum is.

Some of the "airports" were nothing but mud fields. You know, you brushed the willow trees when you took off, that sort of thing; came out with little green marks all over your propellers. I'm making out some of this as though it was a hero's job, which is a bunch of B.S. It wasn't.

As aircraft proved their worth, they became indispensable and were in demand all year round. In the northern part of the province this meant coping with the difficulties caused by operating in extreme cold.

EARL GEROW: We operated without being tied up too many times. I think one day it got to fifty-five degrees below. We stayed inside that particular day, but it became milder the next day. We flew in thirty-five or forty-five below weather. In order to get our engines going — of course, in those days they were piston-driven engines in aircraft — we had to use a plumber's pot. It's like a big blowtorch, with a little metal shield over the top of it. We put an asbestos blanket over the engine and we put the plumber's pot in there and heated the engine up. Of course, the first thing you did when you landed was drain the oil from your engine while it was hot. [You would] heat it up on the top of a B. C. heater [type of wood stove] and put it back in the oil tank after you had heated the engine up. You'd crank it up until you got momentum up and you wound the engine over two or three times to get the hot oil through the engine. Then you primed it, and all but got out of breath again, cranking up the inertial starter and getting it going. You'd wind the engine up until it had its proper temperatures and away it would go. You had to work as a team, the pilot and the mechanic, when you started. The priming had to be just right, and you'd get the inertial starter wound up, and the pilot would engage it and start it over. If you missed, it meant going over [the procedure] again. Not very often did you miss on having to crank up the inertial starter twice. It was a good health thing. It kept your lungs good because it was a real strenuous exercise.

GORDON BALLENTINE: To deice propellers, you could change the pitch on them. When you started to feel that you were losing power there, you'd put it into fine pitch and start the engines screaming and then throw chunks of ice off [against] the skin of the airplane. On the wings they had these "boots," as they called them, which was really a flat thing like an inner tube, formed to fit the nose contour [leading edge] of the wing. And this was operated by an air pump, which caused this thing to expand and contract at different sections out along the [wing], so that it sort of pulsed here and there. And by no means was this a cure-all, I'll tell you. The only cure-all for ice is to get the hell out of it. Again, you learned that under certain circumstances it's something you can handle; under certain others, no way.

I guess you know a little bit about how an airplane stays up in the air? The smooth flow of air over the wings, right? So: you get ice on the wing and you wait a little while and then you put the boots [pneumatic deicers] to work, and they break the ice off it. It only breaks it off on the [leading edge]. What's left? A nice, little sharp ridge on which the next accumulation of ice forms. So pretty soon you got a two-by-four lying across the top of your wing, and it ceases to be a wing. I was flying over pretty ice-laden mountains. Canadian Pacific Air Lines's Vancouver–Prince George–Fort St. John run was a great place for ice if you wanted it. My procedure was, if ice started to come on and it wasn't coming on too quickly, I would wait until I got maybe an eighth of an inch or a quarter of an inch of ice on and then turn the boots on. If it started to shed ice over the whole top of the wing, I would turn the boots off and carry on again, break it off. But if it broke off only on the boots, I would get the hell out of there as quickly as I could. Up, down or back, one way or another, because I never found any way of forecasting how quickly ice could come on.

I remember this one occasion — something that sticks in my memory, I'll tell you. We were flying across the Rockies between Prince George and Fort St. John; that's the lowest part of the Rockies. We were flying over there at about eleven thousand feet. We were flying on instruments; nice smooth air, just flying in milk. I was eating lunch. We got a smattering of ice, and I sat there and looked at it for a minute or two. Then another splatter, just sprinkles. I set my lunch down on the floor of the cockpit, and as I did that, it was just as though we'd been driving behind a dump truck full of stucco. In thirty seconds the airplane stalled going at 145 miles an hour, fell off on one wing and started down. There were four inches of ice there, just like that. And it ceased to be an airplane, right then. So I grabbed a hold of it, and the first officer, his job was to keep the engines going. We had everything up against the firewall, engines absolutely wide open, just screaming in fine pitch, and [we were] sinking and falling off on one side or another. We flew through the Rockies below the peaks and never saw a bloody thing. When we came out the other side, the ice all melted off before we got to Fort St. John, so nobody else could ever see it. That was the most horrible sight I ever saw. It just didn't look like an airplane. Gee, it was a horrible looking sight.

When I got back to Vancouver, I promptly went to the [weather] office and said "This is what happened. What did I do wrong?" And we couldn't find any reason in the weather maps which would justify it. About a month later the same thing happened to a TCA pilot over Crescent Valley. So I got a hold of him, and we compared symptoms. You know, similar things: all of a sudden you were a chunk of ice and down you were coming. We both decided that God just decided that once a year He had to teach you who was boss.

Notes on Editing and Sources

A Note on Editing

Many of the reminiscences in this book were recorded years after the events that are described. Some readers, therefore, might question the accuracy and legitimacy of this type of historical information. It is quite true that the human memory is fallible; remembrances of events as they actually happened may lose clarity or even be reconstructed. However, with the careful use of corroborative techniques, such as talking to several witnesses, checking against other contemporary sources, an accurate overall impression can be achieved. In recreating the commonplace but nonetheless historically interesting experiences of the past, oral history has no equal. Furthermore, it is often the case that in examining the past, that what people *thought* happened is just as important as what *actually* did happen.

Some of the interviews have been extensively altered by editors. Editorial licence has been taken to delete completely the words of interviewers and to provide for more continuity and readability in the interviewees' words. This style of editing necessitates the addition of a few words in some cases, deletions and alterations in others. For example, where a key word or phrase was used in a question but not the response, they have been reintroduced as the words of the interviewee. On the other hand, verbal crutch words such as "well" and "you know" have been eliminated, except insofar as they were judged to add to the flavour of the interview. Some of the articles in this book are shorter or rearranged versions of those originally published in the *Sound Heritage Series*.

The richness of the remembered past is evident from these interviews. Without them, those interested in the fascinating history of British Columbia would be the poorer. A special debt of gratitude is owed to those who have taken the trouble to record the reminiscences of the province's pioneering era and to those who had the foresight to record and preserve them. The original recordings are held in the permanent collection of the Sound and Moving Image Division of the Provincial Archives of British Columbia and are available for consultation or research.

Derek Reimer
Head, Sound and Moving Image Division
Provincial Archives of British Columbia

The Sound Heritage Series *Editorial Staff, 1974–1984*

William J. (Bill) Langlois	Editor, 1974–1978
Derek Reimer	Assistant Editor, 1974–1978 Editor, 1978–1982 Supervising Editor, 1982–1984
Charles Lillard	Editor, 1982–1983
Janet Cauthers	Assistant Editor, 1974–1980 Associate Editor, 1980–1981
Allen Specht	Assistant Editor, 1976 Associate Editor, 1981–1982
David Mitchell	Assistant Editor, 1979–1980 Associate Editor, 1980–1981
David Mattison	Associate Editor, 1981–1982
David Day	Guest Editor Vol. IV, No. 2 (1975) Vol. V, No. 3 (1976) Vol. VI, No. 3 (1977)
Robert Levine	Guest Editor Vol. IV, Nos. 3 & 4 (1975)

A Note on Sources

All the selections in this book were originally published in the *Sound Heritage Series* by the Sound and Moving Image Division of the Provincial Archives of British Columbia.

PART I   THOSE WHO CAME BEFORE

> "The Flood, a True Story," "How the Animals and Birds Got Their Names" and "Underground Homes of the Lillooet" are from *Lillooet Stories*, edited by Randy Bouchard and Dorothy I. D. Kennedy, vol. 6, no. 1 (1977), 1, 3, 5, 10–13, 62–64.
>
> "How We the Native People Lived" is from *Native Languages and Culture*, edited by Janet Cauthers, vol. 4, nos. 3 and 4 (1976), 18–25.
>
> "The Meeting of Captain Cook and Chief Maquinna" is from *Nu·tka· Captain Cook and the Spanish Explorers on the Coast*, edited by Barbara S. Efrat and W. J. Langlois, vol. 7, no. 1 (1978), 54–55, 59–60.
>
> "Forming Tender Ties: Fur Trader Fred Thornberg" is from *Settling Clayoquot*, edited by Bob Bossin, no. 33 (1981), 7–10.
>
> "The 'Romantic' Missionary: Robert Tomlinson," "Indian Memories of Mission School" and "Nursing Sisters" are from *Now You Are My Brother: Missionaries in British Columbia*, edited by Margaret Whitehead, no. 34 (1981), 7–14, 57–66, 77–82, 88.

PART II   SETTLING THE FRONTIER

> "Into a Wild Country: Norwegians at Bella Coola," "No Paradise, No Utopia: Danes at Cape Scott" and "Away from the Outside World: Danes at Sointula" are from *Dreams of Freedom: Bella Coola, Cape Scott, Sointula*, edited by Gordon Fish, no. 36 (1982), 1–2, 6–16, 19–26, 31–40.
>
> "Toil and Peaceful Life: Doukhobors in the Kootenays" is from *Toil and Peaceful Life: Portraits of Doukhobors*, edited and translated by Marjorie Maloff and Peter Ogloff, vol. 6, no. 4 (1977), 12, 16–17, 19–20, 61–72.
>
> "Ranches on the Open Range" and "Grow Fruit and Grow Rich" are from *Bright Sunshine and a Brand New Country: Recollections of the Okanagan Valley, 1890–1914*, edited by David Mitchell and Dennis Duffy, vol. 8, no. 3 (1979), iii, 1–6, 9, 11–12, 53–54, 56–59, 64, 66–68.
>
> "Packing Along the Telegraph Trail" is from *Skeena Country*, edited by Allen Specht, vol. 5, no. 1 (1976), 7, 19, 24, 26, 28–29.

"In Search of Silver and Gold" and "Andy Daney, a Rough and Ready Man" are from *Where the Lardeau River Flows,* edited by Peter Chapman, no. 32 (1981), 2, 4–5, 9–13, 14–15.

"Whatever the Weather: Red-Shirt Bill and the Royal Mail" is from *Floodland and Forest: Memories of the Chilliwack Valley,* edited by Imbert Orchard, no. 37 (1983), 39–42.

"Free and Fearless: Children of the Backwoods" is from *Growing Up in the Valley: Pioneer Childhood in the Lower Fraser Valley,* edited by Imbert Orchard, no. 40 (1983), 4, 8–9; *Martin: The Story of a Young Fur Trader,* edited by Imbert Orchard, no. 30 (1981), 13, 23–24, and *The Gulf Islanders,* edited by Derek Reimer, vol. 5, no. 4 (1976), 21, 27–29.

"Greenhorns, Mudpups and Remittance Men" is from *Bright Sunshine and a Brand New Country: Recollections of the Okanagan Valley, 1890–1914,* edited by David Mitchell and Dennis Duffy, vol. 8, no. 3 (1979), 31–38, 44–46.

"The Squire of Saltspring Island" is from *The Gulf Islanders,* edited by Derek Reimer, vol. 5, no. 4 (1976), 17–19.

"Dream Isle: Fred Tibbs and His Castle" is from *Settling Clayoquot,* edited by Bob Bossin, no. 33 (1981), 2, 35–47.

"Swiss Climbing Guides in the Rockies" and "Expeditions to Mystery Mountain" are from *In the Western Mountains: Early Mountaineering in British Columbia,* edited by Susan Leslie, vol. 8, no. 4 (1980), 4, 7, 10–14, 52–61.

"Victoria: A City of Mud and Dust" is from *A Victorian Tapestry,* edited by Janet Cauthers, vol. 7, no. 3 (1978), 1, 7–11.

"Chinatown and the Chinese," "Chasing Cows and Chickens in the City," "Hobo Jungles and Hopping Freights," "Bootleggers and Gamblers in Hogan's Alley" and "The Internment of the Japanese" are from *Opening Doors: Vancouver's East End,* edited by Daphne Marlatt and Carole Itter, vol. 8, nos. 1 and 2 (1979), 1–2, 6, 15–23, 55, 58, 80, 83, 105–7, 140–44.

PART III   HOPES HIGH, DOLLARS FEW — WORKING PEOPLE

"Those Days in the Woods" and "Roughhouse Pete and Other Characters" are from *Men of the Forest,* edited by David Day and Howie Smith, vol. 6, no. 3 (1977), 3, 5–9, 31–33.

"In and Out of Camp" is from *Sound Heritage,* edited by Derek Reimer, vol. 3, no. 2 (1974), 25, 28–32.

" 'The Big Strike' of 1912" and "Sixteen Tons a Day" are from *Fighting for Labour: Four Decades of Work in British Columbia, 1910–1950,* edited by Patricia Wejr and Howie Smith, vol. 7, no. 4 (1978), 11, 13–21, 38–39.

"Gill Netters on the Skeena" is from *Skeena Country,* edited by Allen Specht, vol. 5, no. 1 (1976), 40–44.

"Trolling off the West Coast" is from *Settling Clayoquot,* edited by Bob Bossin, no. 33 (1981), 25–26, 53.

"Hunger Marches, Relief Camps and the On-to-Ottawa Trek" and "The 'Bloody Sunday' of 1938" are from *Fighting for Labour: Four Decades of Work in British Columbia, 1910–1950,* edited by Patricia Wejr and Howie Smith, vol. 7, no. 4 (1978), 5–6, 42–59.

PART IV   ON LAND, OVER WATER AND THROUGH THE AIR

"The Glacier Slide," "Post Office on Wheels" and "The CPR Motor Car on Rails" are from *Railroaders: Recollections from the Steam Era in British Columbia,* edited by Robert D. Turner, no. 31 (1981), iii, 1, 9–15, 63–64, 66–67.

"Swift Water: Upriver by Canoe and Riverboat" is from *Skeena Country,* edited by Allen Specht, vol. 5, no. 1 (1976), 4–5, 11–18.

"Passengers and Freight of Every Description" and "Navigating by Whistle and Echo" are from *Navigating the Coast: A History of the Union Steamship Company,* edited by Peter Chapman, vol. 6, no. 2 (1977), 1, 24–27, 29–30, 34, 48–51, 55–59.

"The Life of a Lighthouse-Keeper" is from *The Gulf Islanders,* edited by Derek Reimer, vol. 5, no. 4 (1976), 65–71.

"The Spirit of Adventure," "Crash Landing," "Barnstorming to Make a Dollar" and "Bush Pilots" are from *The Magnificent Distances: Early Aviation in British Columbia, 1910–1940,* edited by Dennis Duffy and Carol Crane, no. 28 (1980), 15–29, 47–51, 53–56.